FACT AND FICTION

BERTRAND RUSSELL

with a new Introduction by
John G. Slater

London and New York

First published 1961
Second impression published 1979
by George Allen & Unwin Ltd.

First published in paperback 1994
by Routledge
11 New Fetter Lane, London EC4P 4EE

Simultaneously published in the USA and Canada
by Routledge
29 West 35th Street, New York, NY 10001

© George Allen & Unwin Ltd.
New introduction © John G. Slater

Printed and bound in Great Britain by
Redwood Books, Trowbridge.

British Library Cataloguing in Publication Data

A catalogue record for this book is available from the British Library

Library of Congress Cataloging in Publication Data

A catalogue record for this book has been requested

ISBN 0–415–11461–6

CONTENTS

Introduction

From time to time throughout his long writing career Russell gathered together some of his essays into collections, selecting those he thought had enduring value. *Fact and Fiction*, which was published on 26 October 1961, is one of these books. Its immediate predecessor in this unofficial series is *Portraits from Memory and Other Essays*, which had come out in 1956. So *Fact and Fiction* gathers together the best of Russell's shorter works written during the latter half of the 1950s. The contents of the volume, when compared to that of *Portraits*, reflects the sharp turn which his activities had taken at the end of 1954 with his famous broadcast, 'Man's Peril from the Hydrogen Bomb'. The anxiety which that broadcast uncovered in the general population thrust Russell into a leadership role in the peace movement, work that took up most of his time during the period covered by this book. But his old writing interests did not all dry up at once as an examination of the book's contents reveals.

After his return to England from the United States in 1944 Russell became a popular guest on the BBC, speaking on a wide variety of topics. His was a voice from the Victorian past, articulating for his listeners the vast changes to which he had been witness and of which they were perhaps only dimly aware. Listener response to his broadcasts was overwhelmingly favourable and led to more invitations than he could accept, so he was careful to select, from among those received, only the ones with special appeal. Starting at about the time of his eightieth birthday, on 18 May 1952, he made a large number of broadcasts in which he described what it was like to grow up in Victorian England in a household consisting of his grandmother, Lady

John Russell, Uncle Rollo and Aunt Agatha, both unmarried, and himself, with eleven servants to do the work; the liberation he felt when he went up to Cambridge; the extraordinary personalities with whom he came into contact there; the enormous delight he experienced when he discovered that he was regarded by his teachers and his fellow students as a man of great intellectual ability; the near delirium of falling in love with Alys Whitall Smith, who became his first wife; the sheer joy he felt in his work on logic and the foundations of mathematics; the delightful memories of his contacts with some legendary personalities, such as George Bernard Shaw and D.H. Lawrence, most of whom were now dead; and the great sorrow he experienced when the First World War brought this delightful period of his life to an abrupt end. Most of these autobiographical broadcasts were included in *Portraits from Memory*, but *Fact and Fiction* reprints a fascinating set broadcast in 1957, in which he recalls the impact which certain books, and therefore to a certain extent, their authors, made upon him in his formative years. The six talks in 'Books that Influenced Me in Youth' clearly fall under the 'fact' part of the book.

Two other parts, 'Politics and Education' and 'Peace and War', are also intended by Russell to be considered as 'fact', but now surely 'fact' must be interpreted to mean 'non-fiction', because much of the argument of the essays in these parts is hortatory in nature, trying to get his readers to accept his view of the world, and not just to accept it, but also to prepare themselves to act on it in the way Russell himself was acting during this period. As a philosopher Russell agreed with Hume that logic forbade arguments from 'is' to 'ought'. Fact was one thing and value another, and no number of facts, reported by sentences in which 'is' is the verb, could ever establish a normative rule, a sentence in which 'ought' is the verb. A normative sentence recommends a course of action which will bring (it is claimed) about a certain value, the assumption being that the person addressed wants to see that value realized. So even when Russell is most passionate in these essays and addresses, the reader should not conclude that he is guilty of this elementary fallacy. He knew exactly what he was doing. For after all he had honed his persuasive skills during the First World War when, as a member of a tiny band opposed to the war, he had churned out tens of thousands of words in a vain attempt to alter the opinions of others, especially those in positions of power. Compared with that time, the late 1950s and early 1960s, when he headed organizations with hundreds, perhaps thousands, of members, were like coming out into the blaze of sunlight from a dark cave.

From very early in his life Russell had taken an active interest in public affairs. His grandmother had planned his education on the assumption that he would enter politics and (she hoped) become Prime Minister as his grandfather, Lord John Russell, had done. The sense of public duty which she instilled in him dominated much of his life. Even during the ten years or so that it took to write *Prinicipia Mathematica*, with the indispensable help of Alfred North Whitehead, he engaged in the controversies surrounding the Boer War, free trade, and votes for women. But it was his anti-war work in the period from 1914 to 1918 that made him master of some of the techniques of public controversy. During the period between the two world wars he continued to offer his opinion—in pamphlets, articles and letters to the editor—on nearly every matter of public debate. In 1936 he even published a book, *Which Way to Peace?*, giving his ideas on the way the Hitler menace should be faced. But when war did come he supported the Allies. After the war he resumed giving unsolicited advice; for a brief period even advocating the threat of war against the Soviet Union to prevent that country developing the atomic bomb. But his most active political period started in late 1954 with his Christmas broadcast, 'Man's Peril from the Hydrogen Bomb'. Thereafter he focused most of his energies on that menace.

But as the part on politics and education in this volume shows, he did not stop writing about other social problems facing policy makers. The positions he still advocates on most of these issues reflect his deep and very long-lasting commitment to the liberal democracy he had imbibed at his grandmother's knee; it was the position he returned to, almost instinctively, after brief flirtations with other political theories. During his lifetime he wrote hundreds of articles urging change upon his readers. They are usually dominated by the idea that if people would only act rationally life on earth could be a paradise, a term he did not shrink from using. But obviously life on earth was not paradisiacal, for the reason, as he so often pointed out, that people, especially those with political power, do not act rationally. This oddity in his views led John Maynard Keynes to observe that Russell ascribed the world's troubles to the fact that people acted irrationally, but that the way to set matters right was for them to act rationally.

Russell's frequent references to paradise are indicative of the very strong role the imagination played in his thinking. Without it he probably would not have made his important and lasting contributions to logic and philosophy generally. But in these explorations it was coupled with an equally strong passionate nature—'the search for knowledge' being determinate—which drove him on long after others would have given up the attempt to solve some particularly knotty problem. His *Autobiography* brings vividly to life those important intellectual efforts. When he first used his imagination alone, uncoupled from a guiding passion, to write a novel the result was not successful. This occurred when he was most under the influence of his love for Lady Ottoline Morrell and everyone agreed that *The Perplexities of John Forstice*, which has now been published in Volume 12 of *The Collected Papers of Bertrand Russell*, did not measure up to his other writings; in his *Autobiography* he noted that the last part 'seems very dull to me'. He did not try his hand again at fictional writing until 1951 when he published, anonymously as a competition, 'The Corsican Ordeal of Miss X;' no one, it should be noted, correctly identified the author. This was the first effort in a binge of fictional writing, which resulted in two books, *Satan in the Suburbs and Other Stories* (1953) and *Nightmares of Eminent Persons and Other Stories* (1954). In his *Autobiography* he justified his fictional writings in this way: 'I could state in fiction ideas which I half believed in but had no good solid grounds for believing. In this way it was possible to warn of dangers which might or might not occur in the near future.' In a speech he delivered in 1953 he joked about it: 'Some of you may perhaps have heard that I have devoted the first eighty years of my life to philosophy. I propose to devote the next eighty years to another branch of fiction!'

The last of his fiction is contained in this book, but the reader should be warned that not everything under 'Divertissements' is fictional. In a letter to his publisher while the contents of the book were being settled Russell remarked: 'One question arises as to the "Dreams" in the section called "Divertissements": these dreams are exactly as I dreamt them, but the second of them, relating a meeting with God, may perhaps be thought offensive, and, if that is your view, I should wish that dream omitted.' Sir Stanley Unwin did not think it offensive. The reader will have to sort the writings of this section according to their contents. Most of them are definitely fictional, but what about 'Cranks'? It seems to me to have the ring of truth about it, even though I have not been able to identify with confidence the footnote in Arthur Balfour's book. The final hurdle in this book's production was the writing of a blurb. Unwin asked Russell to do it, but Russell had to concede defeat: 'I am finding difficulty in constructing a blurb for *Fact and Fiction*. In happier days you used to do the blurb for a new book of mine. Could you possibly get the most junior of your assistants to do the blurb for this book? If you could, I should be infinitely grateful.' Unwin obliged him.

Fact and Fiction is the next to last collection that Russell made of his essays; it stands seventh in a line beginning with *Philosophical Essays* in 1910. That book, and its immediate successor, *Mysticism and Logic and Other Essays* (1918) are, with one exception, purely philosophical in content. The exception is 'A Free Man's Worship', which is included in both books. By the time he made his next collection in 1928 his transformation into a wide-ranging and popular author was complete. *Sceptical Essays* discusses a delightful mixture of topics, all subjected to that besom of reform, a sceptical wit. *In Praise of Idleness and Other Essays* (1935) reflects Russell's concern with the urgent political perils of the 1930s both on the left and on the right but, following the tradition set by its predecessor, there is a sprinkling of essays with a lighter and sparkling touch. Russell did not collect again until 1950 when he published *Unpopular Essays*, which contains some of his funniest writing, especially that devastating account of human folly called 'An Outline of Intellectual Rubbish'. Mixed amongst these witty put-downs, however, there are serious essays on philosophy and politics and other topics. The sixth member of this set has already been mentioned, namely *Portraits from Memory and Other Essays* (1954), which is the most autobiographical of them all, and reflects his reminiscent mood in the period following the awards of the Order of Merit in 1949 and the Nobel Prize for Literature in 1950, and his eightieth birthday and fourth marriage in 1952, not to mention his lionization by the BBC. But his mood was to change with the increasing world tension, and that change is reflected vividly in this book. Moreover, this mood would dominate for the rest of his life. There would be no more sparkling writing to illuminate the gloom. His last collection, *War Crimes in Vietnam* (1967), is exclusively devoted to its topic; it vividly documents his preoccupation with that war during the last years of his life and the despair he felt about the future.

Fortunately for his readers, there had been brighter days filled with the hope that better times lay ahead. The Victorian belief in progress, although he often disavowed it, was never completely stilled in his breast; it was the engine driving some of his most sparkling writing. He did sincerely believe that his readers had within themselves the ability to turn their lives around, if only he could hit upon the right words to move them. The essays in *Fact and Fiction* engage the intelligence, imagination, and feelings of his readers in yet another attempt to alter their outlook on the world, and for many of them reading him will make a difference in their lives. This would have pleased him.

PART ONE

Books that Influenced Me in Youth[1]

I

The Importance of Shelley

I AM beginning a series of talks on books that influenced me
when I was young—that is to say, broadly speaking, from the
age of fifteen to the age of twenty-one. I have not found in
later years that books were as important to me as they were
when I was first exploring the world and trying to determine
my attitude to it. In those days a book might be a great
adventure, expressing ideas or emotions which one could
absorb and assimilate. In later life one has more or less decided
upon a fundamental outlook that seems congenial and only
something very rare can effect an important change.

But when the great books of the world were new to me,
when I first learnt what had been thought and felt and said by
men who had thought and felt profoundly, there was a great
liberation in the discovery that hopes and dreams and systems
of thought which had remained vague and unexpressed for
lack of sympathy in my environment had been set forth in
clear and shining words by men whom the world acknowledged
to be great. From books I derived courage and hope and
freedom in arduous endeavour.

DESIRE TO UNDERSTAND THE WORLD

In my adolescence, as is not uncommon, a number of very

[1] From a series of talks given in the BBC Overseas Service, 1957.

11

strong emotions jostled each other in my feelings, and in spite of apparent incompatibility none yielded to any of the others. I liked a number of books of very different kinds because I found in them expressions of the different kinds of feelings that tossed me hither and thither on contending waves. I cared for beauty, especially in poetry and in nature. I wanted some kind of vivid hope for the destiny of mankind. I was filled with revolt against what Blake calls 'mind-forged manacles'. Underneath all these emotional attitudes and more compelling than any of them was the desire to understand the world, which I hoped to do as far as was possible by means of mathematics and science.

Here I propose to speak about poetry. My education in this respect had been old fashioned even for that time. When I began reading poetry for myself I was at first somewhat circumscribed by this upbringing. I read Shakespeare and Milton and all Byron's longer poems except *Don Juan*; I read Tennyson, but was repelled by his sentimentality; and then one day I came upon Shelley, whose very name was unknown to me. I took out from a shelf the Golden Treasury volume of selections from Shelley and opened it at *Alastor or the Spirit of Solitude*. I read on and on entranced. Here, I felt, was a kindred spirit, gifted as I never hoped to be with the power of finding words as beautiful as his thoughts.

It was only at a later time that I became interested in Shelley the political rebel; it was Shelley the lyric poet who attracted me. He attracted me as much by what I now consider his weaknesses as by what I still consider his merits. I learnt most of his shorter love-poems by heart, and longed to experience the emotions they expressed even when they were painful. I liked his despair, his isolation, his imaginary landscapes that seemed as unreal as scenery in sunset clouds. He did not offend my intellectual taste by accepting conventional beliefs for which there seemed to be no good evidence.

COMPLETE OUTLOOK OF A ROMANTIC

My friend and collaborator Whitehead, not without some consciousness of paradox, used to praise Shelley for scientific accuracy and cited a line in *Prometheus Unbound* in which Earth says: 'I spin beneath my pyramid of night.' It would not be difficult to find many other instances, but I will give only one, from *Hellas:*

> Worlds on worlds are rolling ever,
> From creation to decay,
> Like the bubbles on a river,
> Sparkling, bursting, borne away.

This might be a poetic paraphrase of any modern scientific treatise on the stars. But what attracted me most to Shelley was what made him a typical romantic, for I myself, in adolescence, had the complete outlook of a romantic. I agreed passionately when he said:

> I love waves and winds and storms,—
> Everything almost
> Which is Nature's and may be
> Untainted by man's misery.

The scenery in *Alastor* I should now feel might be criticized for its vagueness, which is like that of scenery in dreams, but at that time it suited me completely. I liked the 'lone Chorasmian shore', and had no wish to know where it was on the map. One thing that now seems to me somewhat surprising is that like many adolescents I had a very vivid sense of a happy past now lost, and of this I found many expressions in Shelley, such as, 'Like the ghost of a dear friend dead is time long past'. I revelled in his romantic gloom, and welcomed the poetic despair of his little poem called *Time:*

> Unfathomable Sea! whose waves are years,
> Ocean of Time, whose waters of deep woe
> Are brackish with the salt of human tears!

Thou shoreless flood which in thy ebb and flow
Claspest the limits of mortality,
And sick of prey yet howling on for more,
Vomitest thy wrecks on its inhospitable shore!
Treacherous in calm, and terrible in storm,
Who shall put forth on thee,
Unfathomable Sea?

I shuddered with mingled awe and sympathy as I read his sonnet:

Lift not the painted veil which those who live
Call Life: though unreal shapes be pictured there,
And it but mimic all we would believe
With colours idly spread,—behind, lurk Fear
And Hope, twin Destinies, who ever weave
Their shadows o'er the chasm sightless and dread.
I knew one who had lifted it—he sought,
For his lost heart was tender, things to love
But found them not, alas! nor was there aught
The world contains the which he could approve,
Through the unheeding many he did move
A splendour among shadows, a bright blot
Upon this gloomy scene, a spirit that strove
For truth, and like the Preacher found it not.

If I were writing about anybody but myself, I should treat the youthful emotions aroused by this sonnet with kindly sympathy; but as the emotions were mine I will say only that they now seem to me somewhat absurd. I should be unjust to my adolescent self, however, if I were to omit other things that struck me in my reading of Shelley. I noticed the similarity and difference between Shelley's 'The flower that smiles today Tomorrow dies'; and Herrick's 'And this same flower that smiles today, Tomorrow will be dying'. I noticed that although one is tragic and the other gay, the difference is wholly one of rhythm.

As I was already anxious to learn to write well I noted the effect of rhythm in whatever good literature I read, more especially in Milton. It was largely the jingling, mechanical metres of Byron that prevented me from admiring that poet. I loved Shelley for his rhythm as much for his sentiment. It was not only Shelley's despairs that I liked among his sentiments but also his apocalyptic hopes. The vision of a world suddenly transformed when 'the banded anarchs fled' entranced me, and I was enraptured by the chorus at the end of *Hellas*, of which I will quote the first stanza:

> The world's great age begins anew,
> The golden years return,
> The earth doth like a snake renew
> Her winter weeds outworn:
> Heaven smiles, and faiths and empires gleam,
> Like wrecks of a dissolving dream.

I have never quite overcome this point of view. Although I am intellectually convinced that any great improvement in human life must be gradual, I still find my imagination dominated by the hope of a general change of heart.

Shelley dominated my imagination and my affection for many years. When I went to Italy in 1892 my first place of pilgrimage was Casa Magni, where Shelley spent the last months of his life. I loved him not only for the reasons I have already mentioned but also for an extraordinary quality of light, like sunshine after a storm. I have spoken of his landscapes as unreal, but this same quality is to be found in some actual landscapes, especially those on eastern shores of the Atlantic. I have found it in Cornwall, in Connemara, and on the mountains of Skye, and sometimes in north Wales: a magical, transfiguring beauty which seems not of this world but like a glimpse of an imagined heaven. It was this transfiguring quality in Shelley's poetry that I found intoxicating. In this respect, I do not know of any other poet to equal him.

15

Although I have learnt reluctantly to admit some weaknesses in Shelley, he has remained important to me for the purity of his passion, the intensity of his love of beauty, and the scope of his constructive imagination. I wondered in adolescence whether I should have the good fortune to meet someone like him. I still feel that if this had happened it would have been a supreme event in a not uneventful life.

II

The Romance of Revolt

TURGENEV, who will be my subject, had a profound influence upon me in various different ways. Tolstoy and Dostoevsky I did not read until some years later, and although both seem to me now to have more genius than Turgenev had, neither of them ever influenced me greatly. Turgenev was my first contact with anything Russian, and I found his novels at once immensely impressive and immensely attractive. Some of his books excited me as poetic love-stories at a time when I knew of love only through literature. His characters, both those whom he loved and those whom he hated (for he did not pretend to any detachment), seemed to me to be both more interesting and more delicately portrayed than those of English novelists. I read him in German because Mrs Garnett's translation did not yet exist, and his novels impressed me as few books of literature have done.

My grandmother had often spoken to me of some Russian friends in the Russian diplomatic service in Paris who called themselves, and whom she called, Tourgeneff. I asked her whether she knew of the novelist and whether he was related to her friends. She replied that they had mentioned having a cousin who wrote novels, and, indeed, she had once met him and he had given her one of his books, but she had never read it and did not know what sort of books he wrote.

EAGER AND HOPEFUL YOUNG PEOPLE

I found in Turgenev, first of all, a society of eager and hopeful young people such as I could have loved if I had known them, and infinitely more sympathetic to me than any young people whom I knew before I went to Cambridge. They combined hope and indignation in proportions which were entirely congenial to me. They were oppressed or seduced by cynical aristocrats who made me shudder. They attempted heroic tasks, and came to grief heroically. They won my heart and retained it down to the moment of their final defeat by the Bolsheviks.

Romantic rebellion inspired the young and some of the old throughout the generations from 1789 to 1918. Throughout this long period many of the most talented people in every country of Europe and the western hemisphere believed that the cruelties and oppressions existing in many parts of the world were due to small cliques of wicked men against whom, sooner or later, the people would rise in noble wrath and establish a heaven on earth. One generation after another was disappointed, but new crops of young men perpetually took the place of the 'Lost Leaders'.

This long procession of romantic rebels began with the French Revolution. Wordsworth, after he had been disillusioned, recounted the emotions of his youth, which he recollected in very complete tranquillity. They are to be found in the sonnet with the somewhat unpromising beginning: 'Jones! As from Calais southwards you and I went pacing side by side . . .' and more poetically in the well-known lines: 'Bliss was it in that dawn to be alive but to be young was very heaven.' The guillotine and the Reign of Terror obscured in men's memories the hopes inspired by the first years of the French Revolution, but the romantic tradition survived and was kept alive by romantic facts.

18

AMERICA—A LAND OF PROMISE

Tom Paine was preserved from Pitt's minions by the judicious advice of Blake, and embarked at Dover twenty minutes before those who had come to arrest him arrived. He had been elected by Calais as its representative in the Convention and was hailed by the French with a frenzy of acclamation. He survived the hatred of Pitt, Washington, and Robespierre, all of whom wished him dead. But though they failed to kill him they succeeded in killing his hopes.

Nonetheless, America remained a land of promise for lovers of freedom. Even Byron, at a moment when he was disgusted with Napoleon for not committing suicide, wrote an eloquent stanza in praise of Washington. Admiration of America as the land of democracy survived through the greater part of the nineteenth century. Richard Cobden, who was in most respects the opposite of a romantic, cherished illusions about the United States: when admirers presented him with a large sum of money he invested it in the Illinois Central Railroad and lost every penny. When my parents visited America in 1867 it still had for them a halo of romance. This survived even for me through Walt Whitman, whose house was the first place that I visited when I went to America.

But except for Walt Whitman the New World was not the favourite of the poets. In the time of Byron and Shelley Greece was the country that inspired the Muse, and the Turk was the symbol of tyranny. After Greece had won independence it was the turn of Italy. Browning and Swinburne sang the praises of Italian patriotic exiles, of whom Mazzini was the most eminent symbol. It was the abomination of the Neapolitan régime that finally turned Gladstone from a Peelite into a Liberal. Mazzini's history was very typical: he inspired the enthusiasm which created united Italy; but Cavour harnessed this enthusiasm to the House of Savoy, and the result was profoundly disgusting to the man who had done so much to bring it about.

There was nothing peculiar to Italy in this series of events. In one country after another the old régime was overthrown, and the momentum which produced the overthrow was generated and at first led by romantic idealists. Everywhere the régime which emerged from successful revolution was disillusioning to the idealists. But their hopes did not wholly die; they only travelled on to some new land where present oppression was certain and future glory still seemed possible.

When I was young it was the Russian revolutionaries, above all, who were the inheritors of the tradition of romantic revolt. Czarist Russia was viewed with shuddering horror by Liberals throughout the world. The very word 'Siberia' froze their blood. Ever since the Decembrists in 1825 heroic Russians had struggled to overthrow the régime. No Liberal doubted that they would succeed some day and that the result would be a splendid growth of freedom in regions where the human spirit had hitherto been enslaved. I shared these hopes; and I found in Turgenev's books imaginative portraits of the men who were to create the new world.

Political revolutionaries are the subject-matter of *Virgin Soil*, a book by which I was greatly moved. But the best of Turgenev's books, and the one which affected me most, was *Fathers and Children*. The hero of this book, Bazarov, is not much concerned with politics, but is a rebel of every other imaginable sort. He calls himself a Nihilist, a word which Turgenev invented in this book, and which was afterwards universally adopted as a symbol of hope to some and terror to others. Bazarov professes to believe in nothing at all, but has, in fact, a somewhat reluctant belief in science. He is training to be a doctor and tells everybody that medicine is all nonsense, but he works assiduously to acquire all the medical knowledge available. He carries his dislike of humbug and his cult of sincerity to a point which makes him brutal and unfeeling in his conversation even with those who love him deeply. He has a disciple, an aristocratic young man named Arkady, who is amiable and kindly and finds Bazarov's pronouncements delightfully horrifying.

DID TURGENEV BETRAY THE LIBERALS?

When I read the book I read it with the feelings of Arkady. I had grown up in a world in which good manners were regarded as of supreme importance, and in which very grave social evils remained rampant because any mention of them was repugnant to good taste. When Bazarov behaved like a boor, I supposed that this was really very admirable, but in spite of the worst intentions I remained much more like Arkady: I admired ruthlessness but could not bring myself to practise it. Much subsequent experience of Bazarov's imitators has made me more tolerant of politeness than I was when it still held me in a kind of prison. It is natural to groping youth to admire opinions too extreme to command complete agreement.

For example, I admired but did not share Bazarov's ethical destructiveness when he says: 'There are no general principles —you've not made out that even yet! There are feelings. Everything depends on them. I, for instance, take up a negative attitude by virtue of my sensations; I like to deny—my brain's made on that plan, and that's all about it! Why do I like chemistry? Why do you like apples?—by virtue of our sensations. It's all the same thing. Deeper than that men will never penetrate.' When Bazarov begins to get tired of Arkady, he says: 'You're a capital fellow; but you're a sugary, Liberal snob for all that.' I trembled at the thought that Bazarov might consider me a 'sugary, Liberal snob', which I thought very probable. Bazarov dies of blood-poisoning acquired in dissecting a corpse. The grief of his parents, who adore him, is one of the most affecting things that I know in literature.

Turgenev was taken to task by Liberal Russians for representing Bazarov as a typical revolutionary. They said he was a caricature. They said that it was a soft heart and not a hard

21

head that made them revolutionary. They felt that he had betrayed the cause, and attacked him with great bitterness. He defended himself with vigour. I quote from Edward Garnett's introduction to his wife's translation of a passage from a letter of Turgenev to a Russian lady: 'What, you too say that in drawing Bazarov I wished to make a caricature of the young generation. You repeat this—pardon my plain speaking—idiotic reproach. Bazarov, my favourite child, on whose account I quarrelled with Karkoff; Bazarov, on whom I lavished all the colours at my disposal; Bazarov, this man of intellect, this hero, a caricature! But I see it is useless to protest.'

No one at that time foresaw the Russian future with any accuracy, but it must be said that those who emerged victors in the Russian revolution bore more resemblance to Bazarov than to his critics. Perhaps, nevertheless, Bazarov, if he had survived, would have felt about the victors as I did.

III

Revolt in the Abstract

IBSEN, who is the subject of this talk, presents for me a difficulty which did not exist in the cases of Shelley and Turgenev. The difficulty is that I no longer admire him except to a very limited extent, and that it is only by an effort that I can recall what he meant for me at one time. I first heard of him from a friend of my family, a Unitarian minister named Philip Wicksteed, whom I admired for his work on economics.

I next came upon the name of Ibsen through Shaw's laudatory writings on him. The third thing that predisposed me in his favour was a hostile criticism in the *Cambridge Review*, a periodical mainly designed (or so I thought then) to keep dons feeling comfortable. This criticism was brought to my notice by Whitehead who for years afterwards quoted from it with delight a sentence saying: 'Life presents no problems to serious and well-conducted persons.' Given such credentials, I naturally had high hopes of Ibsen's plays.

The moment at which I first saw his plays on the stage helped not a little to deepen the impression which they made upon me. In June, 1893, I had just come of age. I had also just finished the mathematical tripos for which I had been preparing during the previous ten years under a willingly accepted discipline almost as severe as that of an athlete in training, and more prolonged. The two events coming together gave me an exhilarating sense of liberation and a readiness for adventure. Just at this time a number of Ibsen's plays were being acted in London and when I saw them they excited me in a very high degree.

WHEN THE PILLARS OF SOCIETY RAVED

I think, in retrospect, that this was partly due to the leading lady, Elizabeth Robins. Of her, Edmund Gosse wrote at the time: 'Of Miss Robins' impersonation of Hilda (the heroine of *The Master Builder*) there could be no two opinions even among those who disliked the play. The spirit of April laughed and leaped with her; the inconscience, the spontaneity of unreflected youth were rarely presented and sustained with such extraordinary buoyancy.' I expressed my enthusiastic admiration for Elizabeth Robins to a maiden aunt who knew her, but my aunt very prudently did not enable me to meet the lady.

It is not easy at this date to realize the passionate admiration and the passionate hate that Ibsen inspired. All the people who could consider themselves pillars of society raved against Ibsen as immoral, subversive, and anarchical. Their attacks upon him would have sufficed of themselves to put the enthusiastic young on his side. Rebels, as I have come to realize, are never quite emancipated from the people against whom they rebel. Whatever these people have admired they have to decry; whatever these people have decried they have to admire. Their opinions are thus dictated in reverse by their enemies. It only gradually becomes apparent that there is no such simple way of arriving at the truth. To assume that Mr So-and-so is always wrong is almost as bad as it is to assume that he is always right.

IBSEN'S WOMEN—'BRAWNY AND ARROGANT'

This, however, is not what I felt when I was twenty-one. I felt then that anything hated by conventional, middle-aged people must be good. Ibsen's heroines do things which are considered criminal or immoral but are held up by the dramatist as nevertheless worthy of enthusiastic respect. I was very full of rebellion against the subjection of women. I read with delight

Walt Whitman's praise of 'the brawny and arrogant woman I love'; and Ibsen's women seemed to approximate to this type. Conventional morality, I thought, is very apt to be wrong; these women sin against conventional morality; therefore they are probably right.

Put in such terms this outlook seems almost unbelievably simple minded, but it was in those days very widespread. I re-read some of his plays, among them *Hedda Gabler*, for purposes of this talk, and found the heroine of that play absolutely intolerable, a heartless, intriguing, over-sexed snob. But it was in common with many other people that I thought otherwise at the time. Hedda Gabler goes everywhere with pistols, and finally shoots herself with one of them. I knew a lady who did exactly that, chiefly I think through an imitative impulse. Before she reached this disastrous climax I had entirely ceased to admire Hedda. But when I first saw the play acted I thought her a noble, courageous rebel, thinking, feeling, and acting freely out of her own impulses, not slavishly in obedience to the herd.

Ibsen has certain clichés which I now find tiresome. Whenever any character—a drunkard, a forger, or a prostitute—infringes conventional morality somebody in the play is sure to remark that he, or she, has had the courage to live his, or her, life in his, or her, way. This is all very fine if it is seen as the rare exception in a stable society. But when it is regarded as a general rule for everybody to follow it leads either to disaster or to the establishment of a tyranny in which only a few people at the top can, in Ibsen's words, live their own life in their own way.

Ibsen is a somewhat belated romantic and shares with the romantics both what is true and what is false in their outlook. There are two extreme views as to how human life should be lived, neither of which can be accepted in its entirety. You may think of it as a minuet in which a certain ordered pattern is produced by rigid adherence to rule and spontaneous impulse has no place; or you may think of it as a witch dance in a Voodoo incantation in which excitement is stimulated until it issues in atrocious cruelty. The former suits the classicist; the latter, the romantic. Neither is quite adequate. The classical outlook produces the rebel. The romantic outlook, when it is widespread, necessarily generates the tyrant.

The cruelty inherent in the romantic outlook is quite evident in Ibsen's plays. Rebecca West drives an unfortunate lady to suicide. Hedda Gabler, from jealousy, drives a reformed dipsomaniac back to his former failing and destroys the manuscript of the book which he has written while reformed. Hedda Gabler holds up to the contempt of everybody her well-intentioned, hard-working husband, whose sole defect is that Providence has not provided him with first-rate wits. Helda Wangel, finding that the master builder grows dizzy at great heights and therefore always avoids them, persuades him by taunts to climb to the top of a tower from which he falls to his death while she exults in this proof of her power over him.

Ibsen's ethic is essentially the same as Nietzsche's. He seems to think that the superman (who is, as in Shaw, usually a woman) is so much more splendid than the average run of human beings as to have no duties whatever towards them and to have the right to bring them to destruction in the pursuit of what is considered to be heroic passion. The outcome must inevitably be a régime of Nazi despotism and cruelty. Everyone will struggle to be the superman and will be deterred by nothing but superior force or cunning on the part of some other claimant for this exciting role.

CONTEMPT FOR WELL-CONDUCTED PERSONS

All this was not foreseen sixty years ago by those who were dissatisfied with things as they were. 'Serious and well-conducted persons' roused our contempt both because they were dull and because most of them upheld everything bad that was established. Those of us who made fun of them failed to realize that they also upheld some very essential good things which we took for granted and therefore thought unexciting. Most people in an ordered community have never committed a murder. Most people have not made false accusations against their parents who consequently perished miserably in concentration camps. Most people have not built lethal chambers in which they have exterminated millions of innocent victims. Most people have not driven large sections of mankind to the brink of insanity by hunger and cold and misery and terror. To have abstained from such acts is not to have reached a very high level of virtue, but to have committed them is to have reached a very high level of wickedness.

We have seen the influential part of whole populations guilty of this high level of wickedness, and the spectacle has compelled us to feel respect for the humbler, everyday merits which Ibsen and Nietzsche despised. The brute in man lies nearer to the surface than we used to think. There is a strange excitement in yielding to what Baudelaire calls the nostalgia of the slime; and the faster we fall the more persuaded we become that we are rising. All these dangers are implicit in the romantic outlook because it values strong feelings without regard to whether the feelings are good or bad. The homicidal maniac, one must suppose, has strong feelings, but we do not on that account admire him. If you love your neighbour it is well to love him strongly; but if you hate him it is less bad to hate him weakly.

But Ibsen is not merely a preacher of bad morals: he is also a creator of good drama. The best of his plays are admirably constructed and very exciting—more so on the stage than one would know from reading them. He has the art of letting past events become gradually known as the action proceeds. But I do not think that he reaches quite the first rank even as a pure dramatist. His characters, like Shaw's, tend to be embodied arguments or points of view, not rounded individuals with all

27

the little, irrelevant peculiarities that help to make real people endearing or hateful. They are dry like tinder, not full of sap like living trees. For this reason I find now that their joys and sorrows do not move me as do those portrayed by the greatest writers; and this, I suppose, is the reason why, now that his crusades are outmoded, his works are sinking into oblivion.

I am not sure how far this criticism is valid in regard to his verse dramas, *Brandt* and *Peer Gynt*. *Brandt* especially has passages of terrifying sublimity in which the howling wind of the dark, Arctic night seems to penetrate to the very soul. *Brandt* still seems to me worthy to be remembered.

IV

Disgust and Its Antidote

IT IS, I imagine, common in youth to feel in quick succession a number of different attitudes towards life and the world, and to feel each in turn as strongly as if it had no competitors. I loved the imagined beauty that I found in Shelley; I rejoiced in the ardent revolutionaries portrayed by Turgenev; and I was excited by the bold voyages of adventure that made the subject-matter of Ibsen's plays. All these in their various ways satisfied optimistic moods; but I had other moods for which quite different literature found expression, moods of despair, disgust, hatred, and contempt. I never gave wholehearted assent to these moods, but I was glad when I found in literature anything that seemed to sanction them.

I read in adolescence a great deal of Carlyle. I thought his positive doctrines foolish, but his virulent denunciations delighted me. I enjoyed it when he described the population of England as 'twenty-seven millions, mostly fools'. I was delighted by his remark: 'Fancy that thou deservest to be hanged (as is most likely), thou wilt feel it happiness to be only shot!' But I came to feel that his attitude to life and mankind was peevish rather than tragic. It was not in his writings but in *King Lear* that I found the fullest satisfaction for black moods.

EARLY PREFERENCE FOR 'KING LEAR'

At that time I preferred *King Lear* to all the rest of Shakespeare, even to *Hamlet,* and it was because of its vast cosmic despair

that I liked it. 'When we are born, we cry that we are come
To this great stage of fools.' This seemed to me at moments
to express ultimate wisdom. I liked, also: 'As flies to wanton
boys, are we to the gods; They kill us for their sport.' There
was a kind of bitter satisfaction in imagining that the tortures
human beings endure give pleasure to the gods and are therefore not wholly purposeless. I revelled in Lear's comment when
he and Kent and the Fool meet Edgar, naked, in the storm:
'Ha! here's three on's are sophisticated; thou are the thing
itself; unaccommodated man is no more but such a poor, bare,
forked animal as thou art. Off, off, you lendings! Come;
unbutton here.'

I exulted in the heroic magnificence of Lear's defiance of
the storm:

> Blow, winds, and crack your cheeks! rage! blow!
> You cataracts and hurricanoes, spout
> Till you have drench'd our steeples, drown'd the cocks!
> You sulphurous and thought-executing fires,
> Vaunt-couriers to oak-cleaving thunderbolts,
> Singe my white head! And thou, all-shaking thunder,
> Strike flat the thick rotundity o' the world!
> Crack nature's moulds, all germens spill at once
> That make ingrateful man!

Lear's speeches in the scenes on the heath make the romanticism
of the romantics seem thin and paltry by comparison. There is,
however, a more fundamental difference: the romantics believed
it all, whereas Shakespeare put it in the mouth of a man going
mad.

THEN FOR 'GULLIVER'S TRAVELS'

On a lower plane of tragedy I enjoyed King Lear's subversive
sentiments, such as 'Through tattered clothes small vices do
appear, Robes and furred gowns hide all'. I liked, too, his
comment on bureaucracy: 'Thou hast seen a farmer's dog bark

at a beggar?' 'Ay, Sir.' 'And the creature run from the cur? There thou might'st behold the great image of authority; a dog's obey'd in office.' In the same scene King Lear makes a pleasant remark about the perspicacity of statesmen: 'Get thee glass eyes; And, like a scurvy politician, seem To see the things thou dost not.'

But in *King Lear*, even in the blackest and most despairing passages, there is a redeeming sublimity. One feels in reading that, though life may be bad and the world full of unmerited suffering, yet there is in man a capacity of greatness and occasional splendour which makes ultimate and complete despair impossible. It was not in Shakespeare but in Swift that I found the expression of the ultimate and complete despair.

It was largely by accident that I came to read Swift. The room that was my schoolroom had been my grandfather's library. The shelves were filled with great tomes, but I was solemnly warned not to read them. This had the effect which ought to have been anticipated but was not. Among the tomes that I took down from the shelves was an unexpurgated Swift. I read first *The Tale of a Tub*, which delighted me because it treated theological controversies with a flippancy of which nowadays not even the most arrant free-thinker would dare to be guilty. I then went on to *Gulliver's Travels*, a book which has had the curious fate of being regarded as one for the amusement of children, although it is the most biting and devastating and completely black of all the satires ever penned by embittered men.

The account of Laputa is an early example of science fiction; not, by any means, the first, since it had been anticipated, for example, by Francis Godwin and Cyrano de Bergerac. But it is, I think, the first to represent a scientific community in the manner familiarized for our generation by Huxley's *Brave New World*. Other writers, until nearly our own day, had thought of science optimistically as a liberator. Swift was, I believe, the first to think of it as affording a means of ruthless tyranny.

I imbibed this point of view at the age of fifteen, and it left
my imagination well prepared for the shock of nuclear bombs.
I realized then, and have remembered ever since, that science
in itself is ethically neutral. It confers power, but for evil just
as much as for good. It is to feeling not to knowledge that we
must appeal if science is to be beneficent. Laputa showed me
the possibility of scientific horrors and made me realize that,
however scientific, they remain horrors. Abominations are
abominations even if the utmost skill is required to contrive
them.

But it was, above all, the Yahoos that impressed me. I read
with growing horror the skilful pages in which the reader
is gradually enticed into the belief that the Yahoos are just
ordinary human beings, ending with the appalling climax in
which on Gulliver's return home he shrinks from his wife in
horror because he sees her as a Yahoo. In the land of the
Houyhnhnms, where horses are rational and lord it over the
rest of the animal kingdom as men do with us, there are hordes
of wild and horrid creatures, human in form and called Yahoos,
who are regarded by the Houyhnhnms much as we regard
hyenas. Gulliver at first is viewed with suspicion by the wise
horses, but in the end they admit that he has some glimmerings
of reason and virtue, and they consent to listen to his account
of the world from which he has come.

The Houyhnhnms have, of course, all those merits which
Swift believes that he would like men to possess, while the
Yahoos have in a supreme degree all the demerits which his
spleen inclines him to find among human beings. It does not
occur to the reader at first to think of the Yahoos, in spite of
their human shape, as like the people that he knows. It is only
Swift's diabolical skill that insinuates this horrid idea into his
disgusted mind. This terrible indictment had a profound effect
upon me, and it was only with an effort that I shook off its
paralysing influence.

AND SO TO THE ANTIDOTE

I found the antidote to Swift in a place which may, perhaps, seem surprising: I found it in Milton's prose. I did not fail to appreciate his verse—indeed, at that time I learnt a great deal of it by heart—but in his verse it was not the philosophy that pleased me: it was more purely poetic merits such as those of diction and metre. The philosophy left me unmoved: *Paradise Lost* did not diminish my taste for eating apples. But in his prose at its best I found not only splendid writing from the purely literary point of view but also doctrines that were wide and free and ennobling. I had known the sonnet beginning, 'Avenge, O Lord, Thy slaughtered saints, whose bones Lie scattered on the Alpine mountains cold'. But I had not known until I read his prose works that in his capacity of Foreign Secretary he sent paraphrases of this sonnet to many of the governments of Europe. Never since that time has the Foreign Office spoken in such accents.

But, above all, I admired the *Areopagitica*. I treasured such sentences as: 'As good almost kill a man as kill a good book: who kills a man kills a reasonable creature, God's image; but he who destroys a good book, kills reason itself.' This was an inspiring sentiment for an intending writer who devoutly hoped that his books would be 'good books'. And more especially encouraging to a budding philosopher was the statement: 'Where there is much desire to learn, there of necessity will be much arguing, much writing, many opinions; for opinion in good men is but knowledge in the making.' This might almost be taken as the sacred text for free speech and free discussion. 'Opinion in good men is but knowledge in the making', says in few words what is essential for the condemnation of censorship. Alas, I did not know in those days that to cure Milton of opposing censorship they made him a censor. This is the almost invariable logic of revolutions: while in the making they praise liberty; but when successful they establish tyranny.

But it was not only the justice of Milton's opinions that I valued: it was also, and more especially, the pomp and majesty of his finest passages. Though they are very well known I cannot refrain from quoting two sentences which inspired me then and which I still cannot read without intense emotion: 'Methinks I see in my mind a noble and puissant nation rousing herself like a strong man after sleep, and shaking her invincible locks. Methinks I see her as an eagle mewing her mighty youth, and kindling her undazzled eyes at the full mid-day beams.' In spite of growing blindness Milton was happy while he could so feel about England. For the time his hopes ended in disappointment, but something shining and noble descended from them to later generations.

V

An Education in History

HISTORY, or at least English history, was part of my education
from a very early age. Constitutional history especially was
implanted in me before I was ten years old. The instruction
that I had in this subject was unadulterated indoctrination with
as little attempt at impartiality as under any totalitarian régime.
Everything was treated from a Whig point of view, and I was
told, only half in joke, that history means 'hiss-Tory'. There
was a simple rule for deciding who was right; in a quarrel
between Church and King one sided with the King, except in
the case of the seven bishops prosecuted by James II; when
the King had a dispute with anybody other than the Church
one took the side against the King.

Parliament was always glorified, and its powers in early
times were exaggerated. For instance, I was told that in the
wars of the Roses one should side with the Lancasters because
their claim was derived from Parliamentary sanction, whereas
the claim of the Yorkists was merely dynastic. I was taught as
a matter of course that the Americans were right in the war of
independence, and although I was allowed a childish pleasure
in the victories of Trafalgar and Waterloo I was told to
deplore the British Empire and to abhor the makers of the
Afghan and Zulu wars which occurred when I was beginning to
be politically conscious.

CHARLES II BEHEADS THE FAMILY HERO

From the time of Henry VIII onward English history came to me as bound up with the history of my family. This was especially the case as regards the conflict with the Stuarts. My ancestor whose head was cut off by Charles II was the family hero, whose life my grandfather had written. History, as I was taught to think of it, ended in 1815. After that one knew of it from those who had taken part in it and not from books. My grandfather, who had been in Parliament since 1813, and whom I remember as continually reading Hansard, made the whole nineteenth century personal and lively to me. Great events had not the impersonal and remote quality that they have in the books of historians. Throughout the nineteenth century these events intimately concerned people whom I knew, and it seemed to me a matter of course that one should play some part in the progress of mankind.

The vast democratic nations of our time have generated an unfortunate sense of individual impotence in the majority of their citizens. This sense of individual impotence was totally absent in my upbringing. I believed in my very bones, hardly consciously but all the more profoundly, that one should aim at great achievement in the full conviction that such achievement is possible.

The time came, however, when I began to read history on my own account, and when this happened my reading was largely guided by the accident of what I found on the shelves. My bedroom had been treated as a cemetery for books which no one would wish to disinter. I studied their titles but never looked inside them. They were an odd collection: Sugden on *The Law of Property*, Cox's *Pelham Administration* (Pelham, I thought, was an adjective), *The Scottish Nation* (in three volumes), *The Dispatches of Field Marshal the Duke of Wellington, K.G.*, and (a totally mysterious item) Mohan Lal's *Life of Dost Mohammad Khan*. All these books remained dark to me, but the books in my schoolroom were more hopeful. There were *The Annals of Ireland* by the Four Masters, from which I learnt about the people who went to Ireland before the Flood and perished in that cataclysm.

There was a book called *Irish Pedigrees* which gave the genealogy of the British Royal Family all the way to Adam. The genealogy went by way of Robert Bruce, and as my own genealogy up to Robert Bruce was known I felt this adequate as a prop to self-importance. Then there was *L'Art de Vérifier les Dates* in two enormous volumes. For years I supposed that this book contained something like the tables for finding Easter at the beginning of the Prayer Book. At last, when I grew big enough to support the weight, I took one of the volumes out of the shelf and found that the only art consisted of looking up the date in the book.

I read with delight a book then famous though now forgotten: Buckle's *History of Civilization*. I liked in this book the emphasis on the influence of climate, not because I especially believed in this theory but because it suggested to me the possibility of scientific treatment of history. I contemplated with a certain reverence a sixteenth-century edition of Guicciardini, and I read large parts of the works of Machiavelli. I sought out eagerly books dealing with the conflict between theology and science. There was one such book that especially roused my enthusiasm: it was Draper's *Intellectual Development of Europe*. From this I was led on to an interest in ecclesiastical history: I studied Dean Milman's *History of Christianity*.

But all my previous reading of history was eclipsed when at last I came to Gibbon, whose many volumes I read and re-read while still adolescent. Gibbon had many merits in my eyes, both great and small. To begin with the minor merits, his narrative was interesting, his jokes were amusing, and his characters were often very queer. For instance, in dealing with the sixth century he speaks of 'the polished tyrants of Africa', and my imagination played round the question as to what sort of people these were.

To come to more important matters, I was immensely interested by his account of œcumenical councils and theological disputes from the time of Constantine to the time of Justinian. It seemed to me then strange that whole populations should have passionate party feeling on minute points of theological doctrine. This now seems less strange, since we have been educated by Stalin's metaphysical niceties on the subject of dialectical materialism. Gibbon's greatest merit, however, of which I am now even more aware than I was in youth, is his capacity for presenting world history as a stately procession in which one sees as on a stage the 'sages of Greece and Rome' swept away for a time by a tide of barbarism but gradually recovering their influence on the minds of men and giving rise to the highly civilized prose and periwigs of the eighteenth century. I could imagine in those days that the victory of culture over barbarian hordes had been achieved once for all. Subsequent events, however, have made this seem much less certain.

Already in youth I felt an interest, which has remained with me, in solitary outposts of civilization, and men or groups who were isolated in an alien world. I did not then have the knowledge that I have since acquired about such matters, but I already wished to have it. This interest has led me in later years to read about the Bactrian Greeks, separated from the mother-country by deserts and alien monarchies, losing gradually most of their Hellenism, and finally subdued by less civilized neighbours, but passing on as they faded away some part of the cultural heritage of Greece in the Buddhist sculpture which they inspired.

I contemplated with vivid interest the civilization of Ireland that was destroyed by the Danes. This civilization, which was created by refugees from the barbarian invasions of the fifth and sixth centuries, kept alive in one corner of the extreme West the knowledge of the Greek language and of Greek philosophy, which elsewhere in the West had become extinct;

and when at last the Danes began their destructive inroads France was ready to accept the heritage at the hands of John the Scot.

I liked to think of St Boniface and St Virgilius, two holy men engaged in the endeavour to convert the Germans, meeting in the depths of the Teutonic forest, glad for a moment of each other's society but quarrelling desperately on the question whether there are inhabited worlds other than our own. I liked to think of the last lingering remnant of pagan antiquity among the aristocratic families of Rome, and of how their outlook, as expressed by Boethius, conquered the Catholic world owing to the accident of his being put to death by the Arian heretic, Theodoric.

INDESTRUCTIBILITY OF CULTURAL VALUES

From such contemplations I derived a belief in the indestructibility of certain things which I valued above all others, the things which make up our cultural heritage, and which have as yet persisted through all the various disasters from the time when the Minoan civilization was destroyed until our own day. I valued above all the gradually increasing power of intellect and knowledge, beginning in the tiny city-states of Greece, spread by Alexander throughout the Middle East, handed on by Alexandria to the Arabs, passed on by them to western Europe—and more especially, to Spain and Italy—and, when those countries were condemned to intellectual death by the Inquisition, acquired new life in France and Holland and England.

The love of free inquiry and free speculation has never been common. When it has existed, it has existed in only a tiny minority and has always roused furious hatred and opposition in the majority. There have been times when it has seemed wholly extinct, but over and over again it has revived. Although the life that it inspires is arduous and dangerous the

impulse which leads some men to adopt it has been so overwhelming that they have braved all the obloquy to which they
were exposed by devoting themselves to the greatest service
that man can do to man.

It is this indomitable quality of the human mind at its best
that gives hope for mankind, and that causes me in spite of
the unprecedented dangers of our age to believe that the
human race will emerge as it has emerged from other dark
times with renewed vigour and with a more confident and
triumphant hope of overcoming not only the hostile forces of
nature but also the black nightmares inspired by atavistic fears
which have caused men, and still cause them, to create and
endure great worlds of sorrow and suffering for which there is
no longer any reason except in human folly. We know as never
before the road to a happy world. We have only to choose
this road to lead our tortured species into a land of light
and joy.

VI

The Pursuit of Truth

THROUGHOUT the early period of my life almost all my serious working time was devoted to mathematics. I supposed in those days that I was more interested in the application of mathematics to the explanation of natural phenomena than in pure mathematics for its own sake. This emphasis changed with time, and it was the purest of pure mathematics that finally claimed me. This change had various causes but one of the most important was a desire to refute Kant, whose theory of space and time as *a priori* intuitions seemed to me horrid. All this, however, belongs to a later date, and so do the revolutionary discoveries and theories which distinguished the physics of our century from the physics of Newton and his successors.

All these great discoveries and theories came after my formal education was completed. Faraday and Maxwell, it is true, had laid the foundations for one part of the advance beyond Newton, but I did not read their work until I had finished with Triposes. The first modern advance that I found exciting was Hertz's experimental manufacture of electro-magnetic waves, from which wireless and broadcasting sprang. The next exciting event was Becquerel's discovery of radio-activity. Then came Planck's discovery of the quantum; and next Einstein's special theory of relativity. All these revolutionary events occurred within about a decade. Theoretical physics has remained ever since immensely exciting and important. When I was learning

41

mathematics it had not this character but was still statuesquely Newtonian.

THE STIMULUS OF MATHEMATICS

What delighted me about mathematics was that things could be proved. The pleasure that I derived from demonstrations burst upon me as a new kind of joy when I began Euclid—for in those days one learnt geometry from Euclid himself and not from modern adaptations. It is true that Euclid was in some respects disappointing. Some of his axioms seemed questionable, and a good deal of his reasoning was rather slipshod; but these defects appeared to me remediable and did not destroy my belief that it is possible to rear an indestructible edifice of deductive reasoning. When I was fourteen I had a tutor who told me about non-Euclidean geometry, and although I did not study it until some eight years later it remained as a stimulus to my imagination, and as something which I would investigate as soon as I had time. It was, in fact, the subject of my first serious original work. Meantime I read with enthusiasm W. K. Clifford's *Common Sense of the Exact Sciences*, which I still think an admirable book for a budding mathematician.

It was, I repeat, above all the application of mathematics to the real world that I found exciting. Newton's *Principia*, in a three-volume Latin edition of 1760, was on the shelves. I pulled it out and read his deduction of Kepler's laws from the law of gravitation. The beauty and clarity and force of his reasoning affected me in the same kind of way as the greatest music. Tremors ran up and down my backbone, and I rejoiced in having become acquainted with anything so splendid.

From Newton I proceeded in my thoughts to theories very like those of the French mathematicians and philosophers of the eighteenth century. Within the Newtonian dynamics there were two possible pictures of the material world. There was the billiard-ball picture, according to which matter consists of little hard atoms that bump into each other and behave when they collide as billiard balls behave. This doctrine became plausible with Dalton's atomic theory. But there was another possible view, influentially advocated by the philosopher Boscovitch. This might be called the centres-of-force theory. According to this theory every little bit of matter exerted forces of attraction or repulsion upon other bits without touching them, in the kind of way in which the sun attracts the planets.

Both these theories, as we now know, were immeasurably simpler than the truth. The physical world, as our century has discovered, behaves in all sorts of complicated ways that the eighteenth century never suspected, and of which I also, as a boy, had no inkling. I thought then that it should be possible, given enough facts and enough mathematical skill, to calculate all the movements of matter throughout the whole of the past and the future, and I supposed that this must be true also of the motions of living matter, and that the movements of a man's lips and tongue when he speaks must be calculable consequences of the distribution of matter in the primitive nebula.

This hypothesis, of course, disposed of free will and involved a rigid determinism. As to this, I had a twofold emotional attitude: when I thought of the delights of mathematics and of the magnificent possibilities of scientific prediction I found the deterministic theory exhilarating, and this exhilaration was promoted by my reading of Newton and Newtonian dynamics; but when I thought in more human terms, and realized its apparently devastating consequences as regards virtue and vice and the traditional importance of human effort, I found determinism depressing and searched for some way of escape from its rigidity.

This conflict was partly resolved for me, though in a way which I no longer think valid, when I read Spinoza's *Ethics*. Spinoza allayed my suspicion of sentiment by his geometrical method. The apparatus of definitions, axioms, and demonstrated propositions lulled my doubts to sleep. The rigid determinism of his system allowed me to think that there was nothing in him that the most austere scientific rigour need view with distrust. And yet despite all this he arrived in the end at a degree of ethical sublimity which I found unequalled in those who advocated free will for the sake of morals. I still feel that Spinoza was a very great man, whose life was consistent with his belief, and was lived always in a profoundly admirable manner. Morally he still stands for me where he did, but intellectually, in spite of his parade of mathematical cogency, I find his doctrines almost wholly unsatisfactory.

There were even in adolescence some limitations of my unduly mathematical outlook upon the world. I read Mill's *Logic*, and derived without complete agreement a view (not exactly like his) that induction is what is important, and that deduction is little more than an idle amusement of the Schoolmen. I began to give due weight to the obvious fact that deduction is powerless without major premisses, and that its major premisses must therefore have some independent source. I could not accept the theory that the necessary major premisses were supplied by *a priori* intuitions; but I was equally unable to believe Mill's contention that it is induction from experience which persuades us that two and two are four. This dilemma left me in a perplexity which lasted for many years. Indeed, it was the endeavour to resolve this perplexity that led to the attempt to reconcile empiricism and pure mathematics which had been at war with each other ever since the time of Leibniz and Locke. All this, however, belongs to a later date. While still full of uncertainties I became subjected at Cambridge to the assault of German idealism, from which I extricated myself slowly and with much difficulty.

Throughout my adolescent years, as I have suggested, I was torn by a severe conflict between two opposite sets of emotions: on the one side were the emotions connected with mathematics and mathematical physics, which were by no means wholly intellectual; I was also entirely convinced of the benefits to mankind to be derived from science. What may be called the technological view of the road to human welfare was bound up in my mind with science and mathematics, and I did not at that time feel its limitations as acutely as at a later period. I could in some moods contemplate with pleasure a world in which machines did all the work, and food was produced by chemistry, and wise men were built on the pattern of the philosophers of Laputa.

CLAIMS UPON MY ALLEGIANCE

But as against these moods, side by side and wholly unreconciled, were the enthusiasms of which I have spoken in previous talks; and there was a hankering to retain as much as possible of orthodox religious beliefs. I had, as a matter of course, a much closer acquaintance with the Bible than is common among the young nowadays. Beauty, especially beauty in nature, caused me at times to lean towards pantheism. What made things difficult was that these two opposing trends in my thinking and feeling were almost equally passionate and made almost equal claims upon my allegiance. The claims, however, were not quite equal. I resolved from the beginning of my quest that I would not be misled by sentiment and desire into beliefs for which there was no good evidence.

The world is still full of people who when they feel a sentiment that they themselves judge to be beautiful or noble are persuaded that it must find some echo in the cosmos. They suppose that what seems to them to be ethical sublimity cannot be causally unimportant. The indifference to human joys and sorrows which seems to characterize the physical world must, they believe, be an illusion; and they fancy that the painfulness of certain beliefs is evidence of their falsehood. This way of looking at things seemed in youth, and still seems to me, an unworthy evasion.

45

This is recognized where simple matters of fact are concerned. If you are told that you are suffering from cancer, you accept medical opinion with what fortitude you may, although the pain involved to yourself is greater than that which would be caused to you by an uncomfortable metaphysical theory. But where traditional beliefs about the universe are concerned the craven fears inspired by doubt are considered praiseworthy, while intellectual courage, unlike courage in battle, is regarded as unfeeling and materialistic. There is, perhaps, less of this attitude than there was in Victorian days, but there is still a great deal of it, and it still inspires vast systems of thought which have their root in unworthy fears. I cannot believe—and I say this with all the emphasis of which I am capable—that there can ever be any good excuse for refusing to face the evidence in favour of something unwelcome. It is not by delusion, however exalted, that mankind can prosper, but only by unswerving courage in the pursuit of truth.

PART TWO

Politics and Education

I

What is Freedom?[1]

(1) NATIONAL FREEDOM—FREEDOM OF THE GROUP—
INDIVIDUAL FREEDOM

THERE ARE many kinds of freedom. Of some the world has
too little and of others it has too much. But in saying that there
can be too much of any sort of freedom I must hasten to add
that the only kind of freedom which is undesirable is that which
diminishes the freedom of others, for example the freedom to
make slaves.

The world cannot secure the greatest possible amount of
freedom by merely instituting anarchy, for then the strong will
be able to deprive the weak of freedom. I doubt whether any
social institution is justifiable if it diminishes the total amount
of freedom in the world, but many social institutions are justifiable in spite of the fact that they curtail the freedom of some
individual or group.

In its most elementary sense freedom means the absence of
external control over the acts of individuals or groups. It is thus
a negative conception, and freedom alone will not confer any
high value upon a community. The Eskimos, for example, can
dispense with government, with compulsory education, with
traffic regulations, and with the incredible complications of

[1] Originally appeared as a Background Book, by the Batchworth Press,
1952 (revised 1960).

company law. Their life, therefore, has a very high degree of freedom, but nevertheless few civilized men would prefer it to life in a more organized community.

Freedom is a requisite for many kinds of good things; but the good things have to come from the impulses, desires, and beliefs of those who enjoy the freedom. Great poets confer lustre upon a community, but one cannot be sure that a community will produce great poetry merely because there is no law against it. We think it right to compel the young to learn reading and writing though most of them would much rather not. This is because we believe in positive goods which only literacy makes possible. But, although liberty does not constitute the total of social goods, it is so necessary for most of them and so liable to be unwisely curtailed that it is scarcely possible to exaggerate its importance.

National Freedom

There are various kinds of freedom, and at least two different forms of classification of these kinds. First, freedoms may be classified according as they are enjoyed by a nation, a group within a nation, or an individual. And secondly, they may be classified according as they are economic, political, or mental, though this latter division can never be made very sharp.

In the eighteenth and early nineteenth centuries, it was especially national freedom that was emphasized. When it was said that 'Britons never shall be slaves' what was meant was that they should not be under the orders of foreigners. It was not thought that the press gang, for example, interfered with freedom, or that there was any inconsistency in speaking of England as a free country at a time when men were liable to be transported for radical opinions.

It may even be freedom from freedoms which is especially desirable. When Eire acquired freedom, one of the advantages sought and obtained was extinction of the freedom to read books disliked by the Roman Catholic Church—a kind of freedom which the brutal English had insisted upon inflicting upon Ireland.

National freedom will always be energetically sought wherever it does not exist. It is, at present, a dominant aim in North Africa and in those parts of Asia where it has not yet been achieved. The desire for it is so vehement that there is sure to be dangerous unrest wherever one nation attempts to govern another.

It does not follow, although many people seem to think that it does, that a nation should be subject to no control whatever. In so far as nations form an international community, individual nations need the control of law just as individual persons do in a national community. There is as much difference between imperialism and international control as there is between slavery and the control of the criminal law. In the reaction against imperialism, nations which emancipate themselves from the control of a single imperialistic power are apt to make a claim for complete independence of all control which can only be justified on principles which lead straight to anarchism.

It must be said that the great Powers are almost equally to blame. They tend to favour an international authority only so long as they feel sure of dominating it, and they thus make it appear as merely a disguised prolongation of the old imperialism. The problems which are daily becoming more acute in Asia and in Africa require for their solution the general acceptance of a point of view which, so far, has not commended itself either to the great Powers or to the smaller ones.

Take, for example, the question of the Suez Canal: there was no reason why it should be controlled by the British, but there is also no reason why a waterway of such international importance should be controlled by those who happen to live in its neighbourhood. You might just as well say that people who live near a great main road should have a right to erect obstacles upon it whenever they feel so disposed. It is obvious that in reason the Suez Canal should be controlled by an international authority. It is equally obvious that the Panama Canal should be so controlled. In a just system, while the Egyptians would share power over the Suez Canal, they would acquire in return a share of power over the Panama Canal. I do not see such a proposal winning acceptance at the present time, but until it does the Egyptian case can not be fully answered.

Freedom of the Group

Freedom for subordinate groups within a nation raises difficult problems. If the group is geographically concentrated, the matter can be dealt with by devolution within a federal authority. But if the group is scattered this solution is impossible.

Many of the fights for liberty have been concerned with such groups, first with religious communities, then with trade unions, monopolies, trusts, etc. It used to be held that capitalists ought to be free to combine but wage-earners ought not. Now, the opposite view is apt to prevail. Neither is logical and each is only advocated as part of the class struggle.

Rousseau condemned all freedom for subordinate groups since he held that it interfered with loyalty to the State. Totalitarian countries take the same view. In Russia, although trade unions exist in name, they are merely government departments. There is no such thing as the right to strike, and any collective demand for higher wages is practically impossible. In Western countries, on the contrary, trade unions gradually won freedom and have become almost independent powers. It is clear that the power of a trade union, like that of a sovereign State, ought to be subject to certain limitations, but it is now generally conceded in the West that the freedom to form such groups as trade unions and to permit them a wide range of collective activities is an essential part of what we mean by freedom. Western trade unionists who are Communists or fellow travellers would find life unbearable if their unions were as restricted as in Russia.

Throughout the Western world an acute question has arisen as to freedom for groups of which the purpose is to destroy freedom.

Should democracy tolerate attempts to replace it by despotism?

Should toleration extend to those who advocate intolerance?

Should freedom of the Press extend to those who think a free Press an abomination?

And, above all, should a nation permit the formation of powerful groups which aim at subjecting it to foreign domination?

Western nations have given a variety of answers to these questions. Some have allowed more liberty, others less. I do not think there is any clear principle by which such questions can be decided. Broadly speaking, the greater the danger from such subversive groups, the more justification there is for interfering with their activities. The danger is that frightened men will forget the general arguments in favour of liberty and will carry suppression much farther than is necessary in the interests of security. I think that in Britain we have to a great extent avoided this danger. I do not think that it has been avoided in the United States. But since the matter is one in which arguments *pro* and *con* have to be balanced, it is difficult to advocate any clear-cut policy.

Individual Freedom

Freedom for individuals as opposed to groups was formerly the most important part of freedom. But in the modern world very few individuals can have much influence except as members of organizations, and therefore the question of freedom for organizations is becoming more important than that of freedom for individuals.

In the late eighteenth century many men believed in the Rights of Man, meaning individual man, but did not favour the rights of organizations in cases where these organizations had a purpose running contrary to that of the government or majority.

Although freedom for individuals is now relatively less important than it was in former times, it is still much more important than many people realize. Buddhism, Christianity, and Marxism owe their origin to individuals, and no one of them could have arisen in a totalitarian State. Galileo was ill-treated by the Inquisition, but half-heartedly as compared to modern methods. He was not put to death, his books were not burned, and his followers were not liquidated.

It is only in quite modern times, indeed only since the end of the First World War, that persecution has become scientific and effective.

The harm done by persecution of individuals whose views are unpopular is that every progress, whether moral or intellectual, is at first considered shocking. For this reason, a society which cannot put up with unusual opinions necessarily becomes stereotyped and unprogressive.

Suppose, for example, you hold that if a husband and wife hate each other there is no great gain to mankind in perpetuating the legal tie, and divorce by mutual consent ought to be possible. Or suppose you hold that a pregnant woman who, in the best medical opinion, is almost sure to die if her pregnancy is not interrupted, should not be forced to perish. So long as you keep these opinions to yourself no great harm will come to you, but if you give public expression to them vast forces will be set in motion against you.

If you are a teacher in an American college you will very likely not be allowed to go on teaching. If you are a politician, you will not be elected. If you are a journalist, only a few obscure Left-wing journals will employ you. The forces of organized cruelty, disguised as morality, will crush you if they can. They will not succeed if you have private means or happen to be a successful writer, but if you have neither of these pieces of good fortune your life will become very painful.

People imagine that the battle for religious toleration has been won because we tolerate all sects that existed in the eighteenth century, but heresies which have arisen since that time are still viewed with the old horror.

(2) POLITICAL FREEDOM—ECONOMIC FREEDOM— MENTAL FREEDOM

As I remarked before, there is another way of classifying freedoms. In this way of classification the three main kinds may be called political, economic, and mental.

Political Freedom

Political freedom involves two different elements: on the one hand, wherever a common decision is necessary, it should be the decision of the majority; on the other hand, there should be every readiness to avoid a common decision whenever such avoidance is possible.

In Russia at the present day there is no vestige of either kind. Common decisions are made, not by the majority, but by the governing clique. And a great many things are considered matters for common decision which in a freer community would be left to the individual.

There appears to be in human nature an impulse to demand conformity even when it serves no social purpose. This is especially notable in schoolboys. In a school where nobody wears a hat, a boy will be kicked if he does not go bare-headed. Not one boy in a thousand would think that an eccentric in the matter of hats is harmless.

Civilized people gradually grow out of this blind impulse towards enforced uniformity; but many never become civilized, and retain through life the crude, persecuting instincts of the schoolboy. If there is to be political liberty, this feeling must not be embodied in legislation. It was only this feeling which caused hostility to the Mormons. It was not a belief in the conventional moral code, since no one objected to polygamy in Asia and Africa.

I should not like it to be thought that I favour polygamy, but the true test of a lover of freedom comes only in relation to things that he dislikes. To tolerate what you like is easy. It is toleration of what you dislike that characterizes the liberal attitude.

Economic Freedom

Economic freedom is a matter which raises some of the most acute controversies of our time.

It used to be thought obvious that complete *laissez-faire* is the system under which there is most freedom, but gradually opinion has changed in this respect. Extreme anarchists advocate freedom for murderers and thieves, but most of us realize that we should have far less freedom if criminals were in no way restrained. Early industrialism in England, which allowed unrestricted child labour, in the end shocked the conscience of the community. As regards the adult wage-earner also, it was realized that, so long as trade unions were illegal, his liberty consisted only in being free to choose between the employer's terms and starvation. This form of liberty, oddly enough, was not greatly valued by those who enjoyed it.

Economic liberty rightly conceived does not consist in allowing anybody to do anything he likes in the economic sphere, but consists rather in freeing a man from economic compulsion so long as his behaviour does not flagrantly disregard the public interest. This means, in effect, that if a man is law-abiding and willing to work he must not be allowed to starve. *Laissez-faire* cannot secure this result. It has been hoped that Socialism would achieve it, but Socialism in the Russian form does far more to destroy it than was done by capitalism even in its most ruthless days.

A Russian worker whom the authorities dislike can be deprived of his ration book. If this is thought an insufficient punishment, he can be removed to a concentration camp. I do not think that there has ever in past history been so little freedom anywhere as there was in Stalin's Russia.

In England, on the contrary, only those forms of Socialism have been adopted which tend to increase the economic freedom of the wage-earners. I think that the genuine lover of freedom ought to welcome this result in spite of the lessened freedom of capitalists. For the capitalists, like the burglars, are a minority, and are restrained for the sake of the freedoms of the majority. But I will not pretend that the problem of economic freedom has as yet been fully solved either in Britain or elsewhere.

Mental Freedom

Mental freedom, although primarily important only to the minority, is in the long run immensely valuable to the whole community. Mental freedom from a public point of view has two branches: on the one hand, a man should not suffer for holding or proclaiming opinions other than those of the government; on the other hand, education should not be such as to make its victim incapable of ever thinking an original thought.

Consider what happened in Stalin's Russia in both these respects. If you were so rash as to agree with almost all competent geneticists on the subject of heredity, you would be sent to dig canals or mine gold under servile conditions in Arctic wastes. If you had been educated in a Soviet school you would have been subjected year after year to such intensive propaganda that you would probably emerge completely conditioned to Soviet orthodoxy and as incapable of a heterodox thought as of standing on your head.

There are still people in Russia who grew up before the present school system was perfected, and therefore the government still finds it necessary to persecute deviations; but when all the population has enjoyed the full benefits of indoctrination in school, there will no longer be any heretics, and the Soviet Government will be able to point triumphantly at a revival of apparent mental freedom secured at the cost of complete psychological enslavement by the process of education. Everybody will then believe everything that the government thinks it good for the population to believe.

Any State that despises freedom of thought can secure results if it so desires. There will be no limit whatever to the possibilities in the way of exploitation of the majority by the governing minority. There will be no need to punish new ideas, because there will be no new ideas to punish. A nation so enslaved may show for a time a monolithic strength, but will inevitably before very long be outstripped by the nations that have retained intellectual initiative and a capacity for scientific progress—if, that is to say, any such nations remain.

But there is a real danger lest, terrified, hypnotized, and fascinated by such a menace, other nations should so completely forget the value of mental freedom as to share in the stagnation which must inevitably befall a State which has suppressed individual initiative.

I should not wish to be thought to advocate mental freedom solely as a means to success in war. It *is* a means to this end, and this is an important fact. But the chief value of mental freedom lies elsewhere. It is the source of all that is good in art and literature and science, and of much of what is best in individual personality. A world without it would be tame and dull and scarcely more interesting than an ant heap.

There are those who say that war is necessary to bring out the best in men. I do not believe this. But I do think that there are forms of contest which are valuable. The valuable forms of contest are those that do no serious injury to the vanquished. Contests in athletics and politics, rivalries in art and literature, and controversies in intellectual matters are all to the good. (In the case of political contests, however, one must add the proviso that they are to remain within non-violent bounds, for otherwise they partake of the evils of war.) All of these, with the exception of athletic contests, depend upon mental freedom.

(3) PERSONAL LIBERTY—GOVERNMENT AND LIBERTY
—LIBERTY AND IDEAS—LIMITS OF TOLERANCE—
EDUCATION FOR FREEDOM

Let us now consider in a more general way what are the advantages of the various kinds of liberty, and why it is important that there should be as much liberty as is compatible with avoidance of anarchy. And here let us begin with the liberty of the individual.

Personal Liberty

What is important as regards the individual is that he should be able to do what he thinks important, and, if his work is of a public nature, that he should be able to obtain publicity for it. It is not important that he should be rewarded for his work provided he is able to keep alive. It is not even important that he should not be punished, provided he has been allowed to do it. Socrates was very much helped in his work by being put to death. Without this incident he would not have had nearly as much influence as he has had. A modern Socrates, if one were to arise in Russia, would be put to death while still young and would find no Plato to publicize his doctrines.

It used to be said that the blood of the martyrs is the seed of the Church, but that was before the technique of martyrdom had acquired its present efficiency. If nobody knows what you have said and nobody knows that you have been martyred, whatever seed you may have tried to sow has fallen upon stony ground and withered fruitlessly.

Provided a man is able to do his work and to get it known, he will not, if he is truly creative, be very much troubled about his personal fate. But in the modern world, with its higher level of organization and its more efficient police, the loopholes by which in the past great men slipped through the restrictions of petty officials are rapidly ceasing to exist.

The problem of personal liberty, therefore, in degree if not in kind, is a new one. Never before in human history has it been possible to impose such complete mental slavery as is to be found in modern totalitarian States.

Consider Russia in this respect. We used to think the Czarist Government a tyranny. But what an ineffectual and feeble tyranny it was compared to what Stalin created! Turgenev, Tolstoy, and Dostoevsky were all engaged at one time or another in conflict with the government. Dostoevsky was actually sent to Siberia, but was pardoned when he wrote an ode on the Empress's birthday. Turgenev lived abroad in comfort. Tolstoy was so much revered throughout the world that the Czarist Government did not dare to touch him. And so, in spite of tyranny, Russia in the nineteenth century was supreme in literature.

Under Stalin nothing of the sort was possible. Turgenev got into trouble for maintaining that serfs are human beings with feelings and passions not unlike those of their masters. If any Russian literary man in Stalin's day had maintained such an opinion about the inmates of concentration camps, his writings would not have been published. He himself would have learned what it is to be an inmate of a concentration camp. His wife and family would have starved, and not one jot of what he had hoped to do would have been accomplished. And so Russian literature, formerly supreme, became virtually non-existent.

This same sort of thing happens in other spheres. The Doukhobors were disliked by the Czarist Government because, on religious grounds, they refused military service. Tolstoy, as a pacifist, took up their cause and they were allowed to emigrate to Canada. Under the present régime none of them would have been allowed to emigrate, and all those who did not recant would have been made to disappear.

Nations which have been glorious in history, except in the purely military sphere, have always in fact allowed great liberty to individuals either by accident or by design. In the great days of Greece, although many governments were tyrannous, each of them covered such a small area that escape was easy. A very large percentage of Greek thinkers were refugees either from Persia or from their own cities. But the life of a refugee was not necessarily a hard one. If you were expelled by your own city, you took refuge in an enemy city and were acclaimed by all its leading citizens.

The same sort of thing can, of course, happen now to a Russian who is able to escape; but escape is incomparably more difficult from a country the size of Russia than from the territory of a Greek city State which was never larger than an English county. When Rome at last established order in the ancient world, great individuals soon disappeared.

The next age of great individuals in Europe was the Italian Renaissance, which politically resembled ancient Greece since it consisted of a large number of petty States in perpetual conflict with each other. As soon as the Spaniards achieved supremacy and established order, the age of great Italians came to an end.

Apart from the production of great works, there is a more widespread merit in liberty. It makes it possible for a man to retain his self-respect, to stand upright and to do what his own conscience tells him that he ought to do. In the modern world, such liberty belongs to very few.

If a man is not prepared to starve he must find work, probably under some great corporation which has sinister purposes of which every friend of mankind must disapprove. If you are a Socialist and a journalist, you will have to work for a reactionary newspaper. If you are a steel worker and a pacifist, you will have to work for armaments. If you are a friend of Asia and a publicist, you will have to hold your tongue or be thwarted in your efforts to make the facts known. Only those who enjoy an independent income are free from this slavery. I doubt whether Darwin could have overcome the blast of ecclesiastical prejudice with which his doctrine was met if he had been dependent for his livelihood upon academic employment.

Government and Liberty

It is increase of efficiency that causes the gravity of the present situation. Governments almost always and almost everywhere have done what they could to impede mental progress, but in the past they were more apt to fail in this than they are now.

The extent to which governments interfere varies greatly from one country to another. In England the interference is probably less than in most large countries. But even in England much useful knowledge on matters connected with sex is only open to those who have enough education to understand long words, since short words are regarded by police and magistrates as obscene.

In America there is a great deal more interference than there is in England. Everybody who knows China is aware that American policy in China ever since 1945 has been misguided. But many reactionaries are anxious that this fact should not be known. The method adopted to secure this result has been to accuse everybody who knew anything about China of being a Communist or fellow traveller. This has so frightened the administration that American policy has been entirely at the mercy of the ignorant.

Not only so, but any person who is in any way, however remotely, connected with the administration risks dismissal if even in private among friends he ventures to criticize American policy—unless, of course, he criticizes it from the standpoint of MacArthur and McCarthy and the China Lobby. That is to say, the only criticism permitted is such as in the opinion of all who know China would make American policy even more disastrous than it has been.

This is only one example of the public evils that result from lack of liberty. Governments invariably assume that they have a monopoly of wisdom and virtue, and that whoever opposes them is a fool or a knave or both. Since this assumption is almost invariably false, it does harm.

In America as yet this sort of interference with liberty is still, and I hope will remain, at an early stage. To see it fully fledged one must turn to Nazi Germany and Soviet Russia.

One of the peculiar features of the Stalin dictatorship is that it extended to matters which most people would consider outside the scope of politics. No Western man, unless he were a Communist, would think that the question of the inheritance of acquired characteristics had any political importance, and if, without having heard of the Lysenko controversy, he were asked which is the Right and which the Left in this question, he would be completely at a loss. Nor would he have known off-hand that a composer must be a bourgeois reactionary if he failed to produce tunes that gave Stalin pleasure.

I have no knowledge whatever as to the musical tastes of either Mr Churchill or Mr Attlee, but I do not think that our composers in 1945 would have been altogether pleased if the change of government had obliged them to alter their style.

Lack of liberty is bound sooner or later to lead to ossification. New ideas are unpleasant to the great majority of mankind. They disturb habits. They may alter the balance of power. And there is always a risk that they may be socially subversive.

In the third millennium before Christ much valuable work in mathematics was done in Mesopotamia, but the social system became stereotyped, and further mathematical progress had to wait for the Greeks, who never, except in Sparta, had a government sufficiently competent to prevent originality.

If one could imagine the Stalinist government lasting for three thousand years, as did the ancient governments of Egypt and Babylonia, it would be obvious that no important new ideas could ever arise in Russia. At the end of the three thousand years Western anthropologists would study Russia, as they now study the South Sea Islands, to see curious survivals of a past that would be dead everywhere else. The Russians no doubt would still be relying on atom bombs at a time when the rest of the world would be viewing these puny weapons as we view bows and arrows.

I do not, however, wish to encourage undue hopefulness. It is by no means certain either that Russia will allow us the necessary time or that we shall ourselves preserve the necessary freedom.

I do not deny that where a matter is of immediate military importance secrecy may be necessary, but I think there is a tendency to exaggerate the amount of secrecy required, and I think the atmosphere in which nuclear research has to be carried on in present-day America is so inimical to progress as to constitute a danger even greater than that of occasional leakages.

Liberty and Ideas

Liberty is no less important in the political sphere than in the sphere of ideas. Where there is not liberty there is some group which has power and which is able to prevent or punish all criticism of itself. The group may, like Cromwell's Saints, believe itself to have a monopoly of virtue and to have no aim except the public good, but, in fact, it is sure to be deceiving itself in so thinking. Those who enjoy irresponsible power will inevitably further, if not their own pecuniary interests, at least their own creed and their own prejudices. In fact, it will only be for exceptional periods that a group in power will abstain from enriching itself at the expense of the powerless.

Of this, again, Russia affords a notable example. Karl Marx, owing to a purely intellectual error, imagined that if private property were abolished economic injustice would cease. He made this mistake because he did not realize that property is only one form of power, and that to abolish private property while concentrating power in the hands of a minority not only ensures an intolerable tyranny, but also must lead to the grossest economic injustice. The percentage difference between generals and privates is greater in modern Russia than in any other civilized country. The gulf between the pay of officers and the pay of privates in the army is such as to horrify Americans, but that does not stop Communists from speaking of America as the home of plutocracy and of Russia as the country where the interests of the proletariat prevail.

A hundred and fifty years ago, when the English were terrified by the French Revolution, the new proletariat in our manufacturing towns were abominably oppressed: they had no voice in the government, they were forbidden to combine, and they were kept illiterate; but even at the worst moments they had a better life than that which fell to the lot of the proletariat in Stalin's Russia. They were not starved to death by artificial famines or sent by the million to rot in Arctic labour camps. They had champions who were allowed to speak for them and, in the end, they were able to secure political rights and economic security.

For the Russian proletariat in Stalin's day there was no hope except the despairing hope of defeat by an external enemy. I do not think there has ever in human history been such a vast organized hypocrisy as the pretence that the Stalin government represented the interests of the proletariat. What it did represent was the arbitrary power of a clique supported in comparative affluence and comfort by a subsidized army and police force amid a vast ocean of squalor and misery and torture.

Democracy in the sense of a legislature and executive chosen by the votes of the people does not of itself ensure liberty. There is democracy in Ireland, but a very large percentage of the books that intelligent people wish to read are forbidden by the censorship. In the days before 1922, when the Irish sent members to Westminster, Ireland enjoyed the blessings of full democracy, but, since the majority in Parliament came from England or Scotland, the Irish were never free to realize their desires. It is important to remember that democracy does not

E 65

necessarily involve liberty, and that, of the two, liberty is if anything the more important.

Modern democracies are exposed to certain dangers which did not exist in former times. The most important of these dangers comes from the police. When the Communists were acquiring control of satellite countries, they were willing to enter into coalitions provided they had control of the police. Given control of the police, they could arrest anybody they disliked and concoct fantastic stories of plots. It was largely by this method that they passed from participation in coalition governments to exclusive control.

The same sort of thing, though on a lesser scale, can easily happen elsewhere. Who, in America, would wish to fall foul of the FBI? And who, not in America, can deny that the FBI has a corporate interest and a corporate bias which may be quite out of harmony with the interests of the American people?

Apart from the police, important pressure groups can cause individuals and even whole sections of opinion to be unjustly condemned. Accusations often repeated are in the end believed by all but an exceptionally sceptical minority.

This evil is one which it is not very easy to deal with. In England the libel laws are so strict that even perfectly just accusations can only be made with great risk. It is not altogether easy to draw the line between preventing unjust accusations and permitting just ones.

What is perhaps even more important is that where public opinion is intolerant a man may be gravely damaged by the publication of something which is in no way to his real discredit. If you have lived in Russia and studied Russian opinion, your mere knowledge makes you suspect, and you will have to walk very warily if you are not to be regarded as a fellow traveller. There cannot long be liberty without tolerance, for liberty without tolerance leads to civil war. The ultimate basis of liberty, therefore, lies not merely in political institutions, but in the general diffusion of a conviction that all opinions have their rights, and that however convinced you may be it is nevertheless possible that you may be mistaken.

This is one of the things that ought to be secured by education, whereas in fact most education at present does exactly the opposite. It ought to be the aim of education to produce open-mindedness and a willingness to listen to arguments without growing angry because they tend to conclusions that we dislike. Wherever there are mass prejudices, whether of nationalism or of race or of religious bigotry, the schools ought to set themselves consciously to the softening of such prejudices.

I would have the schools in India teach the virtues of Mohammedans, and the schools in Pakistan teach the virtues of Hindus. I would have Zionists taught the merits of Arabs, and Arabs taught the merits of Jews. I would have the West taught that even Russians are human beings, and the Russians taught that not all Westerners are lackeys of capitalism.

All such large collective prejudices are harmful. It is they that make war seem not a destructive madness. It is they that cause comparatively decent people to acquiesce in persecution. It is they that inhibit the impulses of humanity. It is they that make it seem practical and reasonable to organize vast communities for purposes of mutual homicide rather than for co-operation in the common tasks of mankind. All this would be different if the schools were different, but the schools will not be different until the governments are different; and the governments, I fear, will not be different until by touching the very depths of misery mankind have learnt the folly of their present divisions.

Limits of Tolerance

Tolerance, like all other virtues, has its limits. I should not wish to see it carried to the point of thinking that any one system is as good as any other.

But looking further afield to a time when fanaticism has grown less, and when co-operation among nations has become more possible than it is at present, it becomes obvious that the anarchic liberty at present claimed by national States is as much to be condemned as the anarchic liberty claimed by burglars and murderers. There are liberties which, if tolerated, diminish the total amount of liberty in the world.

If there were no law against murder, we should all have to go armed and avoid solitude and be perpetually on the watch. Many liberties which we now take for granted would disappear. It is, therefore, in the interests of liberty to curtail the liberty of would-be murderers.

The argument is exactly the same in the case of the liberty of States. But in this case it is very much more difficult to enforce the necessary restrictions. Nevertheless, if a civilized way of life is to continue, it will be necessary to arrive at a method of preventing aggressive war.

I do not know of any way of securing this result except the creation of an international government with a monopoly of all the major weapons of war. Such a government, if it existed, should have only such powers as are necessary for the prevention of war, and should leave separate nations free except as regards armaments. If such a government existed, it would be possible to inaugurate such a system of education as I spoke of a moment ago. Such a system, instead of teaching nationalism, would teach consciousness of what men in different nations have in common and of what they can achieve by working together instead of working against each other. Gradually, under the influence of such a system of education, bigotry and intolerance would diminish and social liberty would gain as much as political liberty.

In the course of education the young should be exposed to opinions that they would be likely to regard with horror. I do not mean that they should be asked to accept them, but that they should be asked to consider them and to find, if they could, arguments of reason and not of mere prejudice for rejecting whatever they continued to reject.

I met a man once who spent half an hour inveighing against race prejudice, in which he had my hearty concurrence. He spent the next half hour telling me that all Filipinos are scoundrels. If he had been properly educated he would have seen the inconsistency.

Education for Freedom

Education is not at present designed with a view to eliminating prejudice. Large-scale education is conducted, as a rule, by either a State or a church. In the former case, it teaches nationalism; in the latter case, bigotry.

In the present state of the world, nationalism is the greater danger. School children are taught to reverence the national flag, and by the time they leave school, they have become incapable of realizing what worship of the national flag means.

The national flag symbolizes belief in the superior excellence of one geographical group. If the geographical group is large enough, the school children will be expected to consider that it is justified in putting members of other groups to death whenever they interfere with its desires. The justification is derived from the pre-eminent merit of the group to which the school child belongs. And this pre-eminent merit is taught so pervasively and hypnotically that at the end of the school years hardly any child is able to question it.

You may reply: 'But at any rate so far as my country is concerned, the belief is true. My country is immeasurably better than any other. It has stood always for. . . .' And then will follow a long list of virtues.

Let it be granted, dear reader, that in the case of your country there is not a word to be said against the claims of nationalism. It then follows logically that in all other countries the doctrines of nationalism are unjustified, and even if you belong to the largest country in the world, other countries comprise the immense majority of mankind. The teaching of nationalism in schools is therefore far more frequently a teaching of lies than a teaching of truth. You know, of course, that in your own country it is a teaching of truth, and therefore, if it is the purpose of education to teach truth, school children in all other countries should be taught to salute *your* flag.

But how is this to be brought about? Other countries are, unfortunately, so benighted that they will not admit your superiority except at the point of the bayonet. Perhaps it might be wiser to forgo some part of your own nationalistic teaching in exchange for an equal forbearance in other countries.

The analogous behaviour in private life is taken for granted. Even if an individual really is a very superior person, he is not expected to go about boasting of it, and everybody realizes that, if he does, he will become unpopular. But where nations are concerned there is no corresponding code of good manners, and the man who does not boast offensively about his country's superiority is thought a poor creature—except, of course, when his country's armed forces are not very formidable.

This fact is concealed by ideological talk. The Russians think that they stand for Communism, while the Americans think that they stand for democracy. But, in fact, these ideological labels, although they have an element of truth, are very largely cloaks for nationalism.

Russian foreign policy differs very little from what it was under the czars. British foreign policy ever since the Crimean war has been anti-Russian at all times when fear of Germany was not paramount.

If liberty is to survive in this closely-knit scientific community in which mankind now have to live, it will be absolutely necessary to give up the plan of indoctrinating the young with mutual hatreds and with the belief that murdering each other is a sacred duty.

(4) THE FUTURE OF FREEDOM

Social liberty is intimately bound up with certain intellectual virtues. It can hardly exist in a world where large groups of people feel dogmatic certainty about matters which are theoretically doubtful. It is the nature of the human animal to believe not only things for which there is evidence, but also very many things for which there is no evidence whatever. And it is the things for which there is no evidence that are believed with passion.

Nobody feels any passion about the multiplication table or about the existence of Cape Horn, because these matters are not doubtful. But in matters of theology or political theory, where a rational man will hold that at best there is a slight balance of probability on one side or the other, people argue with passion, and support their opinion by physical slavery imposed by armies and mental slavery imposed by schools. So accustomed do people become to feeling certain where they ought to feel doubtful that they become incapable of acting on a probability.

If you come to a fork in the road at a point where there is no signpost and no passer-by of whom to inquire, and if you have no map to tell you which is the right road, you will if you are rational choose one of the two roads at haphazard, but inquire as soon as you come upon anybody likely to know. If, on the other hand, you have lived always in a dogmatic atmosphere, you will either stay still in hopeless bewilderment, or, if you choose at haphazard, you will become dogmatically convinced that you have chosen rightly and will never stop to inquire when opportunity occurs.

The Future of Freedom

If liberty is to survive in the world and if mankind is not to perish in futile suicide, it will be necessary to learn to act like our rational man at the fork in the road, and not like the devotee of geographical dogma.

In the realm of science the correct intellectual attitude is taught in the West. But in the realm of ethics and politics it is still thought nobler to indulge in blatant, blaring dogmatism of the sort most likely to cause the death of millions. If I say that perhaps there are parts of the world where democracy is unworkable, I shall be viewed in America as a fellow traveller. If I say in Russia that perhaps there are parts of the world where democracy is good, I shall be viewed as a lackey of capitalism or perhaps as a 'rotten bourgeois humanitarian'.

I do not wish to be led by love of symmetry into an appearance of neutrality as between Russia and the West. The West has more than Russia of everything that I think valuable, and, first and foremost, it has more liberty. But I think it of the highest importance, if liberty is to survive in the West, that we should be conscious of its value, conscious of its intellectual conditions, and conscious of the danger that in a desperate contest it may be lost. I cannot admit that, in pointing out unnecessary infringements of liberty in the West, one is showing disloyalty. On the contrary, those who have kept alive a knowledge of what it is that makes us prefer Western systems to that of Russia are doing something absolutely necessary to the victory of what they value.

What the West professes to stand for fundamentally is the belief that governments exist for the sake of individuals, not individuals for the sake of governments. It is this principle that is at stake.

II

What is Democracy?[1]

(1) DEMOCRACY—WHAT IT MEANS—HOW IT BEGAN—
REPRESENTATIVE GOVERNMENT—AMERICAN DEMOC-
RACY—THE ROLE OF POLICE—THE STATE AND THE
ARMY

THERE ARE, at the present day, two different views as to
what is meant by the word 'democracy'. West of the Iron
Curtain it is generally taken as implying that ultimate power
is in the hands of the majority of the adult population. East
of the Iron Curtain it means military dictatorship by a certain
small minority of people who have chosen to call themselves
'democrats'. This difference of meaning, if it could be viewed
from a merely linguistic point of view, would be quite interesting, but, unfortunately, it is bound up with the whole tension
which is threatening the world with another Great War.

Differences in the meanings of words are, of course, common.
Italians who wish to address me politely call me 'The Egregious
Sir Russell', which, to English ears, seems unduly accurate.
Originally the words 'orgy' and 'theory' meant the same thing,
namely 'divine intoxication', which, when Bacchus was the
Divinity, was not very sharply distinguished from ordinary
intoxication. But fortunately these linguistic curiosities did not
lead to an armed conflict.

1 Originally appeared as a Background Book, by the Batchworth Press,
1953 (revised 1960).

73

It must be said that the present Russian use of the word democracy diverges widely from previous usage, and is merely designed to conceal Russian failure to carry out the provisions of Yalta and Potsdam. There were to be democratic governments in what are known as the 'satellite States', and the Russians decided that they would establish dictatorships and *call* them democracies. This simple device, being backed by the largest army in the world, proved to be regrettably successful.

It must, however, be confessed that what in the West is called democracy, is not quite what the word originally meant.

How It Began

Democracy, both the word and the thing, was invented by the Greeks. So far as is known, nobody conceived of it before their time. There had been monarchies, theocracies, and aristocracies, but nobody had imagined a system in which all the citizens should have a voice in government. Even the most extreme forms of democracy developed by the Greeks were limited in certain respects; women and slaves had no part in government. As far as women are concerned, Plato thought this limitation unjust, but he had few followers in this matter.

Where democracy prevailed in ancient Greece the individual citizen had, in many ways, more power than he has in a modern democratic State. He could vote on every proposed law, judges were chosen by lot from among the citizens, and there was no powerful bureaucracy to place obstacles in the way of the popular will. Such a system was only technically possible in a city State, since it presupposed that the citizens could assemble and vote directly on each measure, a thing which, in a large modern State, is not possible.

It cannot be said that the system was very successful. It arose in opposition to aristocracy, which itself had arisen in opposition to monarchy. Aristocracy, in most Greek city States, was defeated by democracy, but democracy itself, as a rule, gave way to tyranny. A tyrant, as the Greeks understood the word, was not necessarily a bad ruler; he was merely a man who had acquired the powers of monarchy by force or the popular favour, and not by heredity. He generally made himself the champion of the people against aristocrats and plutocrats, and when he acquired sufficient popularity he represented that his enemies were plotting to assassinate him and that he needed a bodyguard if his life was to be preserved. When once he had got the bodyguard, he only had to favour the men who composed it, and the people were forgotten.

The Greeks never discovered any method of making democracy secure against this sort of thing. Democracy, however, lingered until the time of Alexander the Great, who, before embarking upon his Persian war, forced treaties upon the Greek city States compelling them to keep the democrats in subjection.

Rome, on a larger scale, repeated the Greek experience. There was a long period of strife between the aristocracy and the populace. Julius Caesar won favour as the champion of democracy, which he abolished as soon as he was securely established. After his day, democracy disappeared from the world for a long time. It rose again very slowly and very gradually as a result of the new commercial prosperity that began in Lombardy in the eleventh century, and spread northward to such great centres of trade as the Hanse towns.

Modern Liberalism begins in Milan in the conflicts of that city with its Archbishop and the Emperor. It was a very limited form of democracy, consisting chiefly of independence from feudal magnates and ecclesiastical dignitaries. It had immense historical importance as giving opportunity for revival of political speculation and freedom of thought. Democratic forms of government, it is true, did not last very long. They gave way in Venice to aristocracy, and in Milan and Florence to the rule of plutocratic bosses. But there were always limits to what these men could practise in the way of abominations, since they had no traditional claim to power and were liable to be expelled if they behaved too badly.

Representative Government

Meanwhile, a new institution had been established in various countries north of the Alps—I mean the institution of representative government. To us this seems an essential part of democracy, but the Ancients never thought of it, and, in its earlier forms in the Middle Ages, it was not very democratic. Its immense merit was that it enabled a large constituency to exert indirect power, and thus made possible the distribution of political responsibility throughout the great States of modern times, whereas formerly such distribution had only been possible in single cities.

Although representative government seems to us intimately connected with democracy, it need not be so, since the constituency that elects can be very restricted. Scottish Peers elect representatives to the House of Lords, but this is hardly an example of democracy. It would, however, be quite impossible, apart from representative government, to find a mechanism by which the ordinary citizen could acquire any degree of control over the policy of a geographically large State.

Representative government brings with it certain new dangers to democracy different from those which tyranny brought in ancient times. It is possible for a representative assembly to treat itself as absolute and to forget that it owes its position to popular election. The first thing the Long Parliament did in its contest with Charles I was to decree that it could not be dissolved except with its own consent. It could, therefore, constitutionally remain in power indefinitely, however much it might come to be out of sympathy with those who had elected it. This was one reason why Cromwell was compelled to act unconstitutionally, since there was no constitutional method by which he could get rid of the Long Parliament.

Rousseau, who professes to be a believer in democracy, considers that this word is only rightly applicable to the ancient form in which every citizen votes on every legislative act. When the power is delegated to elected representatives, Rousseau calls the system 'Elective Aristocracy'. He admits what is obvious, that it is impossible to have democracy in the ancient sense in such countries as France or England. Such a system, he says, is too perfect for our imperfect world, except in his own city of Geneva. There alone it is possible to have the sort of government that he thinks really good. In view of this conclusion, it is odd that his books caused such a commotion.

Democratic theory, in the modern sense, was not invented by Rousseau but by the progressive element in Cromwell's army. These men failed at home, but carried their doctrines across the Atlantic where, after a period of incubation, they at last gave birth to American democracy. The success of America was largely influential in spreading democratic ideas in France and also, though less directly, in England.

American Democracy

The character of a democracy is very largely determined by the forces which it regards as its enemies. American democracy at first was directed mainly against England. French democracy was directed in 1789 mainly against the large landowners. English democracy in the first half of the nineteenth century was engaged in acquiring power for the middle class, but, after that, was seeking power for wage-earners and was regarding large employers as the enemy.

American democracy underwent a great transformation when Andrew Jackson became President. Until his time presidents had been cultivated gentlemen, mostly with a settled position as landowners. Andrew Jackson represented a rebellion against these men on the part of the pioneers and immigrants. He did not like culture and was suspicious of educated men since they understood things that puzzled him. This element of hostility to culture has persisted in American democracy ever since, and has made it difficult for America to make the best use of its experts.

At the present day this trouble is peculiarly acute, but it cannot be said that such hostility is any essential part of democracy. It has never existed in England, and, in France, has been absent except at the height of the terror during the French Revolution. It was, at first, very dominant in modern Russia and is, I suppose, one of the excuses that the Soviet Government offers to itself for thinking itself democratic.

One of the problems which every modern democracy has to face is that of the utilization of experts. There are many matters of the utmost importance which are too difficult for ordinary citizens to understand. Of these, perhaps finance is the most obvious. Jackson abolished the Bank of America, chiefly because he could not understand banking. The problem is to secure that, when expert opinion is necessary, it shall be in accordance with a popularly chosen policy and not covertly such as to favour some minority policy. A good example of this has been Trade Union legislation in England. Urban working men acquired the vote in 1867, and since then it has been necessary to persuade trade unionists that their interests were being considered. Repeatedly Acts have been passed which were thought to have secured the objects of trade unionists, but the House of Lords, in its judicial capacity, has discovered that the Acts did not mean what they seemed to mean. This has only somewhat delayed matters, since the working-class vote was sufficient to secure the passage of new Amending Acts, but it shows what legal experts can do to defeat the popular will.

In America, when people in Jackson's time became conscious of this danger, they decided that State judges, though not federal judges, should be elected. This remedy, however, proved worse than the disease. It increased the power of the political boss who had secured the election of his favourites to judgeships and could be tolerably certain that his favourites would decide cases as he wished, and not in accordance with the law. In fact, the political boss acquired a position not wholly unlike that of the Greek tyrant. There was, however, an important difference. It was possible to remedy the evil by wholly constitutional methods without the need of revolution or assassination.

In Latin America, which also adopted democratic theory, this has not proved nearly so uniformly possible, and many dictators have risen on the ruins of democracy.

The Role of Police

There is one matter in which many democracies have been unsuccessful, and that is the control of the police. Given a police force which is corrupt and unscrupulous, and judges who are not anxious to discover its crimes, it is possible for ordinary citizens to find themselves at the mercy of a powerful organization which, just because it is supposed to enforce the law, has exceptional facilities for acting illegally. I think this is a danger which is much too little realized in many countries.

Happily it is realized in England, and most English people regard the policeman as a friend. But in many countries he is viewed with terror, as a man who may, at any moment, bring grave trouble upon any person whom he happens to dislike or whom the police, as a whole, consider politically objectionable.

When the Communists were acquiring control of what are now satellite States, they always aimed, first of all, at control of the police. If they acquired that, they could accuse their enemies of plots or other crimes and terrify everybody into subservience.

The State and the Army

A danger which is much more realized is that of military rule. States need armies, and armies can take control of government if individual soldiers are willing to obey their officers when their officers give orders that are illegal.

This danger was so present to the minds of British politicians in the time of William III that they only consented to the creation of a standing army on condition that the penalties for mutiny should be enacted afresh by Parliament every year. This provision continues down to the present day, and, if at any moment Parliament should become suspicious of the armed forces, it might refuse to pass the Mutiny Act, and every soldier would be absolved from obedience to the orders of his officers. In the time of William III it was the experience of Cromwell that inspired caution, but in many countries at many times this caution has been absent.

Perhaps it has not always been a lack of legislative caution that has brought about military dictatorship where it has replaced democracy. Sometimes the cause has been that the armed forces came preponderantly from a minority section of the population, and saw no reason why they should submit to an unarmed majority. It cannot be hoped that democracy will succeed except where, among political opponents of the majority, there is, nevertheless, a profound sense of the importance of legality.

(2) EVILS OF POWER—DEMOCRATIC FREEDOM— DEMOCRACY AND WAR

Two opposite forces have caused, in our time, an undue diminution in the respect which people feel for democracy. On the so-called Left, there are admirers of Russia who think that, since dictatorship is adopted by Russian Communists, democracy must be in some way reactionary. On the Right, there are those who fear Socialism and who wish to preserve ancient privileges.

In addition to these two kinds of opinion there are people who are conscious that all is not well, and imagine impatiently that some other system would be better. For my part I think it extremely dangerous, so far, at least, as Western civilized communities are concerned, to imagine that there are better systems than democracy. It is not so much that democracy is positively good as that it makes impossible certain great evils which are apt to exist under other systems. When people imagine some undemocratic system introduced as a reform, they always implicitly or explicitly think of themselves as the holders of power in the new régime, and oneself, of course, is all-wise and perfectly virtuous.

This, however, is not how things work out in practice.

Evils of Power

Holders of power, always and everywhere, are indifferent to the good or evil of those who have no power, except in so far as they are restrained by fear. This may sound too harsh a saying. It may be said that decent people will not inflict torture on others beyond a point. This may be *said*, but history shows that it is not true. The decent people in question succeed in not knowing, or pretending not to know, what torments are inflicted to make them happy.

Lord Melbourne, Queen Victoria's first Prime Minister, was just such a decent person. In private life he was charming. He was cultivated, well read, humane, and liberal. He was also rich. His money came to him from coal-mines where children worked for long hours in darkness for a pittance. It was by the agony of these children that he was enabled to be so urbane. Nor is his case in any way exceptional. Analogous things affect even the origins of Communism. Marx lived on the charity of Engels, and Engels lived by exploiting the proletariat of Manchester during the hungry '40s. The polished young men in Plato's dialogues, whom English classicists have held up as models to the British upper-class youth, lived on slave labour and on the exploitation of the short-lived Athenian

F   81

Empire. Injustices by which we profit can always be justified by some kind of sophistry.

People are horrified, and rightly so, by Mau-Mau atrocities, but how few reflect that these, in their entirety, are not a thousandth part of the atrocities that white men inflicted for centuries upon negroes by slavery and the slave trade. The City of Bristol contains rich men of the very highest moral integrity, but the wealth of the city was acquired originally chiefly through the slave trade.

When Stalin was introducing collectivization, he encountered the stubborn opposition of the peasants. He met this opposition with a ruthlessness which would have been impossible in a democratic régime. He caused some five million peasants to die of hunger and several millions more he transported to labour camps in the Arctic. All this was done in the name of 'scientific agriculture'.

Much the same thing, though on a smaller scale, was done in England in the late eighteenth and early nineteenth centuries. Parliament, in which both Houses at that time represented the landed aristocracy, passed Enclosure Acts which took away from the rural poor the rights they had enjoyed on common land. The result in de-populating the countryside is vividly described in Goldsmith's *Deserted Village*. The rural population was compelled to migrate to the towns, where they rendered possible the growth of industrialism at the cost of long hours and starvation wages.

Not only adults worked these long hours, but children also. Children worked in the mills for twelve hours a day or even more, and not infrequently fell asleep at work and rolled into the machines where they were mangled.

We do right to be horrified by Stalin's ruthlessness, but we are wholly mistaken if we think that, given opportunity, we should be any better. It is only democracy that makes us better. While the English upper class had a monopoly of political power, it was just as bad as Stalin. Democracy is to

82

be valued because it prevents such large-scale atrocities. This is its first and greatest merit.

Democratic Freedom

It has, however, others only slightly less important. It makes possible a degree of intellectual freedom which is not at all likely to exist under a despotic régime. In Russia at the present day no literature is permitted which might instil a doubt as to the wisdom and virtue of the Masters.[1] Despotic monarchs have always suppressed, as far as they were able, every suggestion that their power was excessive. Churches have been equally to blame in this respect.

I have no wish to enter upon a theological argument, but anyone who cares to examine the theological innovations introduced by Protestants in the sixteenth century will find that practically every one of them was such as to diminish the income of the clergy, and I think it would be contrary to all that we know of human nature to suppose that this had nothing to do with the opposition offered by the Catholic Church to the heretics.

The clergy caused many thousands to be burnt at the stake, believing, no doubt, that their motive was wholly laudable. In this they resembled Stalin and the British landowners who passed the Enclosure Acts, but in all cases alike, the fury which gave momentum to the movement had a very egotistical source, though one which perhaps remained subconscious.

It is, of course, possible for persecution to occur in a democracy, but it can only be persecution of a rather small minority. Quakers were persecuted in New England, but only for a short time. Mormons were persecuted in the nineteenth century because polygamy shocked the immense majority of the population. But, in this case also, persecution was short-lived. Under an undemocratic régime, persecutions of this sort can continue unabated for centuries. In czarist Russia, the Old

[1] Written in 1953.

Believers suffered persecution of greater or less intensity until the revolution. Since the revolution, until Stalin's death, every deviation from Communist orthodoxy, however minute, exposed the deviators to death or life-long torture.

Democracy and War

Another advantage of democracy is that it is likely to be less war-like than an autocratic government. The advantages of war, such as they are, fall only to the eminent in victor nations. The disadvantages fall upon the common people. I have little doubt that if the will of the Russian people could prevail at the present moment the danger of war between East and West would be at an end.

Consider the motives which make the Russian Government such a source of danger to Western countries, and vice versa. These are of various sorts. There is first, on both sides, a fanatical creed which it is thought desirable to spread. There is next a possibility of glory. And, perhaps more powerful than either of these, there is the sheer lust for power. These are not motives which have anything like the same potency in the lives of ordinary men and women as they have in the thoughts of eminent statesmen. For this reason, where ordinary men and women have power there is much less likelihood of a war-like policy than there is under a despotic régime.

Although it cannot be said in any absolute way that democracies are against war, I do think it can be said that they are less apt to be war-like than autocracies are.

It is still a more or less controversial question how the blame for the First World War should be apportioned, but I think almost anybody would agree that the greatest share of blame is to be divided among the three Empires, Germany, Austria, and Russia. As to the Second World War, no doubt is possible that the whole blame falls fairly and squarely upon Hitler, whose régime was the very reverse of democratic.

If a third world war should break out—which Heaven forbid

—it is clear that the unfriendliness and aggressiveness of Russian policy ever since 1945 will have been a main cause, whatever may be the final spark that brings the explosion. I think, therefore, we may fairly claim that a greater love of peace is one of the advantages of democracy over the other forms of government.

In spite of what is often said to the contrary, a very great merit of democracy has been that it gave increased strength in war. This was not perhaps true in the first months of a war, especially if, during those months, the initial victories could be won by an autocracy. But it was true in the long run. Anyone who will take the trouble to survey the important wars that have occurred during the last 250 years will find that, in every case, they have been won by the side which made the nearer approach to democracy.

The main reasons are, I think, two. The first is that a democratic nation at war feels its own pride and self-respect involved, whereas if it has been led into war by a tyrant or an absolute monarch, it does not feel the same responsibility, and is, therefore, less steadfast. The other reason is that where there is democracy, the government has to submit to criticism, and it is therefore much more difficult to encourage gross incompetence or to discourage wise initiative.

One of the most disturbing views about the undemocratic witch-hunt in which some Americans are indulging is that it is diminishing the capacity for serving the public, both on the part of eminent men of science and on the part of those who have any knowledge that is irritating to the China Lobby.[1] Nevertheless, even at the height of the witch-hunt, experts have a very great deal more freedom of expression and action in America than they have in Russia. We might hope that this would produce a technical supremacy in weapons of war on the

[1] The name applied to the body of opinion and pressure in American politics which strenuously opposes recognition of the Communist régime in China, and advocates support of Chiang Kai-shek.

side which has the more democratic régime, but it must be confessed that so far there is little evidence of such a result.

(3) THE GEOGRAPHICAL PROBLEM—TOLERANCE IN DEMOCRACY—DEMOCRACY AND NATIONALISM— THE TEACHING OF HISTORY

A democratic government raises various problems, some of which are sometimes very difficult. Consider first the problem of the right area for a government. In the days when Ireland was united with Great Britain in electing a single Parliament, the Irish felt that they had a grievance, and I think they were justified in this feeling. Although there was democracy so far as definition goes, there was, in fact, a form of government in which the Irish were in a permanent minority. The only way in which they could get Parliament to listen to them was to make themselves a nuisance.

Wherever there is a sharp division, as there was between Great Britain and Southern Ireland, democratic principle demands that each group should be in a position to settle its internal affairs independently of the other group—that is to say, there must be devolution so far as home affairs are concerned. On this ground, I think the Southern Irish were entirely justified in demanding their own Parliament. Oddly enough, they failed entirely to see that the same arguments justified the Protestant Irish of the North in claiming independence of the Southern Irish. This claim has never been recognized by the Southern Irish. I think that psychologically, though of course not explicitly, their argument would be: 'From the time of Henry II to the time of Lloyd George, we had to endure oppression by the English. Surely it is only fair that we should have our turn in inflicting oppression, and who are we to oppress unless it be the Northern Irish?' This argument is human, but not, I fear, strictly logical.

But I do not wish to seem to give all my sympathies to

Northern Ireland. When it comes to the counties of Fermanagh and Tyrone, the Northern Irish show exactly the same failure of logic as the Southern Irish show towards them. And if the counties of Fermanagh and Tyrone were allowed to join Southern Ireland, they would certainly make few concessions to the Protestant part of the population of those two counties.

The Geographical Problem

It is difficult to arrive at a clear principle in such matters, since it is evident that there must be a limit of size below which the group cannot be admitted to self government. What this limit of size should be it is quite impossible to settle in the abstract. What can be said generally is that where any large group is basically out of sympathy with the rest of the citizens of the State, democracy is apt to become unworkable, except by a use of force which will produce great discontent in the subordinate group, and a harsh temper in the dominant group.

When the dissident minority is geographically concentrated, the matter can be dealt with by devolution, but when it is distributed throughout the population there is much greater difficulty. This is the situation of Jews in a country where popular sentiment is strongly anti-semitic. It is the situation of Mohammedans in India, and Hindus in Pakistan. It is the situation of negroes in America. In all such cases the difficulty cannot be solved by *geographical* devolution. Democracy in such cases can only be successful if there is a diffused sentiment of tolerance.

Tolerance in Democracy

Tolerance is, in many ways, absolutely essential to the success of democracy. If people hold their principles so strongly that they feel they ought to die or kill for them, every difference of opinion will lead to war or to a *coup d'état*.

Democracy requires, in fact, a rather difficult combination of individual initiative with submission to the majority. It requires

87

that a man who has strong political convictions should argue for them and do what he can to make them the convictions of the majority, but that if the majority proves adverse, he should submit with a good grace.

There was, some twenty years ago, a small country—I will not say which—in which opposing parties were very nearly evenly balanced. The Members of Parliament of the minority party, in the middle of the session, shot a sufficient number of their opponents to become the majority. This expedient was not adopted by the Conservative Party in England in 1950, nor by the Labour Party in 1951.

Any really fanatical belief tends to be incompatible with democracy. When in 1918 the Russian Constituent Assembly proved to have an anti-Bolshevik majority, the Bolsheviks dissolved it by military force, and ever since then have ruled Russia without regard to popular feeling.

In the sixteenth and seventeenth centuries, the Protestant and Catholic governments acted similarly. Fascist governments in Germany, Italy, and Spain have been indifferent to majority opinion. Wherever any large and important section of a nation has this kind of fanaticism, democracy is hardly likely to survive.

On this ground, believers in democracy ought to do everything in their power to cause a tolerant spirit to be inculcated in education. This is not at all adequately done at present. There are everywhere beliefs favoured by the State, and it is thought proper that the young should be caused to accept these beliefs unquestioningly and dogmatically. The most destructive of these at the present time is nationalism.

The world is divided into a number of areas, and in each area the young are taught that the inhabitants of that area are virtuous, while the inhabitants of other areas are degraded and wicked. This does not make for the peace of the world.

Democracy and Nationalism

Nationalism is one of the matters in which democracy, so far, has proved least satisfactory. In the old days when wars were dynastic and were conducted for the glory of individual rulers, the bulk of the population often regarded them with indifference or hostility.

Throughout the Napoleonic wars, English people of the lower classes took no interest in English victories and were quite ready to believe that the French were as good as the English. This belief did not exist in the upper class. Nelson, for instance, taught his midshipmen that they should hate a Frenchman as they would the Devil. But the upper class had the government. In France, equally, there was no enthusiasm for that war except upon the part of those who were encouraged by Napoleon's victories. Napoleon acquired power on the 18th Brumaire[1] by promising peace, just as Lenin acquired power in 1917 by the same promise.

The unpopularity of wars in the past set a limit to their intensity. When they became too serious, there was discontent —even mutiny. But in a democratic country, the ordinary voter feels that the war is *his* war. His ego is involved in it in a way that does not occur under an autocracy.

This has the good point that it makes a democracy more likely to win, but it has the bad point that it makes it possible for a democratic government to wage war to the bitter end, and, before war has taken place, to be threatening and bellicose in its policy. But within the compass of democratic government, there is only one cure for this evil, which is that by agreement among the nations, education should dwell more upon the common tasks of mankind than upon rivalries between different States.

In the eighteenth century war could be a profitable business. With the exception of the War of American Independence, England emerged from the wars of that century with a balance

[1] The 18th day of 'Brumaire'—the second month in the French Republican calendar, established in 1793. Napoleon's *coup d'état* of that date was in 1799.

of profit from a merely financial point of view. Nowadays, things are different. We have been brought to the verge of ruin by complete and absolute victory in two successive wars, and it is no longer difficult to persuade English people that war is not good business, though in America this lesson has still to be learned.

The Teaching of History

To make democracies peaceable rather than war-like is mainly a matter for the schools. History should be taught as the history of the rise of civilization, and not as the history of this nation or that. It should be taught from the point of view of mankind as a whole, and not with undue emphasis upon one's own country. Children should learn that every country has committed crimes and that most crimes were blunders. They should learn how mass hysteria can drive a whole nation into folly and into persecution of the few who are not swept away by the prevailing madness.

They should be shown movies of foreign countries in which the children, though aliens, would be enjoying much the same pleasures, and suffering much the same sorrows, as those enjoyed and suffered by children at home. All this could be done by UNESCO if the national governments permitted. All this, if it were done throughout the world, would immensely diminish the war-like proclivities of democracies.

(4) REVOLUTION—WORLD GOVERNMENT—EXCESS OF GOVERNMENT—DEMOCRACY AND LIBERTY

To return to the question of devolution. As we saw, devolution presents difficulties where a group is geographically distributed and not concentrated in one area. I think, however, that it should be possible, and is certainly desirable, to have for certain purposes constituencies which are not geographical but occupational or ideological.

Consider, for example, some country in which practically every geographical constituency contains five per cent of Jews. As things stand, these Jews will be everywhere out-voted, and their interests may be quite inadequately represented in Parliament. It might be better if they voted separately, and had in Parliament a number of representatives proportional to their numbers in the general population. I should not advocate this particular measure except where anti-semitism is strong. What I think more important is an industrial application of the same sort of principle.

Socialists have always advocated nationalization of railways and mines. The late Labour Government carried out this programme, but the difference to the employees was not quite so great as Socialists had hoped. The place of the capitalists was taken by State officials, and there was almost the same possibility as before of a clash between employees and management.

I should like to see the internal affairs of any great industry, such as railways or mining, determined democratically not by the State, but by the employees of that industry, leaving only the external affairs in the hands of the State. The modern State is so vast, and even in a democracy officials are so remote from voters, that very little sense of personal initiative remains to the employees of a large nationalized industry.

I think lack of opportunity for personal initiative is one of the great dangers of the modern world. It leads to apathy, to a sense of impotence, and thence to pessimism. There should be, for everybody who is energetic and who has strong convictions, some sphere, great or small, where he may hope to be effective, and this is only possible by means of much more devolution than exists at present.

Before the First World War this idea was advocated in somewhat different forms by syndicalists in France and by guild Socialists in England, but the Russian Revolution captured their imaginations and they went helter-skelter for

State Socialism, and bureaucratic autocracy. They thought, rather foolishly, that if the bureaucrats were former rebels all would be well. The result was not only Russian autocracy, but also a complete failure of movements of the Left in the West to stand for things that they had formerly valued. It is time to revive the aims which progressive people set before themselves in the days before the Russian Revolution. It is only in so far as this is done that Western democracy can be sure of remaining democratic.

World Government

The question of devolution is vital in considering the problem of world government. It is obvious that if there were a world government there would only be certain limited functions that it would have to perform, and that most of the functions at present performed by national governments would remain in their hands.

It may be thought needlessly Utopian to consider world government, since it remains totally impossible so long as the East–West tension continues. It is, however, an urgent problem, since, unless it is solved within the next generation, it is unlikely that the human race will survive. A statement of this sort is found annoying, because people do not like changing their mental habits, and hating certain foreign nations is one of the most deeply engrained of these habits. They do not like to think that old habits are incompatible with survival, and there are very few people who are more anxious to survive than not to think.

It does not, of course, present itself in this way to their minds. What presents itself consciously is a quick conviction that any unusual thought is absurd. The conviction is so quick and firm that they never look to see whether it has a rational basis. I think, however, that anybody who can resist this unreasoning impulse must perceive that the survival of the human race depends upon the abolition of war, and that war

92

can only be abolished by the establishment of a world government.

What powers would such a government need? Primarily those involving peace and war. It would need a monopoly of all the more important weapons of war. It would need the right to revise treaties between nations, and to refuse to recognize any treaty to which it would not give assent. It would need a firm determination to make war upon any nation which rebelled against its authority or committed a hostile aggression against any other nation. But it would not need to control nations as regards their internal economic development, as regards their education or their religious institutions, or any of the matters that could rightly be regarded as internal.

What, in fact, it should take away from a nation is what has long ago been taken away from an individual—namely, the right to kill. Individual citizens, unless they are gangsters, do not feel their liberty unduly hampered by the fact that they cannot shoot their neighbour whenever he plays the piano too loudly.

Individual nations ought to learn that a similar limitation upon their liberty is equally unobjectionable. They ought to be content with liberty to control their own affairs, and not demand the opportunity to shoot foreigners whenever the whim takes them. It is this opportunity of which a world government would have to deprive them. But it need not deprive them of any liberty that a decent person could desire.

Excess of Government

Within a national State, there are certain matters which should be left free from governmental control. It is now generally recognized that religion is one of these matters. In the sixteenth and seventeenth centuries this was not recognized, and violent persecutions were carried out to ensure theological uniformity.

In the modern world it is not theology, but politics, that rouses the persecuting spirit. In Russia this spirit is in absolute control. In America it is much stronger than it ought to be. The excuse is, of course, that political dissidents are a danger to the State, but this excuse also existed in the sixteenth and seventeenth centuries. Queen Elizabeth persecuted Jesuits, but Jesuits maintained that she was not the lawful Sovereign and acted as fifth columnists for the Spaniards.

There is the same excuse in the present day for objecting to Communists in non-Communist countries. But in the one case as in the other, people are subversive because of persecution as well as being persecuted because of subversiveness. Any lessening of the one also lessens the other. No English Jesuit of the present day wants the new Queen Elizabeth dethroned for the benefit of some Jacobite heir. And this is no doubt partly because Jesuits are no longer persecuted.

Democracy and Liberty

The connection of democracy with individual liberty is not as close as is sometimes thought. Theoretically, and as a matter of definition, democracy is compatible with a complete absence of liberty for minorities. There is nothing that can be called strictly undemocratic in outlawing Communists in a country where the majority dislikes them.

In New England colonial communities, there was at first theological uniformity enforced by persecution, and it would not be verbally correct to regard this as an infringement of democracy. Nevertheless, there is an important psychological connection between democracy and individual liberty, for where individual liberty is not respected there will be people inclined to violent rebellion, and where many people are inclined to violent rebellion democratic processes of government become very difficult.

The most difficult kind of liberty to preserve in a democracy is the kind which derives its importance from services to the community that are not very obvious to ignorant people. New intellectual work is almost always unpopular because it is subversive of deep-seated prejudices, and appears to the uneducated as wanton wickedness. Luther thought Copernicus a mere paradox monger who wished to be known for his eccentricity. Calvin took the same view, and so did the Catholic Church in the time of Galileo. Democracy would not have saved Galileo from persecution.

In present-day America, while a teacher is not likely to suffer legal penalties for his views, he will probably suffer very severe economic penalties if he teaches history or economics or social science and does not agree with intolerant and ignorant men.

It has frequently happened in the past that important men have been protected from popular fury by undemocratic rulers. Aristotle was safe in Athens so long as Alexander was alive to protect him, but when Alexander died Aristotle had to flee. Averroes was protected by Mohammedan rulers from the fury of the mob until near the end of his life, when popular pressure became too great for the government to resist. Hobbes was befriended by Charles II when Parliament decided that Divine anger at his impiety was the cause of the Plague. When Tennessee decided against evolution, the decision was not undemocratic. As these examples show, intellectual liberty is not rendered secure by democracy alone.

But it would be quite unhistorical to conclude that intellectual liberty is, in general, safer under an undemocratic régime. There have been a few examples of enlightened autocrats, but the immense majority of autocrats have been completely unenlightened and completely willing to restrain intellectual liberty even more completely than the worst democracies. At the present day Russia is, of course, the supreme example. Stalin thought he knew more about genetics than any geneticist, and those who ventured to disagree suffered very extreme penalties.

In eighteenth-century France, the government was completely obscurantist. It compelled Buffon, for example, to recant publicly the opinion that not all existing mountains had existed since the beginning of the world.

(5) DANGEROUS IDOLATRY—DIMINUTION OF LIBERTY

Where democracy is combined with party government (which is the case wherever it is vigorous) it has one advantage that perhaps outweighs all others, and that is that nearly half the nation believes the government to be composed of scoundrels. This belief is often well founded, but there is no method, except democracy, which will cause it to be held by large numbers of influential people.

It is an essential element in democracy that any member of the public should be able, without too much trouble, to find out the truth when there is a dispute as to facts. It is generally recognized in the West that this demands freedom of the Press. The authorities must not be at liberty to suppress information merely because they do not like it.

But freedom of the Press, though necessary, is not sufficient. There must be quick methods of correcting gross misstatements. For this purpose the machinery of libel actions is quite inadequate, partly because it is slow, partly because it is expensive, and partly because there are cases when it is inapplicable.

Suppose, for example, that a Right-Wing Republican in the United States were to say that many prominent Democratic statesmen are in the pay of the Kremlin. No action would lie so long as he named no names. There ought to be a judicial body with the right and duty to pronounce on any statement injurious to a man or organization; and, in the event of there being no *prima facie* case for the statement, the journal making the statement should be under a legal obligation to print this fact with the same prominence as the original statement. This is important, for, while freedom of information is essential, freedom to correct misinformation is equally essential.

Dangerous Idolatry

Worship of government is the modern form of idolatry and is exceedingly dangerous. Far the most effective antidote to it is the two-party system. I lived in America under Roosevelt, and most of the people that I met considered him a dangerous lunatic. I did not agree with them in this, but I thought it thoroughly wholesome that people should have this opinion of the Head of State.

Liberty will only exist where there is an effective division of opinion with influential men of both sides. It began in the West with the conflict between Church and State in the time of St Ambrose. It exists at the present day owing to the conflict between Conservatives and Socialists in England and between Democrats and Republicans in America.

Where democracy prevails, it is hardly possible to have that worship of the State as the Garment of God which Hegel sycophantically inculcated as he drew his pay from the Prussian Exchequer.

Diminution of Liberty

A sentiment in favour of liberty is something rather separate from forms of government, but on the whole I think that it is somewhat more often found where there is democracy than where there is autocracy. Although I believe this to be true, I think, none the less, that individual liberty is insufficiently valued in many modern democratic countries.

This is a matter in which there has been retrogression since the nineteenth century. The retrogression is caused by fear, and I cannot say that the fear is irrational, but I do not think that a diminution of liberty is a method of escaping from the dangers that are feared.

In America, for example, the question as to what foreigners shall be admitted is left in the hands of uneducated policemen, who have a general belief that all European physicists are spies who will sell to the stupid Russians the atomic secrets discovered by clever Americans. The result is that international congresses of scientists have become difficult in America, and that American scientists who are not free to travel get out of touch with valuable work done in Europe. An American will not be encouraged to work at nuclear physics unless his politics are reactionary, and this is almost sure to diminish the technical efficiency of America in the next war if it comes.

This suggests a wider problem connected with democracy. Democracy is based historically upon the maxim that all men are equal. But if this maxim is to be true, it must be carefully interpreted. It is not the case that all men are the equals of Newton in mathematical ability, or of Beethoven in musical genius. To say that all men are equal is only true if it means that justice requires an absence of discrimination between one man and another in political matters. It is not true if it is held to imply that, even in the most complex matters, one man's judgment is as good as another's. Yet it is only in this latter untrue form that it can justify the ordinary voter in deciding what shall be taught in a university.

In American State universities the taxes pay the teachers, and the ordinary taxpayer infers that he has a right to object to the teaching of anything that he does not agree with. It does not occur to him that perhaps a man who has devoted his life to a difficult subject knows more about it than a man who has never studied it at all. When democracy is thought to justify such conclusions it becomes absurd.

(6) REDRESSING GRIEVANCES—DEMOCRACY AND THE WEST

I do not think it can be said that democracy, always and everywhere, is the best form of government. I do not think that it can be successfully practised among totally uncivilized people. I do not think it is workable where there is a population of mixed groups which fundamentally hate each other. I do not think it can be introduced quite suddenly in countries that have no experience of the give and take that goes with freedom in government. If every compromise is viewed as a surrender of principle, it is impossible for rival groups to make a bargain representing a middle point between their respective interests.

For such reasons I do not think one ought to advocate the introduction of democracy immediately in every part of the world. But having conceded so much to the opponents of democracy, I should wish to state with the utmost emphasis the arguments in its favour wherever it is practicable. In doing this I will repeat more briefly what I have said earlier.

The first and strongest argument for democracy is human selfishness. When a group of men has power over another group, it will almost always ill-treat the subject group. White men have ill-treated negroes, aristocrats have ill-treated peasants, men have ill-treated women. It is hardly possible to find, except for brief periods in rare circumstances, cases where a dominant group has behaved with tolerable humanity towards one over which it had control.

This was not only true in the past. It is true at least as much in the present. Stalin's Government kept millions of workers in slave conditions, and punished the faintest whisper of opposition in the most savage manner. Hitler's atrocities are too notorious to need recapitulating. I value democracy, first of all, because where it exists such horrors are scarcely possible.

Redressing Grievances

The second great merit of democracy is that it affords a possible method of settling disagreements. Where there is no democracy, if any large section is discontented, it has no remedy except rebellion. Democracy gives a legal method of redressing grievances, and makes possible a respect for law which can hardly exist in an autocracy.

Consider, for example, the plot to murder Hitler in 1944. The men involved in this plot were some of the best men in

Germany, and their motives were wholly laudable. One cannot imagine, at the same time, an English plot to murder Churchill. It is mainly the existence of democracy in England that makes this unimaginable.

Although, as we saw above, there can be democracy without liberty, there can never be secure liberty without democracy. Such liberty as has existed under autocracies has depended upon the whim of the momentary despot, and has been liable to disappear overnight. It is only where there is a recognized orderly process of changing the government, or altering the laws, that liberty can be secure.

If I had to choose between liberty and democracy, I should be hard put to it to know which to prefer, since it is only by means of liberty that progress, whether intellectual or moral, is possible. Fortunately, no such choice is forced upon us.

Democracy and the West

The Western nations are, for the present, the custodians of both democracy and liberty. In neither respect are they perfect, but they are better than any other nations, and it is only by developing what is best in them that mankind can advance.

I think we of the West are sometimes insufficiently conscious of what it is that we have to preserve for the human race. It is not only what we owe to the Graeco-Roman heritage and to Christianity, it is perhaps even more what we have achieved during the last four centuries: the substitution of science for superstition; of a technique capable of abolishing poverty throughout the world; of medical knowledge which, in the West, has put an end to those great plagues that used to devastate whole populations; and, more than any of these, although as yet imperfectly, that respect for the initiative and freedom of individuals whose work is creative and not destructive.

Mankind advanced slowly in the past, largely because all those who suggested advance were persecuted. In modern Western nations this is much less true, and the advance during the last four centuries has been more rapid than at any other period in human history.

Is this advance to be brought to an end by an obscurantist tyranny? I cannot believe it. But I cannot deny that the danger is real. The danger is not only, or chiefly, the danger of military defeat in war; it is even more the danger of spiritual defeat, the danger that in a fierce life-and-death struggle men may forget everything that does not serve for immediate military victory.

For this reason, although no one can deny that war might be forced upon the Western nations, a sane man will feel that war, even successful war,[1] would involve a great loss and a very serious set-back in all the matters as to which the West is in advance of the rest of mankind. Perhaps if we have sufficient patience, the time will come when the countries on the other side of the Iron Curtain will decide to liberalize their régime.[2]

It is up to us in the West to behave in such a manner as to make the merits of our system obvious even to those who have the least desire to admit them. This is a slow, patient, and undramatic policy. To some it may seem unheroic. There are those who, when they become aware of an evil, are convinced that it is right to undertake a crusade against it even by military force. They forget that, in the course of a crusade, the crusaders themselves forget the idealistic purposes with which they embarked upon a war, and remember only the desire for victory.

We shall not be wise if we, realizing what is evil in the Communist system, ourselves encourage a war. The chance of gradual improvement east of the Iron Curtain may, for the moment, seem precarious, but it exists, and so long as it exists it is our duty to remember that it is the best of the possibilities offered by our distracted world.

[1] The H-bomb has made successful war impossible.
[2] To a considerable extent, this has happened since Stalin's death.

III

A Scientist's Plea for Democracy[1]

THE LIBERAL tradition, in which I was brought up, has still, it seems to me, immense importance for human welfare. It is true that, on the economic side, the growth of vast industrial organizations has necessitated a new approach to the problem of distributive justice, but in other respects I have found no reason to abandon the ideals that I imbibed in youth: freedom of speech, toleration, democracy, and respect for the individual so far as the need of maintaining public order permits. These ideals are, in the political sphere, the counterpart of scientific method in the intellectual sphere, and where either is abandoned the other suffers. It is this connection between democracy and the scientific outlook that I am now concerned to make clear.

Ever since ancient Greek times there have been two views as to the way of producing true beliefs, and two corresponding views as to the best form of government. Although these two connected controversies have existed for over two thousand years, they are as vigorous in the present day as at any former period. The two ways of producing what are deemed to be true beliefs may be distinguished as the way of authority, and the way of discussion and investigation. Similarly the two forms of government are that of authority and that of discussion followed by a majority decision. Where the way of authority is adopted as the method of producing true beliefs, certain opinions are inculcated as having been proclaimed by the wise

[1] Talk on BBC Third Programme, 1947.

and good: those who controvert these opinions are held to be
foolish or wicked or both, and are subjected to penalties which
have varied in kind and in severity according to the age and
the country. Sometimes the supporters of orthodoxy rely
wholly on tradition, but in most cases there is a sacred book
with which it is impious to disagree. In Christian countries
men were burnt for questioning the official interpretation of
the Bible; in Mohammedan countries it was very rash to
throw doubt on any part of the Koran; in modern Russia, you
risk liquidation if you disagree with Marx or Engels as
expounded by the Kremlin. In all such cases the government
upholds a collection of dogmas, and spreads belief in them, not
by argument or appeal to evidence, but by shielding the young
from contact with adverse opinions, by censoring literature,
and by punishing, usually by death, such heretics as nevertheless have the temerity to proclaim their subversive views. As a
rule, under such a system, the government, having the habit
of authority, becomes gradually more and more tyrannical
until, in the end, it is brought to destruction in a fierce
revolution.

Empiricists, who owe their influence mainly to the rise of
science, have a quite different view of the way of arriving at
true beliefs. Science has developed a method of controlled
observation interpreted by careful reasoning, which, where it is
applicable, has led to general agreement among competent
people. When controversies occur on scientific matters, as
they frequently do, they are decided sooner or later by the
proof that the weight of evidence is on one side, not by
burning or liquidating those who hold what is at the moment
the minority opinion. In the sixteenth and seventeenth centuries,
and even in the eighteenth, science had to fight for its life
against the weight of traditional dogma. Giordano Bruno was
burnt, Galileo's Copernican arguments were condemned, and
Buffon was compelled by the Sorbonne to recant the opinion
that the mountains and valleys of the present day had not

103

existed since the Creation. In Western countries, science was victorious in this conflict, largely because of its economic and military usefulness. When nations had to decide whether they would be poor, defeated, and orthodox, or rich, victorious, and latitudinarian, only the most bigoted, such as Spain, decided for orthodoxy and ruin. The pragmatic advantages of science were irresistible, but the attitude of indifference to authority which it inculcated could not be confined to strictly scientific matters. The American Revolution, the French Revolution, and the growth of democracy in England were its natural consequences.

The connection between science and democracy is closer than is sometimes thought, and the common link is the emphasis on free discussion as opposed to authority. In an unscientific age or community, there are official repositories of wisdom, such as Egyptian priests and Tibetan lamas. The men who possess official wisdom are—or are closely connected with—the men who hold political power. Resistance to what they enjoin is an offence against the gods, and rouses popular detestation, even when to an outsider it seems to be in the popular interest. In such a mental atmosphere, despotism or oligarchy is easily established and perpetuated, for authority in matters of opinion is naturally combined with authority in practical affairs. But where the scientific outlook has become fairly common, it becomes customary to demand something more than emphatic assertion or appeal to ancient tradition before assent is given. There is, of course, still authority: few of us have examined the evidence that the distance of the sun is 93,000,000 miles, of that light travels 186,000 miles a second. We accept these statements because we have heard them made by people whom we consider worthy of belief. But we consider them worthy of belief, not because they hold an opinion which has been held from time immemorial, or because they can quote from a sacred book, or because if we disagree they will cut off our head or put our families into concentration camps. Any man is entirely free to hold what opinion he likes about the velocity of light, and the only penalty he incurs for an unusual opinion is that of being thought a fool. As a result of free discussion all who are capable of forming a judgment have come to agree, and their authority is not enforced but based on reason.

The habit of basing opinions on reason, when it has been acquired in the scientific sphere, is apt to spread to the sphere of practical politics. Why should a man enjoy exceptional power or wealth merely because he is the son of his father? Why should white men have privileges denied to those with other complexions? Why should women be subject to men? As soon as these questions are allowed to come into the light of day and be examined in a rational spirit, it becomes very difficult to resist the claims of justice, which demands an equal distribution of ultimate political power among all adults, with the exception of those who are insane or criminal. It is, therefore, natural that the progress of science and the progress towards democracy have gone hand in hand.

Conversely, those who attempt in the modern world to reintroduce despotic forms of government, whether in Germany or in Russia, are hostile to the scientific point of view. The Nazis maintained that one should think with the blood rather than with the brain, and this habit had very odd results. They held, for example, that Einstein's general theory of relativity was not put forward by him because he believed it to be true, but only because he thought it would puzzle Gentiles. Jews, of course, were not taken in, but were accomplices in his game. For my part, I consider this view somewhat insulting to the brains of Gentiles, but not perhaps to those of Nazis. The same sort of thing happens in Russia: the way to ascertain truth—for example, as to how to obtain a breed of wheat that will resist the cold—is not by making experiments, but by examination of the inferences to be drawn from Marx's metaphysical doctrine of dialectical materialism. This doctrine, being difficult, has to be interpreted by a priestly caste, and heretical interpretations must suffer the traditional penalties of heresy. Where such an ideology has been widely accepted, it is not difficult to preserve the dictatorship of a minority.

What are the advantages of scientific democracy over dogmatic dictatorship? At the basis of all other advantages is the purely intellectual one that in a scientific community doctrines are accepted because, as a result of untrammelled discussion, they have emerged as the most likely to be true, whereas under a dictatorship doctrines are accepted either because they are traditional or because they are convenient for the holders of power. From this difference a multitude of consequences flow. When the official opinion is not the one that would result from free discussion, free discussion has to be prohibited and intelligent thinking has to be discouraged. The government, therefore, has an interest in inculcating stupidity. Furthermore, where there is no free discussion it is impossible to point out the occasions on which the holders of power sacrifice the general interest to their own, so that they soon become able to practise with impunity cruelties and injustices which, in a freer community, would be quickly stopped by the universal indignation that they would arouse. History shows what the study of human nature would lead us to expect: that any set of men, entrusted with power over others, will abuse their power unless they have reason to fear that they may lose it. Perhaps the greatest advantage of democracy over all other systems of government, is not that the men who have come to the top are exceptionally wise, but that, since their power depends upon popular support, they know that they cannot retain their position if they are guilty of more than a certain modicum of injustice.

It has been customary in recent decades, among certain persons who profess to have the interests of the wage-earners at heart, to sneer at intellectual freedom as a matter concerning a small minority of highbrows, who can be liquidated without serious loss to anybody but themselves. This point of view shows an equal ignorance of history and of human nature: where free discussion is prohibited it is not only intellectuals who suffer, but all except those who regulate official propaganda. Consider, for example, the rise of women to equality with men. The movement for women's equality had its origin, it is true, among a few intellectuals, mostly male, and at first the majority of women were as shocked by it as men were. If free discussion and free speech had been prohibited, the movement could never have made any progress; women's earnings would still belong to their husbands, and men would still have the right to beat their wives with a stick no thicker than their thumb. The change in these respects is not one by which only intellectuals profit. Or take again the rise of trade unionism: this would have been quite impossible but for the liberal atmosphere of free discussion which hampered the activities of those who wished unions to remain illegal. Free publicity is by far the best safeguard against arbitrary injustice, as well as against ancient and traditional folly.

In our day one of the most important aspects of the claim for political equality between different human beings is the increasing but as yet very inadequate recognition that there is no justice in the claim to the supremacy of white men over other races. Here also free discussion plays an essential part in refuting those who use a pseudo-scientific pseudo-Darwinism to support indefensible racial doctrines. The modern revolt against democracy on the part of certain sections of Left opinion is necessarily, whether by intention or not, anti-scientific. Marx laid it down that the interests of wage-earners were in some mysterious way bound up with materialism. As a philosophy modern physics makes materialism very unplausible, therefore modern physics is a bourgeois invention. But modern physics had led to the atomic bomb, which cannot be ignored, therefore some theological subtlety has to be invented to reconcile quantum theory with dialectical materialism. In the long run, however, this sort of thing produces a time lag, just as the condemnation of Galileo by the Inquisition caused astronomy to flourish mainly in Protestant countries. Any despotic and dictatorial system, though it may at first be abreast of scientific opinion, is sure to fall increasingly behind as time goes on; and as it falls behind the result will be disastrous, not only in theory, but in technique. It is only in an atmosphere of freedom that progress can long be maintained, even in such matters as military technique which governments are most anxious to promote. New opinions are almost always distasteful to the authorities, but where they are suppressed, communities ossify. I should, therefore, confidently expect that the countries which preserve scientific and intellectual freedom will be more efficient in war than those which submit to dictatorship.

Dictatorship not only tends to stereotype opinion and prevent intellectual and technical progress; it also tends to generate dishonesty in experts. The medical officer at Dachau was ordered to invent something as good as penicillin, and presently professed to have done so. He poisoned prisoners and proved that those whom he injected with his new substance survived while the others died. But it turned out that those whom he wished to survive had been only very lightly poisoned, so the Nazis executed him. Under a reign of terror this sort of thing is sure to be common.

I should not wish, however, to base the argument for freedom and democracy upon success in war; I would base it rather on general considerations of human welfare. Free discussion tends to promote a tolerant spirit, and a tolerant spirit tends to prevent war. Where grievances can be publicly stated they are more likely to be remedied, and less likely to generate implacable hatreds. Wherever a rigid system of government exists, it encourages ruthlessness and cruelty in those who believe their power to be secure. In the end, the forces of resistance become overwhelming, and, maddened by the long endurance of intolerable suffering, they burst their bonds in savage reprisals. Such violent upheavals are unavoidable wherever minorities cling to despotic power, but, however necessary, revolutions inspired by hate are not the best means of creating a better world, since those who hate their oppressors are apt, when they can, to imitate the crimes against which they have rebelled. It is only in a régime of democracy and free discussion that evils can be remedied without an extreme of violence that is apt to generate new evils as great as those that it sweeps away. Democracy embodies justice, free discussion embodies rationality, and it is only through justice and rationality that an issue can be found from the dangers with which modern war is threatening the human race.

IV

The Story of Colonization[1]

THERE ARE various different aspects from which the history of mankind may be viewed. One of the most important of these concerns the spread of civilization. In its earliest phases, this is marked by the presence or absence of certain skills and techniques. The domestication of animals, agriculture, writing, and the use of metals are the most important of these. The beginnings of agriculture are prehistoric, but its gradual spread, after a beginning in certain river valleys, occurred in historical times and was not complete until our own day. The use of metals spread with almost equal slowness. The Iron Age in some countries began thousands of years earlier than it did in others. The art of writing, which seems to have developed slowly out of pictures and not, originally, as a representation of spoken language, can be traced through many early stages in Egypt, the Hittite Empire, and Phoenicia, to Greece. Writing in China, which was not alphabetic, appears to have developed independently. It would seem that in Mediterranean countries, but more especially in Egypt, writing was for a long time a mystery understood only by the priests. In the Dark Ages this had again become the case in Western Europe. It was only gradually that kings decided to teach their children to read and write. As late as 1807 the President of the Royal Society vehemently opposed the extension of literacy to wage-earners on the ground that,

[1] Talk on B.B.C. European Service, 1956.

if they could read, 'it would enable them to read seditious pamphlets, vicious books and publications against Christianity'. The long stretch of time from Egypt in the Fourth Millennium, BC, to the English Education Act of 1870 illustrates, in the case of writing, the extreme slowness which has characterized the spread of culture.

Various agencies have been favourable to the growth of civilization. I think the most important have been military conquest, commercial intercourse, and missionary zeal. In regard to all three a very important part has been played by colonies, which form the theme of these talks. A colony, as the word was understood by the Greeks, consisted of a small group of sea-faring men accompanied by their families, all coming from some one Greek city and settling on the sea-coast of some comparatively uncivilized country. Such cities were founded at an early period of Greek history in Asia Minor, Southern Italy, and Sicily. Before very long they spread farther afield to Spain and Marseilles. Wherever they went, they carried with them the institutions of the parent city, with which they retained close ties in spite of political independence. They were maritime commercial cities, and many of them achieved great wealth, which has become proverbial in the case of the epithet 'sybarite'. They did not aim at conquest of the hinterland, although many of them maintained considerable armies of mercenaries. The Phoenician colonies, especially Carthage, were essentially similar; and, before the rise of Rome, the Mediterranean from Sicily westward was dominated by the rivalry of Carthage and Syracuse. It was owing to the Roman victory that Greek and not Phoenician culture became prevalent throughout the West.

A different kind of colonization was inaugurated by Alexander the Great. The Greek colonies which he planted from Egypt to the Indus came in the wake of conquering armies, and not as an incident of commerce. Where Macedonian or Roman armies preserved their supremacy, these colonies remained centres for the diffusion of Hellenic culture. But where, as in

Persia, Afghanistan, and Northern India, the Macedonians lost their power, the trickle of Greek culture became gradually less and less, like a river losing itself in the desert. Even in India, however, it left important traces: its influence on early Buddhist art is generally acknowledged.

Northern Europe, including Germany, Scandinavia, and Poland, owed its civilization mainly to missionaries, except for the conversion of the Saxons by Charlemagne. Buddhism, quite as much as Christianity, affords examples of the spread of culture by missionary zeal. China, at about the beginning of the Christian Era, acquired Buddhism from India and with it learnt important elements in Indian culture. But this movement, important as it was, owed its success rather to saintly pilgrims than to colonizers, and therefore hardly falls within our theme.

Military conquest has played a very great part in the spread of culture. But here there is a broad division between cases where the conquerors were more civilized than the conquered, and cases where they were less civilized. And the cases in which the conquerors were less civilized, again, fall into two classes: those in which the conquerors swept away the conquered civilization, and those in which they absorbed it and carried it on. The barbarians who invaded the Western Roman Empire degraded the level of Western civilization for centuries, but the Arabs, in the East, assimilated Greek science and philosophy. Many centuries later, the West regained from them what it had destroyed when the Western Roman Empire fell.

Over and over again in history an advanced culture has been overthrown by barbaric conquerors. Sometimes, as when the Greeks overthrew the Cretans, the barbarians have quickly surpassed those whom they had overthrown. Sometimes, their destructiveness has proved more permanent. The Mongols in Persia did irreparable damage, but, in China, in the course of two generations, they learnt everything that the Chinese had to teach. The Danes in the eighth and ninth centuries wiped out the civilization of Ireland and gravely impaired the nascent civilization of Yorkshire monasteries. But their kinsmen, the Normans, at a slightly later time, became, when they had finished conquering, the leaders in all that was best in the West.

Much the largest example of colonization known to history was the settlement of the Western hemisphere by white men. This proceeded on somewhat different lines in tropical and in temperate latitudes. In temperate latitudes the Indians were gradually driven out or confined to reservations. In one way or another they ceased to play any vital part in the life of the community, which became almost as dominantly white as in Europe. In tropical latitudes, on the contrary, where white men 'elt unable to undertake severe physical labour, they remained an aristocracy. In many regions they tried to employ Indian labour, but the Indians often proved recalcitrant and the white men fell back upon negro labour imported by the slave trade. In many parts of Latin America, a large Indian population survives. Latin America, consequently, has not, except in the far south, produced a more or less pure white civilization. Nevertheless the language, religion, and culture of all Latin America are those which were brought by the Spaniards and Portuguese.

North American colonists were of two different sorts. There were those who went for gain, and there were those who went to escape religious persecution and to found communities on new political principles. These principles, developed by discussions in Cromwell's army, were suppressed in England, first by Cromwell and then by the Restoration. But, after a somewhat obscure persistence, they burst upon the Western hemisphere in the American Revolution, and upon Europe in its French sequel.

The acquisition of the Western hemisphere by white men was one of the causes of the supremacy in world affairs which they enjoyed for some centuries. They can hardly recover this supremacy by new colonizing efforts after the old pattern, because there are no longer large regions that are empty or nearly empty awaiting the coming of vigorous and enterprising men. In quite recent times the words 'colonial' and 'colonialism' have acquired new meanings. They are now habitually used to denote regions where the governing class is white but not Russian, and the bulk of the population is of some non-white race. Western ideals of freedom have been propagated throughout the world by Western instructors and have produced an unwillingness to submit to alien domination which in former times was either non-existent or very much weaker. Although only military conquest compelled Gaul to become part of the Roman Empire, its population, after conquest, acquiesced completely and did not welcome the separation from Rome that came in the fifth century. National independence, which has become an obstacle to colonization, seems to modern men a natural human aspiration, but it is, in fact, very modern and largely a product of education. If the human race is to survive, nationalism will have to come to terms with a new ideal—namely, internationalism. I do not see how this new ideal, which will concede to each nation internal autonomy, but not freedom for external aggression, can be reconciled with the formation of new colonies, because empty regions can no longer be found. Perhaps the Antarctic continent will be made habitable, and this might prove an exception, but I think it is the only one.

Perhaps internationalism, as a principle, may sometimes be compelled to over-ride even what might seem to be the internal affairs of a country. This may be illustrated by the problems which have arisen in relation to the latest serious attempt to found a new colony. I mean the creation of the State of Israel. This has raised difficult and bitter controversies in which each side, for different reasons, has claimed the support of outside opinion. I do not wish to express any view on these controversies on the present occasion, but their bitterness is likely to make statesmen wary of similar experiments in any foreseeable future.

Throughout history colonies have been among the most powerful agents for the spread of the arts and science and ways of life that constitute civilization. For the future, it seems that mankind will have to learn to do without this ancient and well-tried method. I think mankind will have to depend, not upon force or domination, but upon the inherent attractiveness of a civilized way of life. The Romans when they overcame the Greeks were at a much lower level of civilization than those whom they defeated, but they found Greek civilization so attractive that, from a cultural standpoint, it was the Greeks who were the victors. Those among us who value culture and a humane way of life must school ourselves to learn from the Greeks rather than from the Romans. If this is to be done successfully, we shall have to eliminate those harsher features of our way of life which have repelled many alien nations with whom we have had contact. Missionary and soldier have hitherto played equal parts in the diffusion of civilization. For the future, it must be the missionary—taking this term in a large sense—who will alone be able to carry on the work.

V

Pros and Cons of Nationalism

NATIONALISM has various aspects, some good and some bad. The first broad cleavage is between cultural aspects and those which have to do with economics and politics. From a cultural point of view there are very strong arguments in favour of nationalism, but from a political or economic point of view nationalism is usually harmful.

Nationalism is regarded in our age as a part of human nature and a perennial fact which it would be folly to overlook. This, however, is not historically true. Nationalism began with the decline of the medieval system and hardly existed at any earlier time. Its origin, everywhere, has been resistance to alien domination or the threat of it. It began, in France, with Joan of Arc's resistance to the English. It began in England with resistance to the Spanish Armada and found its first literary expression in Shakespeare. It began in Germany with resistance to Napoleon, and in Italy with resistance to Austria. In the early nineteenth century, it was acclaimed by liberals and decried by reactionaries. Metternich, who governed a polyglot empire containing a great mixture of races, was the most vehement and powerful opponent of nationalism, while the movements for German and Italian unity and for the liberation of Greece from the rule of Turkey commanded the enthusiastic support of all whose politics were progressive.

But a new era was inaugurated by Bismarck. Bismarck unified Germany by three successful wars of aggression and made nationalism militaristic rather than democratic. It is this new form of nationalism that has dominated Western Europe ever since.

The development of nationalism outside Western Europe has been interesting and unfortunate. Socialism, as Marx conceived it, was to be international, and it retained this internationalism in the minds of Lenin and Trotsky, both of whom had lived in the Western world and, on the whole, thought better of it than of their own country. But Stalin, in a new way, did for Russia what Bismarck had done for Germany. He made Communism nationalistic. Russians who supported him felt that they were supporting Russia. It is this change that enabled Russian Communism to acquire a degree of strength which Lenin could never have given it.

Nationalism triumphant becomes imperialism. This transformation occurred in England, in France, and in Germany. After the Second World War, it occurred also in Russia. Eastern Europe outside Russia contained a large number of small countries lately emancipated from foreign rule. Most of these countries hated most of their neighbours and were stultified by their rivalry. Stalin subdued them all except Turkey and Greece and, after a certain interval, Yugoslavia.

With remarkable propagandist skill, Russian Communism, while enslaving most of Eastern Europe, still posed successfully as the liberator of Asia and Africa. Nationalism in Asia and Africa has still the liberal flavour that it had in Western Europe in the early nineteenth century. It is inspired by resistance to Western imperialism and tends to be friendly to Russia because Russia supports this resistance. To an impartial observer it seems highly probable that any independence acquired by Asia and Africa with the help of Russia will be as temporary as the vanished independence of Poland and Czechoslovakia and Hungary. There is every reason to think that Russian imperialism will swallow up the dainty morsels that Western imperialism has been compelled to drop. But it is unlikely that Asia and Africa will realize this danger until it is too late.

What gains and losses are to be expected from the spread of nationalism to these new regions? The question has two aspects, one political and one economic. I do not think anybody can deny that the aspiration for freedom from alien domination is a sentiment deserving of respect and that those who have to bow down before a foreign master suffer a damage which is very great and very undesirable. It is not a good thing that one nation should dominate another and, in so far as nationalism opposes such domination it must be reckoned to be doing a good work. But as the world develops technically there is a continually increasing need of agreement and co-operation between different nations. The claim to national independence is just where only internal affairs are concerned, but becomes disastrous when it is supposed to involve the right to inflict damage on other nations. The world cannot be saved from its present troubles by unlimited nationalism, but only by the development of internationalism. It is a great misfortune that in Asia and Africa co-operation between different regions occurred mainly as the result of foreign imperialism. The consequence has been that newly emancipated States have rejected forms of co-operation even when the common benefit was entirely obvious. One very clear example of this was the fate of the scheme drawn up by the British for the irrigation of the Punjab. When India and Pakistan became separate States, neither could agree to let the other have any share of its waters and therefore both had to adopt very inferior schemes.

But it is not only in Asia and Africa that nationalism inflicts economic damage. All the countries of the world would be much richer than they are if all of them abolished tariffs. A hundred years ago, it seemed as if this might happen, but national passions proved too strong.

Political theory at the present time has no clear principles by which to decide the delimitation between the sphere of nationalism and the sphere of internationalism. The need of hitherto unrecognized principles has been made particularly

118

evident by the dispute about the Suez Canal. Taking the matter first in the abstract and without regard to current disputes, it is invident that mankind as a whole have an interest in keeping open the routes of commerce and that, where a general interest is involved, it is not right or just that any one nation, or even any two or three, should have exclusive control. But this is never evident to those who, at any moment, have such control. The British had control of Suez and in some degree of Gibraltar; the Americans have control of Panama. It did not occur to us that there was anything unjust in this. On the contrary, we felt ourselves so wise and good that everybody ought to rejoice in having anything so important in our hands. The view which Colonel Nasser has proclaimed is, from the standpoint of principle, the same as that which Britain formerly proclaimed: namely, that there is no injustice in having the canal managed by one Power. It should be generally admitted that anything so internationally important as the Suez Canal or the Panama Canal should be under an international authority. The claim that those who happen to live on its banks should have the right to inflict enormous damage upon those who live elsewhere is one in which there is no justice. One might as well claim that two people who live opposite each other in Fifth Avenue should have the right to put a wall across the street. But there is another over-riding principle more important than the rights and wrongs of any particular dispute. It is that in a world of nuclear weapons no dispute must be settled by war except when a decision has been reached by an international authority and resistance to its decision is easily quelled. These conditions do not exist in the Suez dispute and therefore whoever threatens war as a means of deciding it is an enemy of mankind.

But while there ought to be some body with international authority in such matters, there is at present no such body. In saying this I do not forget the United Nations but, so long as the veto exists in the Security Council, the United Nations does not constitute a government except when all the members of the Security Council are agreed, which does not happen often. It is entirely right that the question of the Suez Canal should be submitted to the Security Council, but it is extremely unlikely that that body will reach a solution, since either Russia or the Western Powers may be expected to veto any suggestion. It will be useful to submit the dispute to the Security Council for two reasons: the first, that the period of deliberation will give time for heated feelings to cool; and the second, that the deadlock which is to be expected will show the necessity for some more effective method of reaching international decisions. I should like to see the Security Council decide in advance to agree to any solution of a dispute commended, after impartial inquiry, by a Committee appointed *ad hoc* containing equal numbers of the two sides of the dispute with a balance made up of representatives of disinterested nations. This would offer a real alternative to war. At present all sane men know that war must be avoided at all costs. In the absence of some peaceful method of reaching decisions, this puts a premium on insanity, since sane men realize, but insane men do not, that war is always the very worst possible outcome of a dispute.

The limitations of nationalism ought to be much the same as the limitations on the liberty of individuals. Individual liberty is immensely important and its preservation is vital to a good community, but we all recognize that it has its limits. We do not think that murder and theft should be tolerated, and we employ the forces of the State to prevent them. Murder and theft by a nation is more harmful than murder and theft by an individual because it is on a larger scale. Its prevention is therefore more important. The principle of nationalism is equally wicked in an unlimited form. It can oppose nothing to murder and theft by a nation, except warlike resistance on the part of the victim. It is obvious that if war is to be renounced it will be necessary to establish a reign of law between nations as firmly as it has been established between individuals. The complete realization of this ideal is as yet distant, since it will involve the dissolution of national armed forces except to the degree required for suppressing civil disorder. A World Government will have to be Federal and will have to have a constitution embodying the principle which should control all federations, namely, that the Federal Government concerns itself only with the external acts of constituent States or, at any rate, only with such acts as very directly affect interests of other States. In regard to the internal affairs of each State, the principle of nationalism should prevail. Each State should have the right to establish any religion that it might prefer or to remain theologically neutral. Each State should have the right to establish tariffs. Each State should have the right to whatever form of government it preferred: monarchical, democratic, totalitarian, or what not. Each State should have the right to establish whatever kind of education it preferred, or even to dispense with education altogether. I think, however, that in regard to education the Federal Government should have certain supervisory rights. Nelson gave his midshipmen three precepts: to shoot straight, to speak the truth, and to hate a Frenchman as you would the Devil. An international government should have the right to object to this third precept if embodied in the system of national education.

From the cultural point of view, as I said above, nationalism has great merits. The large uniformities which grow up in a cosmopolitan world are inimical to art and literature and tend to be oppressive of young talent. In the great days of Greece and of Renaissance Italy a man could rise to eminence in his own city and be honoured by it as an asset in cultural rivalry with other cities. Ancient Greece and Renaissance Italy, alike, after astounding contributions to culture, collapsed for lack of political unity. If culture is not to suffer, some way must be found of combining cultural independence with political union. I do not know whether the cultural variety which I should like to see preserved will prove possible in a world where industrialism and State education and easy transport have become universal. There have been hitherto distinctive characteristics of Englishmen, of Frenchmen, of Germans, of Italians, and these distinctive characteristics have contributed to the merits of their most eminent men. Leonardo could not have been anything but an Italian; Voltaire could not have been anything but a Frenchman; Goethe could not have been anything but a German; and Shakespeare could not have been anything but an Englishman. If these great men had been ground down by circumstances and early education to a dead level of uniformity, they would not have been as great as in fact they were.

But it is not only in regard to a few eminent individuals that national culture is important. Almost any kind of aesthetic excellence depends upon a long tradition which has produced sensitiveness to nuances of little utilitarian importance. A man who suffers too strong an impact from an alien tradition is apt to lose the merit of his own tradition without acquiring the merits of the other. When I lived in China I was immensely impressed by the beauty of traditional Chinese paintings, but my Europeanized Chinese friends despised these paintings since their painters were ignorant of perspective. Such attempts as I saw by modern Chinese painters to paint in the Western manner appeared to me to have lost the merits of the East without acquiring those of the West. I found the same kind of deterioration in more everyday matters. Traditional Chinese furniture was beautiful, but Westernized Chinese furniture was hideous. Perhaps the political and economic unification, which has become necessary if the human race is to survive, is making an age of universal ugliness inescapable. If this is indeed the case, it is immensely to be deplored. But perhaps, if secure peace were established, the world might revert to less utilitarian standards of what is to be admired, and in the course of time diversities of tradition would again be tolerated and again become beneficent. Meanwhile, the immediate perils are so great that such considerations must remain in the background.

The conclusion to which we are forced is that in the modern world nationalism is a grave evil and a source of appalling danger, and that if we are to escape disaster we must develop internationalism in the sphere to which it belongs; namely, that of economics, politics, and war. All the nations of the world, both great and small, have sinned in placing their own interest above that of the world at large. It is to be expected that they will continue to do so until such time as there are international institutions strong enough to insist upon the decision of vexed questions in accordance with the general human welfare and not with the insolence of this or that particular region. Some may think this a distant hope, but it is the only one that offers a future to our distracted species.

VI

The Reasoning of Europeans[1]

IT IS a curious fact that if you ask a cultivated Western European and a well-informed Asian to characterize Western civilization you will get replies which have almost nothing in common. A Western man is considered by his colleagues to be a worthy representative of European culture if he knows Greek and Latin literature, the philosophy of Plato, and the influence which Christianity is supposed to have had upon Western life. He should also know something of Western literature since Dante and should be well informed about Western painting and music and architecture. If he has these qualifications he will pass muster in any Western academic society and will run no risk of being thought an ignoramus.

But such a man is likely to be completely ignorant of everything that the East regards as important and distinctive in the West. Eastern nations have had art and architecture and philosophy and literature. Some virtues, which it is the custom nowadays to regard as especially Christian, have been at most times more worthily practised in the East than in the West. I am thinking in particular of religious toleration. Christian heretics in the early days of Islam were much more kindly treated by the Mohammedans than by the orthodox Byzantine Emperors. Anti-semitism, of which the most shocking examples are nowadays given by non-Christians, was originally and until the nineteenth century closely associated with Christianity. It

[1] A talk on the BBC Overseas Service, 1957.

is not what it has become common to call 'Western values' that the East regards as typical of the West, for in such matters the record of the East is, if anything, better than that of the West.

PYTHAGORAS AND GALILEO

But there is one respect—and an immensely important one— in which the West has made a contribution to which there has, as yet, been nothing parallel in the East. This contribution is due in its earlier form to the Greeks, and in its later form to the Europe of the sixteenth and seventeenth centuries. The Greeks invented mathematics and the apparatus of deductive reasoning. The Europeans who followed the Renaissance invented the technique of discovering natural laws, more particularly laws of change. We may select as two outstanding representatives of these discoveries Pythagoras and Galileo. Pythagoras is a strange character. His mystical philosophy and his belief in transmigration had, presumably, an Eastern origin and in no way distinguished European from Asian thought. But he and his school, utilizing Egyptian and Babylonian beginnings, developed the science of mathematics and applied it with brilliant success to astronomy. The Babylonians and Egyptians could predict eclipses, but it was Pythagoreans who discovered their cause. What the Greeks contributed to civilization in the way of art and literature and philosophy, however excellent, was not so very different from what was done in other nations, but their contribution in mathematics and astronomy was something new and distinctive, and it is for this, above all, that they deserve to be honoured.

The sudden rise of science in the sixteenth and seventeenth centuries was the work of Europe as a whole. The first step was taken by Copernicus, who was a Pole. Kepler was a German; Galileo, an Italian; and Newton, an Englishman. The Greeks, in the main, were able to deal scientifically only with things that were either unchanging or strictly periodic, like the day and the year. The great step, that was due chiefly to Galileo, was the scientific treatment of changes which were not periodic. This was an intellectual achievement which was new in human history.

UNCONSCIOUS NATURE

The men of the seventeenth century who invented modern scientific method had an advantage over their predecessors in a new mathematical technique. But, in addition to this technical advance, there was another almost more important. Before their time, observation had been haphazard, and baseless traditions were accepted as if they recorded facts. The laws which were invented to account for phenomena were not legitimate inferences from observation, but were infected by a belief that nature conformed to human tastes and hopes and fears. The heavenly bodies were supposed to move in circles or complications of circles, because the circle appealed to aesthetic taste as the perfect figure. Pestilences and earthquakes were sent to punish sin. Refreshing rain was sent as the reward for virtue. Comets foretold the death of princes. Everything on earth and in the heavens had reference to Man or to aesthetic tastes which closely resembled those of human beings.

The scientific temper abandoned this point of view. To find out how nature works, we must forget our own hopes and fears and tastes, and be guided only by careful investigation of facts. Although this may now seem a simple idea, it was, in truth, revolutionary. When Kepler discovered that the planets moved in ellipses, not in circles or epicycles, he dealt a death-blow to the interpretation of nature through the medium of human emotions. The essence of the scientific attitude thus inaugurated is this: Nature does what it does, not what we should wish, nor yet what we should fear, but something blandly unconscious of our existence.

From the realization of this fact, the modern world, for good or evil, has inexorably developed. It is, I repeat, a curious circumstance that most of the men who are thought in the West to be embodiments of Western culture are ignorant of this development, which was due, at first, to a tiny minority and is still, in the main, confined to people whom their literary *confrères* regard as narrow and uncouth specialists.

It is not pure science, however, but scientific technique which represents most fully the influence of the West upon mankind. The Industrial Revolution, which is still in its infancy, began in a humble way in Lancashire and Yorkshire and on the Clyde. It was execrated in the country of its origin by most cultured gentlemen, and was tolerated only because it contributed to the defeat of Napoleon; but its explosive force was so great that, by its own momentum, it spread first to the other countries of the West and, later, to Russia and Asia, which it is completely transforming. It is this, and this alone, that the East is willing to learn from the West. Whether the discovery of this kind of skill is to prove a boon or a disaster is, as yet, an open question. But, whether for good or ill, it is industrial technique that is the main cause of the changes that the world is undergoing.

DIFFERENT SCALES OF IMPORTANCE

There are two very different ways of estimating any human achievement: you may estimate it by what you consider its intrinsic excellence; or you may estimate it by its causal efficacy in transforming human life and human institutions. I am not suggesting that one of these ways of estimating is preferable to the other. I am only concerned to point out that they give very different scales of importance. If Homer and Aeschylus had not existed, if Dante and Shakespeare had not written a line, if Bach and Beethoven had been silent, the daily life of most people in the present day would have been much what it is. But if Pythagoras and Galileo and James Watt had not existed, the daily life not only of Western Europeans and Americans but of Russian and Chinese peasants would be profoundly different from what it is. And these profound changes are still only beginning. They must affect the future even more than they have already affected the present.

For all this the Western world has the major share of responsibility; and, because of this responsibility, it is incumbent upon Western man to supplement his scientific discoveries by the discovery of how to live with them. At present, scientific technique advances like an army of tanks that have lost their drivers, blindly, ruthlessly, without goal or purpose. This is largely because the men who are concerned with human values and with making life worthy to be lived are still in imagination in the old pre-industrial world, the world that has been made familiar and comfortable by the literature of Greece and the pre-industrial achievements of the poets and artists and composers whose work we rightly admire.

It is not the first time in history that a revolution in technique has caused a revolution in daily life. The same sort of thing happened, though much more gradually, with the adoption of agriculture as opposed to a nomadic existence. It is said, and no doubt with truth, that nomads have certain excellences which cannot be preserved in a stationary, agricultural life. Nevertheless, the spread of agriculture has been inevitable, although it was accompanied by ages of serfdom and oppression. Gradually, agriculture has been humanized, and we may hope that industrialism will be humanized more quickly.

GREATER INTERDEPENDENCE

From a political and social point of view, the most important change resulting from industrialism is the greater interdependence of men and groups of men upon one another. Important industrial undertakings require the co-operation of large numbers of men, but what is more important, they require, if they are to be useful, the right kind of relations between the men concerned in the undertaking and the populations which it is to affect. Consider such projects as the St Lawrence waterway, the irrigation of the Punjab, and the high dam at Aswan. All these raise international issues of the utmost delicacy. In a world of international *laissez faire* the issues they raise can be decided, if at all, only after long, turbulent debates and contests of power. In such questions, as in the internal affairs of single States, there is much less room than there used to be for *laissez faire* and much less room for individual enterprise, or even for the enterprise of a single nation.

It is growing increasingly difficult, in the world to which modern technique is giving rise, to preserve for the individual a sphere of initiative sufficient to stimulate his energies and give zest to his efforts. If the individual is not to shrivel and become desiccated through feeling himself merely an unimportant member of vast, impersonal organizations, something that seems both interesting and important will have to be found outside the main economic activities of communities. Many kinds of liberty, both personal and national, have become dangerous and need to be curbed. But liberty must have its place if men are not to lose stature. I am thinking not so much of liberty in the abstract as of the possibility of important achievement through individual effort. I hope that Europe, which has unwittingly created this problem, may also lead the way to its solution.

VII

The World I Should Like to Live in

THE TECHNICAL advances of the last one hundred and fifty years have brought about a new possibility of general well-being such as never existed before, since there first were men on the earth. Primitive man suffered from the cold in winter and the heat in summer. He lived in terror of wild beasts. In good times he obtained just enough food to keep him in health. In bad times he died of hunger. There were terrific visitations of plague and pestilence in which whole tribes were wiped out.

It was a furtive, painful, and precarious existence, owing, at that time, not to the folly and wickedness of man, but to natural facts with which he could not yet cope. Gradually his intelligence transformed the scene. He made weapons which enabled him to cope with lions and tigers, with rogue elephants and furious rhinoceroses. He acquired the art of agriculture which made his food supply fairly secure for about four years out of every five. He learned to keep warm by the use of fire, and dry by the building of houses.

By these means, men in ancient Egypt five thousand years ago reached a level of well-being (if it can be so called) which, until our own day, has scarcely been surpassed among Chinese and Indian peasants. But if this is well-being as compared to the life of primitive men, it is utter misery as compared to the life of ordinary men and women in the West.

The peasant and his wife and his children, as soon as they have the muscular strength, toil from morning till night to secure just as much food as the human frame requires, and that only in good years. In bad years immense numbers die. At all times most children die before they are grown up. Bubonic plague, pneumonic plague, typhus, smallpox, and other diseases sweep through the population leaving behind them a great swathe of death.

All this misery is now unnecessary. Given a little wisdom and a little good-will, there need not be anywhere any abject poverty, there need not be great destructive epidemics, there need not be more than a very small child-mortality, there need not be excessive hours of labour.

How could all this be brought about? Let us for a moment forget all about politics and assume some benevolent dictator sufficiently trusted for men to obey him willingly, and sufficiently wise to make use of all the best technical possibilities. What would such a dictator do? He would realize that hitherto the increase in the productivity of labour has not been used to lighten human burdens. It has been used for two purposes: one, to increase the population of one's own group; the other, to improve the means of killing members of other groups. He would point out that with our present techniques we could, without excessive labour, produce enough food for everybody, provided the population did not increase up to the limits of subsistence.

I think food would be the very first problem that he would tackle. He would see to it that the best methods of agriculture were taught everywhere, that the most destitute were assisted to achieve some kind of economic security, and that the benefits to be derived from better agriculture were not all swallowed up by an increase of population. He would, at the same time, use medical instruction and public hygiene to cut down the death rate. Having secured a population free from abject poverty, overwork, and premature death, he would have leisure to think about problems of what those who have never been hungry call the higher life.

I do not wish to seem in any way to belittle this later part of his task. On the contrary, I think that if the existence of the human race has any value it is not because they are born and eat and sleep and finally die: it is because of mental things for which some degree of physical well-being is a condition. I do not think that in the modern world it is possible for the mental and moral life, even among the fortunate, to be what it should be, while the greater part of mankind still suffers totally unnecessary misery.

Suppose you were a visitor from another planet able to observe the actions of men, but not knowing their languages and, therefore, impervious to their propagandas, their ideologies, and their myths. And suppose that you could only observe them in large masses, so that your view of their proceedings would be summary and statistical. What, broadly speaking, would you see? You would see two vast collections of human beings, the one on the whole prosperous, healthy, not overworked, more or less educated, the other very poor, often starving, mostly dying in infancy, and working such long hours at purely physical toil that no leisure remained for anything mental. You would observe, after a time, that these two opposing groups hate and fear each other and are preparing, with extraordinary skill, schemes of mutual extermination which are only too likely to be successful on both sides.

If, after a time, you learned their languages, you would be told by the richer group that the poorer group have no idealism, that they care only about material things, that they are destructive from envy, and that all that we hold precious can only be preserved if the poorer group lives in constant terror of extermination. On the other side you will be told that all the troubles of the world spring from the greedy possessiveness of the richer group, and that if they were willing to share equally with the victims of poverty, all would be well.

Neither side would be telling you quite the truth. It is not *merely* greed that makes the richer group cling to its advantages.

If there were sudden economic equality at the present moment, the result would be that happy populations would be reduced to the level of the unhappy, not that the unhappy would be raised to the level of the happy. To raise the level of the poorer populations is a task which must take time, and which will require skills only likely to be developed where there are many people not on the verge of starvation. It is true, however, that so long as glaring economic inequality exists between one part of the world and another, there will be envy on the one side and fear on the other, so that genuine co-operation will remain difficult.

What I most wish to emphasize is that the obstacles to universal happiness in the present day are, at bottom, psychological, not physical, and that this is a new fact in human history. If it were possible for the poorer groups not to feel envy and the richer groups not to feel fear, a rapid advance on the part of the poorer groups would be possible without any damage to the well-being of the richer groups.

At the moment, a fundamental change in the existing psychology may seem no more than a Utopian dream. The psychology of ordinary individuals becomes accumulated into the policy of great Powers. The mutual hate and fear are embodied in armaments which, in turn, increase the mutual hate and fear. In a kind of blind fatalism the human race marches on towards a universal disaster, which it foresees but imagines to be inevitable.

But it is not inevitable. There is no need to march towards disaster. There is no need to permit mankind to be politically dominated by hate and fear to the virtual exclusion of all other emotions. I will agree at once that it is not easy to see how to emerge from the tragic impasse in which we seem lost. Especially for us of the West it is not easy, since we are met with a hostility and suspicion which, so far, it has not been possible to break down.

I do not think the way out is either easy or dramatic. The

process required is more like the gradual subsidence of waves in the sea after a great storm. If the cold war remains cold long enough, something of the sort may happen. But if it is to happen, we must remain aware that there are rational hopes not based on violence, and that if only mankind would realize it, there is no conflict between the real interests of one group and the real interests of another.

Happiness is not to be secured by politics alone, but there are certain political conditions without which, in our modern world, happiness must be precarious and temporary. The first of these is that all the major armaments should be under the control of one single authority, so that great wars should no longer be possible. The second is that there should be a continual approach in the poorer parts of the world towards that level of prosperity which has already been achieved in the West. And the third is that the habits of populations everywhere should be such as to prevent a rapid increase of population.

Given these three conditions, fear might cease to dominate our daily lives, and, with the disappearance of fear, other more generous and more creative emotions would take its place.

If once these political problems were solved I should expect an extraordinary renaissance in art and literature, in joyousness of daily life, in kindliness, in social relations, in thought and science. I should hope to see man at last come into his kingdom —the kingdom that he has deserved by his intelligence, and hitherto forfeited by mutual suspicion. The human race has become integrated as it never was before. The Mexican and Peruvian civilizations flourished in complete isolation from other continents until the time of Columbus. The Chinese, except in their conversion to Buddhism, suffered little foreign influence until the nineteenth century. The Russians went their own way until the time of Peter the Great.

Gradually all this has changed. One part of the world inevitably has effects on another part, and what these effects shall be depends enormously upon the dominant feelings in the different parts. Where the feelings are hostile one part can bring death to the other, and the other can probably bring reciprocal death to the one. Where the feelings are friendly they can bring each other prosperity. The older competitive doctrines which have come down to us from the times of tribal warfare are no longer true. Two powerful groups can always prosper more by co-operation than they can by competition.

During the First Great War many English people imagined that after victory England would be prosperous because German trade would have been destroyed. It did not work out so. Two successive victories, though complete in a military sense, have brought us to the verge of destitution, and a third can only complete the process.

I am no prophet, and I cannot tell what mankind collectively will decide. It may decide that it has existed long enough and that it is time to yield the place to the animals we have hitherto called 'lower'. This is the view of most practical statesmen and of those who are called realists. People who, like myself, think that it would be a good thing if the human race continued to exist, expose themselves to liquidation if they are Russians, and to accusations of fellow-travelling if they are Western.

I do not pretend that, while the existing tension continues, either side can be expected to relax its war-like preparations. What I do say is that the way out of the trouble is psychological and consists in making men realize, on both sides of the Iron Curtain, that neither side can hope to win any good thing until there is mutual rapprochement. And, in bringing about such a lessening of tension, I can think of nothing more effective than the realization of the happiness that the whole human race might enjoy if only it would allow itself to do so.

I have spoken mainly about material goods and political measures, but, as I said before and as I must repeat, these belong only to the mechanism and not to what has value on its own account. The things that have value on their own account can, however, hardly flourish, or can flourish only with extreme difficulty, in such an atmosphere as that in which we now live. To take one great example: liberty of thought and speculation, without which there can be no mental or moral progress, is continually hampered where there is an atmosphere of fear. There comes to be a general belief that the only thing worth doing is to increase the fear until it becomes hysteria, and to silence the few who refuse to be carried away.

In smaller disasters people know that this is not wise. When a ship is sinking the captain is expected to remain calm, and those who fail to execute his orders are thought ill of. In politics people do not act in this way. If the captain remains calm he finds himself surrounded by a yelling mob which tells him that he does not realize the peril. In their excitement they refuse to do what he advises, but rush hither and thither complaining of the sea. In the end they all drown because they had not the sense to remain rational in the face of danger.

For this reason, in times of political danger men adopt foolish and destructive doctrines and fail to think straight. They persecute those who do, in greater or less degree according to the intensity of their fear. How far this process has been carried in Russia we all know. There is some reason to fear that in a milder form something not wholly dissimilar may happen in the West.

If, however, the reign of fear can somehow be made to cease on both sides of the Iron Curtain—or, if not to cease, at any rate to grow less virulent—intelligence and skill, which have never before been as great as they are at the present moment, and which are, in fact, the very cause of our present dangers, may be turned into fruitful channels, and our grandchildren may look back to our time as the last moment of the dark ages from which, as from a long tunnel, mankind will have emerged into the sunshine and happiness of mutual harmony.

VIII

Old and Young Cultures

1960 *Sonning Prize Address*

THE STUDY of differing cultures is somewhat modern. It has
been pursued in recent times, with an immense wealth of
erudition, by Arnold Toynbee. There is, however, one aspect
in the history of cultures which he does not seem to me to have
adequately emphasized. I mean the changes which most
cultures undergo with the lapse of time. There are some
features common to young cultures, and others common to
old ones, and these are, to a considerable extent, independent
of the particular characteristics of the cultures in question.
Most cultures begin with a revolt of some class or nation or
creed against what they consider unjust treatment. But after
they have conquered an important place in the world, they lose
their original rebellious features and become a help in the
maintenance of stable government. Perhaps I should say a
few words as to what is to be meant by a 'culture'. I should
mean a system of beliefs, or at least of habits, an artistic or
intellectual tradition, and ways of making social coherence
possible. There are two ways in which a culture may die: one
is by foreign conquest, and the other is by a new native culture.
Foreign conquest destroyed the Minoan and Mycenaean civilization, though important elements of it were incorporated in the
later civilization of Greece. The Aztec and Peruvian civilizations were completely exterminated by the Spaniards and

137

contributed practically nothing to the subsequent culture of the regions in which they had flourished. The most outstanding example of the growth of a new culture from within is that of Christianity in the Roman Empire.

It by no means always happens that victors in war impose their own culture upon the vanquished. When the Romans conquered the Greeks, they adopted Greek culture almost in its entirety; and when the Teutons conquered the Western Roman Empire, they, in turn, adopted the culture of Rome.

In our own day, a new culture has been gradually replacing the Judeo-Hellenic culture which has been connected with Christianity. This new culture is that of science—not, mainly, of science as knowledge, but, rather, of science as technique. Christianity took about three hundred years to acquire control of an important government. Scientific technique has · taken about the same length of time—namely, from Galileo to Lenin. It has, at present, all the characteristics of a young culture, as Christianity had in the time of Constantine. But if, in any large part of the world, it acquires secure supremacy, it is to be expected that, like Christianity, it will gradually acquire artistic and philosophic maturity with all the trappings of cathedrals, church music, sacred pictures, and ecclesiastical potentates.

It may be argued that the scientific culture which is tending to replace that of Christianity is not really a new culture, but an inevitable development, having its source in Greek curiosity about the universe. However, it must be said that the distinction between different cultures and divergent branches of the same culture is largely arbitrary. It might, for instance, very plausibly be maintained that Muslim culture is only a continuation of that of Greece. Such questions have no substance and can be decided in accordance with the taste of the author concerned. However we may choose to decide this question, history shows that what are indubitably different branches of the same culture may display a mutual enmity as implacable as that between completely distinct cultures. An example of this is

138

the hostility between Protestants and Catholics during the first hundred and thirty years after the Reformation.

We, who are accustomed to the heritage of cultural wealth that is associated with Christianity as we know it, have difficulty in realizing how hostile it was to culture while it was still new and fighting for supremacy. St Jerome records a dream which illustrates this point. He had been a deeply sensitive student of the literature of Greece and Rome in their great days. He was sensitive to matters of style and found it difficult to give the same literary approval to the somewhat barbaric Greek of the Gospels as he had given to the objects of his unregenerate literary admirations. The qualms which these hesitations gave rise to found expression in a dream. He dreamt that at the Last Judgment, Christ asked him who he was, and he replied that he was a Christian. The answer came: 'Thou liest. Thou art a follower of Cicero, and not of Christ.' And thereupon, he was ordered to be scourged. Still in his dream, he cried out: 'Lord, if ever again I possess worldly books, or if ever again I read such, I have denied Thee.' The dream influenced him profoundly, and, for some years, his letters were free from quotations of pagan literature. Although, gradually, such quotations reappeared, it was half-heartedly and apologetically.

One can imagine almost exactly the same dream, *mutatis mutandis*, occurring to a brain-washed Chinese scholar in the present day. He might remember in a dream the fable of Po Lo who asserted that he understood the management of horses, and, by means of the bridle and the whip, tamed them until more than half of them were dead. The fable concludes: 'Those who *govern* the Empire make the same mistake.' Or he might remember Tao Ch'ien's poem about *New Corn:*

> Swiftly the years, beyond recall.
> Solemn the stillness of this fair morning.
> I will clothe myself in spring-clothing

And visit the slopes of the Eastern Hill.
By the mountain-stream a mist hovers,
Hovers a moment, then scatters.
There comes a wind blowing from the south
That brushes the fields of new corn.

(*Translation by Arthur Waley.*)

In his dream, he would be summoned before an earthly, not a heavenly, tribunal, and would assert valiantly that he was a Marxist-Leninist. But the judge would frown and say, 'Thou liest. Thou art a disciple of Chuang Tze.' Culturally, there is very little difference between St Jerome and the brain-washed Chinese scholar. Each represents a young culture, hostile to ancient beauty, and not yet sufficiently mature to produce new beauties of its own.

There are certain antitheses between old and new cultures. Broadly speaking, the new value work, while the old value what may, in a large sense, be called play. The new make appeal to the poor, and the old to the rich. The new believe that happiness is only obtainable in another world, the old find *this* world full of things to enjoy. The difference between an old and a new culture is epigrammatically expressed by Marx when he says: 'Philosophers have only *interpreted* the world in various ways, but the real task is to *alter* it.' To any person appreciative of an ancient culture, this is a dusty saying. Such a person, when he contemplates a great painting, a piece of exquisite music, or the verse of some supreme poet, does not think that his real task is to alter all this. St Jerome and Marx do think so. For some centuries the Christian Church continued to take St Jerome's view as to classical learning. As Gregory the Great said: 'The praises of Christ cannot find room in one mouth with praises of Jupiter.'

When the new culture has become established, and the struggle for supremacy is no longer necessary, the worldly successors of St Jerome, Gregory the Great and Marx may allow a place for contemplation as opposed to action, and may concede that a busy-body is not the highest type of human being. But this difference is not a difference between one culture and another; it is a difference between an old culture and a young one. If one reads the objections of Plotinus to Christianity, they are extraordinarily similar to the objections which those of us who are not Communists feel to the doctrine of Karl Marx. Plotinus complains, for example, that the only souls acknowledged by Christians are those of God and human beings, whereas, in his philosophy, the sun has a soul, the moon has a soul, and every separate star has a separate soul. Compared with this philosophy, he says, how jejune and dry and lifeless is the world of Christian theology. If he lived now, he would be saying much the same things, no longer about Christianity, but about Marxism.

History, as based upon written records and not only upon archaeological evidence, begins several millennia sooner in Egypt and Babylonia than it does anywhere else. About the time when history begins elsewhere, great religions which had extraordinary vitality began in various parts of the world. Confucius and Buddha belong to this time, and so, according to some authorities, does Zoroaster. In the Hellenic world, the religion of Bacchus probably began at about the same time. This religion illustrates within a rather short period, and in a very striking way, the development from youth to age. At first the religion of Bacchus, which came from the uncivilized Thracians, was associated with drunkenness and ritual murder. But, before long, in the reformed shape of Orphism, it became the inspirer of much that was best in Greece. Pythagoras and Plato owed much to it and, what is perhaps more surprising, whole chunks of its theology became imbedded in Christian doctrine. At the beginning of Plato's *Republic*, there is an old man who has hitherto been indifferent to religion, but now, from fear of death, has adopted Orphic views as to the future life. What Plato relates of his beliefs is amazingly similar to

141

what was afterwards believed by Christians. It is Orphism, also, that first taught the need to be twice born, once physically and once spiritually. The savage elements of the original Bacchic worship still appear in the *Bacchae* of Euripides, but they are then already a somewhat ancient memory and are in process of disappearing.

I said a moment ago that young cultures emphasize work and old cultures lay more stress upon what, in a certain sense, may be called play. But in saying this I am including under the head of play whatever is not designed for practical utility. I include under this head art and literature and contemplative philosophy, and the pursuit of knowledge when not subservient to technique. The Greeks pursued knowledge in mathematics and astronomy, but, with the exception of Archimedes, they valued knowledge for its own sake and not for its usefulness. This was still largely true in Europe after the Renaissance, but gradually, especially after the Industrial Revolution, knowledge came increasingly to be valued for its economic and military utility. There has been, in consequence, a profound disruption in what it has become customary to call 'Western values'. European civilization, as it existed before this disruption, came from a synthesis of Jewish, Greek, and Roman elements. One may describe the new culture, which is gradually arising, as the result of thrusting out the Greek elements in the synthesis and substituting scientific technique in their place. The result, in its extreme form, is Marxism, but something of the same process is visible in all countries that are industrially developed or hope soon to become so. It is only, however, the contrast between its extreme Eastern form and its more moderate Western developments that is producing the political and military strains from which we are suffering. It is profoundly unfortunate that the process of disruption has divided the civilized world between two hostile cultures. There have been such divisions before: between Christianity and Islam; and between Catholicism and Protestantism. But never before have men possessed such scientific power of inflicting disaster upon each other, and never before has tolerance of cultural diversity been so important. I could wish this diversity to be viewed as the inevitable difference between old and young, and, therefore, as something which the passage of time can be relied upon to soften. The apostles of traditional culture are not without their share of blame, since they have been unwilling to admit that science deserves its place as an enricher of culture and not as a destructive enemy to it. If there is something barbaric in the new creed—*that* has generally been a characteristic of what was new. Christianity was, itself, a successful synthesis, but new elements have become important since that synthesis was established; and these new elements have made a wider synthesis indispensable. We must hope that men will develop sufficient new wisdom to live in the new world that their own ingenuity has created, for, if they cannot, the race will perish.

In the world in which we are living, there is a great danger and a great opportunity—both greater than any at any former time, and both created by our power to realize our wishes. We can, if we choose, destroy the human race. We can, on the other hand, create a happy, prosperous, civilized, and peaceful human family, embracing all nations, all colours, and all creeds. Which we shall do, depends upon collective passions, and collective passions are the sum of individual passions. Each one of us, if he allows himself to be dominated by hatred, envy, pride of superiority, or the pursuit of safety by means of large-scale murder, is contributing his quota towards universal disaster. Each one of us, if he is inspired to action by hope and tolerance and the realization that strife is as foolish as it is wicked, is doing what lies within his power to bring about an earthly paradise, never before possible, but now realizable through scientific technique. The choice lies within the scope of human passions. Life or death? Our century will decide.

IX

Education for a Difficult World

YOUNG PEOPLE who are not completely frivolous are apt to find in the world of the present day that their impulses of good will are baffled by failure to find any clear course of action which might diminish the perils of the time. I will not pretend that there is any easy or simple answer to their bewilderment, but I do think that a suitable education could make young people feel more capable of understanding the problems and of critically estimating this or that suggested solution.

There are several reasons which make our problems difficult to solve, if not to understand. The first of these is that modern society and modern politics are governed by difficult skills which very few people understand. The man of science is the modern medicine man. He can perform all kinds of magic. He can say, 'Let there be light', and there is light. He can keep you warm in winter, and keep your food cool in summer. He can transport you through the air as quickly as a magic carpet in the Arabian Nights. He promises to exterminate your enemies in a few seconds, and fails you only when you ask him to promise that your enemies will not exterminate you. All this he achieves by means which, if you are not one in a million, are completely mysterious to you. And when mystery-mongers tell you tall stories of future marvels you cannot tell whether to believe them or not.

Another thing that makes the modern world baffling is that technical developments have made a new social psychology necessary. From the dawn of history until the present century the road to success was victory in competition. We descend from many centuries of progenitors who exterminated their enemies, occupied their lands, and grew rich. In England this process took place in the time of Hengist and Horsa. In the United States it took place during the eighteenth and nine-teenth centuries. We therefore admire a certain sort of character, namely the sort of character that enables you to kill skilfully and without compunction. The milder believers in this creed content themselves with inflicting economic rather than physical death, but the psychology is much the same. In the modern world, owing to increase of skill, this process is no longer so satisfactory. In a modern war even the victors suffer more than if there had been no war. To the British, who are enduring the results of complete victory in two great wars, this is fairly obvious. What applies in war, applies also in the economic sphere. The victors in a competition do not grow so rich as both parties could by combination. The half-unconscious appreciation of these facts produces in intelligent young people an impulse towards general good will, but this impulse is baffled by the mutual hostility of powerful groups. Good will in general—yes; good will in particular—no. A Hindu may love mankind, but must not love a Pakistani; a Jew may believe that men are all one family, but dare not extend this feeling to the Arabs; a Christian may think it his duty to love his neigh-bour, but only if his neighbour is not a Communist. These conflicts between the general and the particular seem to make it impossible to have any one clear principle in action. This trouble is due to a very general failure to adapt human nature to technique. Our *feelings* are those appropriate to warlike nomads in rather empty regions, but our technique is such as must bring disaster unless our feelings can become more co-operative.

Education if it is to be adapted to our modern needs must fit young people to understand the problems raised by this situation. The imparting of knowledge in education has always had two objects: on the one hand, to give skill; and on the other, to give a vaguer thing which we may call wisdom. The part of skill has become very much larger than it used to be and is increasingly threatening to oust the part devoted to wisdom. At the same time it must be admitted that wisdom in our world is impossible except for those who realize the great part played by skill, for it is increase of skill that is the distinctive feature of our world. During the late war, when I dined among the Fellows of my College, I found that those who were scientific were usually absent, but on their rare appearances one got glimpses of mysterious work such as only very few living people could understand. It was the work of men of this sort that was the most decisive in the war. Such men inevitably form a kind of aristocracy, since their skill is rare and must remain rare until by some new method men's congenital aptitudes have been increased. There is for example a great deal of important work which can only be done by those who are good at higher mathematics, and the immense majority of mankind would never become good at higher mathematics, even if all their education were directed to this end. Men are not all equal in congenital capacity, and any system of education which assumes that they are involves a possibly disastrous waste of good material.

But although scientific skill is necessary, it is by no means sufficient. A dictatorship of men of science would very soon become horrible. Skill without wisdom may be purely destructive, and would be very likely to prove so. For this reason, if for no other, it is of great importance that those who receive a scientific education should not be *merely* scientific, but should have some understanding of that kind of wisdom which, if it can be imparted at all, can only be imparted by the cultural side of education. Science enables us to know the means to any chosen end, but it does not help us to decide what ends we shall pursue. If you wish to exterminate the human race, it

146

will show you how to do it. If you wish to make the human race so numerous that all are on the very verge of starvation, it will show you how to do that. If you wish to secure adequate prosperity for the whole human race, science will tell you what you must do. But it will not tell you whether one of these ends is more desirable than another. Nor will it give you that instinctive understanding of human beings that is necessary if your measures are not to arouse fierce opposition which only ferocious tyranny can quell. It cannot teach you patience, it cannot teach you sympathy, it cannot teach you a sense of human destiny. These things, in so far as they can be taught in formal education, are most likely to emerge from the learning of history and great literature.

Familiarity with great literature has been one of the nominal aims of education ever since the time of Peisistratus. The Athenians pursued this aim wisely: they learnt Homer by heart, and were therefore able to appreciate their great dramatists in spite of their being contemporary. But modern methods have improved on all this. I was given when I was very young a little book called *A Child's Guide to Literature*. In this book the child, guided by some preternatural intelligence, asked about the great English writers in correct chronological sequence beginning, 'who was Chaucer?' I regret to say that I never got any farther in this little book. If I had, I should have been able to say just the sort of thing that Examiners wish you to say without having read a single word of any of the authors concerned. I am afraid that the needs of examinations and of an unduly extended syllabus have made this way of studying literature all too common. You may be the better for reading Chaucer, but if you do not read him, knowing his dates and what eminent critics have said about him it does you no more good than knowing the dates of some obscure nobody. The good that is to be derived from great literature is not derived with any fullness except by those who become so familiar with it that it enters into the texture of their everyday

147

thoughts. I think it is an admirable thing when children at
school act a play of Shakespeare. There is then an obvious
reason for getting to know it well, and the enterprise is
co-operative rather than competitive. I am quite sure that to
take part in acting *one* of Shakespeare's good plays is a better
way of acquiring what is valuable in a literary education than
the hasty reading of the whole lot. In former generations
English-speaking people acquired the same sort of training in
prose through familiarity with the Authorized Version of the
Bible, but since the Bible became unfamiliar nothing equally
excellent has taken its place.

In the teaching of history as opposed to literature a smattering
can be of great utility. For those who are not going to be
professional historians the sort of thing that in America is
called a survey course can, if it is rightly done, give a valuable
sense of the larger process within which things which are near
and familiar take place. Such a course should deal with the
history of Man, not with the history of this or that country,
least of all one's own. It should begin with the oldest facts
known through anthropology and archaeology, and should
give a sense of the gradual emergence of those things in human
life which give man such a place in our respect as he may
deserve. It should not present as the world's heroes those who
have slaughtered the greatest number of 'enemies', but rather
those who have been most notable in adding to the world's
capital of knowledge and beauty and wisdom. It should show
the strange resurgent power of what is valuable in human life,
defeated time and again by savagery and hate and destruction,
but nevertheless, at the very first possible opportunity, emerg-
ing again like grass in the desert after rain. It should, while
youth leaves hopes and desires still plastic, fix those hopes and
desires not upon victory over other human beings, but upon
victory over those forces which have hitherto filled the life of
man with suffering and sorrow—I mean, the forces of nature
reluctant to yield her fruits, the forces of militant ignorance, the

148

forces of hate, and the deep slavery to fear which is our heritage from the original helplessness of mankind. All this a survey of history should give and can give. All this, if it enters into the daily texture of men's thoughts, will make them less harsh and less mad.

One of the great things that education can and should give is the power of seeing the general in the particular, the power of feeling that this, although it is happening to *me*, is very like what happens to others, what has happened through many ages, and may continue to happen. It is very difficult not to feel that there is something quite special and peculiar about one's own misfortunes, about the injustices that one suffers, and the malevolence of which one is the object, and this applies not only to oneself as an individual but to one's family, one's class, one's nation, and even one's continent. To see such matters with impersonal justice is possible as the result of education, but is scarcely possible otherwise.

All this education can do, all this education should do, very little of it education does do.

X

University Education[1]

EDUCATION is a vast and complex subject involving many problems of great difficulty. I propose, in what follows, to deal with only one of these problems, namely, the adaptation of university education to modern conditions.

Universities are an institution of considerable antiquity. They developed during the twelfth and thirteenth centuries out of cathedral schools where scholastic theologians learned the art of dialectic. But, in fact, the aims which inspired universities go back to ancient times. One may say that Plato's Academy was the first university. Plato's Academy had certain well-marked objectives. It aimed at producing the sort of people who would be suitable to become Guardians in his ideal Republic. The education which Plato designed was not in his day what would now be called 'cultural'. A 'cultural' education consists mainly in the learning of Greek and Latin. But the Greeks had no need to learn Greek and no occasion to learn Latin. What Plato mainly wished his Academy to teach was, first, mathematics and astronomy, and, then, philosophy. The philosophy was to have a scientific inspiration with a tincture of Orphic mysticism. Something of this sort, in various modified forms, persisted in the West until the Fall of Rome. After some centuries, it was taken up by the Arabs and, from them, largely through the Jews, transmitted back to the West. In the West it still retained much of Plato's original political

[1] Arkansas University Alumnus, 1959.

150

purpose, since it aimed at producing an educated élite with a more or less complete monopoly of political power. This aim persisted, virtually unchanged, until the latter half of the nineteenth century. From that time onwards, the aim has become increasingly modified by the intrusion of two new elements: democracy and science. The intrusion of democracy into academic practice and theory is much more profound than that of science and much more difficult to combine with anything like the aims of Plato's Academy.

Universal education, which is now taken for granted in all civilized countries, was vehemently opposed, on grounds which were broadly aristocratic, until it was seen that political democracy had become inevitable. There had been ever since ancient times a very sharp line between the educated and the uneducated. The educated had had a severe training and had learnt much, while the uneducated could not read or write. The educated, who had a monopoly of political power, dreaded the extension of schools to the 'lower classes'. The President of the Royal Society in the year 1807 considered that it would be disastrous if working men could read, since he feared that they would spend their time reading Tom Paine. When my grandfather established an elementary school in his parish, well-to-do neighbours were outraged, saying that he had destroyed the hitherto aristocratic character of the neighbourhood. It was political democracy—at least, in England—that brought a change of opinion in this matter. Disraeli, after securing the vote for urban working men, favoured compulsory education with the phrase, 'We must educate our masters'. Education came to seem the right of all who desired it. But it was not easy to see how this right was to be extended to university education; nor, if it were, how universities could continue to perform their ancient functions.

The reasons which have induced civilized countries to adopt universal education are various. There were enthusiasts for enlightenment who saw no limits to the good that could be done by instruction. Many of these were very influential in the early advocacy of compulsory education. Then there were practical men who realized that a modern State and modern processes of production and distribution cannot easily be managed if a large proportion of the population cannot read. A third group were those who advocated education as a democratic right. There was a fourth group, more silent and less open, which saw the possibilities of education from the point of view of official propaganda. The importance of education in this regard is very great. In the eighteenth century, most wars were unpopular; but, since men have been able to read the newspapers, almost all wars have been popular. This is only one instance of the hold on public opinion which Authority has acquired through education.

Although universities were not directly concerned in these educational processes, they have been profoundly affected by them in ways which are, broadly speaking, inevitable, but which are, in part, very disturbing to those who wish to preserve what was good in older ideals.

It is difficult to speak in advocacy of older ideals without using language that has a somewhat old-fashioned flavour. There is a distinction, which formerly received general recognition, between skill and wisdom. The growing complexities of technique have tended to blur this distinction, at any rate in certain regions. There are kinds of skill which are not specially respected although they are difficult to acquire. A contortionist, I am told, has to begin training in early childhood, and, when proficient, he possesses a very rare and difficult skill. But it is not felt that this skill is socially useful, and it is, therefore, not taught in schools or universities. A great many skills, however, indeed a rapidly increasing number, are very vital elements in the wealth and power of a nation. Most of these skills are new and do not command the respect of ancient tradition. Some of them may be considered to minister to wisdom, but a great many certainly do not. But

what, you will ask, do you mean by 'wisdom'? I am not pre- ~ wisdom
pared with a neat definition. But I will do my best to convey
what I think the word is capable of meaning. It is a word
concerned partly with knowledge and partly with feeling. It
should denote a certain intimate union of knowledge with
apprehension of human destiny and the purposes of life. It
requires a certain breadth of vision, which is hardly possible
without considerable knowledge. But it demands, also, a
breadth of feeling, a certain kind of universality of sympathy.
I think that higher education should do what is possible
towards promoting, not only knowledge, but wisdom. I do not
think that this is easy; and I do not think that the aim should
be too conscious, for, if it is, it becomes stereotyped and
priggish. It should be something existing almost unconsciously
in the teacher and conveyed almost unintentionally to the pupil.
I agree with Plato in thinking this the greatest thing that
education can do. Unfortunately, it is one of the things most
threatened by the intrusion of crude democratic shibboleths into
our universities.

The fanatic of democracy is apt to say that all men are equal.
There is a sense in which this is true, but it is not a sense which
much concerns the educator. What can be meant truly by the
phrase 'All men are equal' is that in certain respects they have
equal rights and should have an equal share of basic political
power. Murder is a crime whoever the victim may be, and
everybody should be protected against it by the law and the
police. Any set of men or women which has no share in political
power is pretty certain to suffer injustices of an indefensible
sort. All men should be equal before the law. It is such democracy
principles which constitute what is valid in democracy. But this
should not mean that we cannot recognize differing degrees of
skill or merit in different individuals. Every teacher knows that
some pupils are quick to learn and others are slow. Every
teacher knows that some boys and girls are eager to acquire
knowledge, while others have to be forced into the minimum

153

demanded by Authority. When a group of young people are all taught together in one class, regardless of their greater or less ability, the pace has to be too quick for the stupid and too slow for the clever. The amount of teaching that a young person needs depends to an enormous extent upon his ability and his tastes. A stupid child will only pay attention to what has to be learnt while the teacher is there to insist upon the subject-matter of the lesson. A really clever young person, on the contrary, needs opportunity and occasional guidance when he finds some difficulty momentarily insuperable. The practice of teaching clever and stupid pupils together is extremely unfortunate, especially as regards the ablest of them. Infinite boredom settles upon these outstanding pupils while matters that they have long ago understood are being explained to those who are backward. This evil is greater the greater the age of the student. By the time that an able young man is at a university, what he needs is occasional advice (not orders) as to what to read and an instructor who has time and sympathy to listen to his difficulties. The kind of instructor that I have in mind should be thoroughly competent in the subject in which the student is specializing, but he should be still young enough to remember the difficulties that are apt to be obstacles to the learner, and not yet so ossified as to be unable to discuss without dogmatism. Discussion is a very essential part in the education of the best students and requires an absence of authority if it is to be free and fruitful. I am thinking not only of discussion with teachers but of discussion among the students themselves. For such discussion, there should be leisure. And, indeed, leisure during student years is of the highest importance. When I was an undergraduate, I made a vow that, when in due course I became a lecturer, I would not think that lectures do any good as a method of instruction, but only as an occasional stimulus. So far as the abler students are concerned, I still take this view. Lectures as a means of instruction are traditional in universities and were no doubt useful before the invention of printing, but since that time they have been out of date as regards the abler kind of students.

It is, I am profoundly convinced, a mistake to object on democratic grounds to the separation of abler from less able pupils in teaching. In matters that the public considers important no one dreams of such an application of supposed democracy. Everybody is willing to admit that some athletes are better than others and that movie stars deserve more honour than ordinary mortals. That is because they have a kind of skill which is much admired even by those who do not possess it. But intellectual ability, so far from being admired by stupid boys, is positively and actively despised; and even among grown-ups, the term 'egg-head' is not expressive of respect. It has been one of the humiliations of the military authorities of our time that the man who nowadays brings success in war is no longer a gentleman of commanding aspect, sitting upright upon a prancing horse, but a wretched scientist whom every military-minded boy would have bullied throughout his youth. However, it is not for special skill in slaughter that I should wish to see the 'egg-head' respected.

The needs of the modern world have brought a conflict, which I think could be avoided, between scientific subjects and those that are called 'cultural'. The latter represent tradition and still have, in my country, a certain snobbish pre-eminence. Cultural ignorance, beyond a point, is despised. Scientific ignorance, however complete, is not. I do not think, myself, that the division between cultural and scientific education should be nearly as definite as it has tended to become. I think that every scientific student should have some knowledge of history and literature, and that every cultural student should have some acquaintance with some of the basic ideas of science. Some people will say that there is not time, during the university curriculum, to achieve this. But I think that opinion arises partly from unwillingness to adapt teaching to those who are not going to penetrate very far into the subject in question. More specifically, whatever cultural education is offered to scientific students, should not involve a knowledge of Latin or Greek. And I think that whatever of science is offered to those who are not going to specialize in any scientific subject should deal partly with scientific history and partly with general aspects of scientific method. I think it is a good thing to invite occasional lectures from eminent men to be addressed to the general body of students and not only to those who specialize in the subject concerned.

VALUES

There are some things which I think it ought to be possible, though at present it is not, to take for granted in all who are engaged in university teaching. Such men or women must, of course, be proficient in some special skill. But, in addition to this, there is a general outlook which it is their duty to put before those whom they are instructing. They should exemplify the value of intellect and of the search for knowledge. They should make it clear that what at any time passes for knowledge may, in fact, be erroneous. They should inculcate an undogmatic temper, a temper of continual search and not of comfortable certainty. They should try to create an awareness of the world as a whole, and not only of what is near in space and time. Through the recognition of the likelihood of error, they should make clear the importance of tolerance. They should remind the student that those whom posterity honours have very often been unpopular in their own day and that, on this ground, social courage is a virtue of supreme importance. Above all, every educator who is engaged in an attempt to make the best of the students to whom he speaks must regard himself as the servant of truth and not of this or that political or sectarian interest. Truth is a shining goddess, always veiled, always distant, never wholly approachable, but worthy of all the devotion of which the human spirit is capable.

PART THREE

Divertissements

I

Cranks

I HAVE long been accustomed to being regarded as a crank, and I do not much mind this except when those who so regard me are also cranks, for then they are apt to assume that I must of course agree with their particular nostrum. There are those who think that one should only eat nuts. There are those who think that all wisdom is revealed by the Great Pyramid, and among these there are not a few who think that priests carried its wisdom to Mexico and thus gave rise to the Maya civilization. I have come across men who think that all matter is composed of atoms which are regular solids having twenty faces. Once, when I was about to begin a lecture tour in America, a man came to me and very earnestly besought me to mention in each lecture that the end of the world would occur before my tour was ended. Then there was the old farmer who thought that all government, both national and local, ought to be abolished because Public Bodies waste so much water. And there was the amiable gentleman who told me that, although he could not alter the past, he could by faith make it always have been different from what it otherwise would have been. He, I regret to say, was sent to prison for a fraudulent balance sheet and he found, to his surprise, that the law courts did not take kindly to his application of faith to arithmetic. Then there was the letter sent from a suburb of Boston, which informed me that it came from the God Osiris, and gave me His telephone number. It advised me to ring up quickly since He was about to re-establish His reign on earth when the Brotherhood of the True Believers would live with Him in bliss, but the rest of mankind would be withered by the fire of His eyes. I must confess that I never answered this letter, but I am still awaiting the dread moment.

There was an incident which illustrates the perils of country life: on a very hot day, in a very remote place, I had plunged into a river in the hopes of getting cool. When I emerged, I found a grave and reverend old man standing beside my clothes. While I was getting dry, he revealed the purpose of his presence. 'You,' he said, 'in common with the rest of our nation, probably entertain the vulgar error that the English are the lost Ten Tribes. This is not the case. We are only the Tribes of Ephraim and Manasseh.' His arguments were overwhelming, and I could not escape them as I had to put on my clothes.

Experience has gradually taught me a technique for dealing with such people. Nowadays when I meet the Ephraim-and-Manasseh devotees, I say, 'I don't think you've got it quite right. I think the English are Ephraim and the Scotch are Manasseh'. On this basis, a pleasant and inconclusive argument becomes possible. In like manner, I counter the devotees of the Great Pyramid by adoration of the Sphinx; and the devotees of nuts, by pointing out that hazel nuts and walnuts are just as deleterious as other foods and only Brazil nuts should be tolerated by the faithful. But when I was younger I had not yet acquired this technique, with the result that my contacts with cranks were sometimes alarming.

Rather more than thirty years ago, at a time when I shared a flat in London with a friend, I heard a ring at the bell. My friend happened to be out and I opened the door. I found on the door-step a man whom I had never seen before, short and bearded, with very mild blue eyes and an air of constant indecision. He was a stranger to me, and the English in which he explained his purpose was very halting. 'I have come', he said, 'to consult you on a philosophical question of great importance to me.' 'Well,' I replied, 'come in and let us sit down.' I offered him a cigarette, which was refused. He sat for a time in silence. I tried various topics, but at first extracted only very brief replies. I made out at last, though with considerable difficulty, what he wanted of me. He informed me that he was a Russian, but not a supporter of the then recent Communist Government. He had, so he told me, frequent mystic visions in which voices urged him to do this or that. He did not know whether such voices deserved respect or were to be regarded as delusions. It had occurred to him that he might obtain guidance from eminent philosophers throughout the world. At the moment, it was British philosophers whose advice he was seeking. When he had had such guidance as he could obtain from me, he proposed next to consult Arthur Balfour, at that time Foreign Secretary. I listened with such respect as I could command to his revelations from the spirit world, but in my replies to him I remained, for the time being, non-committal. At last he said that he would wish to read some of my books (an extreme step which he had not previously taken) to see whether they contained anything that would be a help to him. For a moment I thought of lending him some book of my own, but I was doubtful whether I should ever see it again and, also, whether he would really take the trouble to read it. I therefore advised him to go to the British Museum and read such of my books as seemed likely to be helpful. He said he would do so and would return to resume the discussion after he had got a grip on my general outlook.

Sure enough, he came back a few days later. Again I invited him into my study, and again I tried to set him at his ease. But he looked more dejected and defeated than ever, shabby and hopeless, a drifting waif, who seemed almost insubstantial. 'Well,' I said, 'have you been reading my books?' 'Only one of them', he replied. I asked which, and found, after some trouble, that it was not a book by me, but a skit on my philosophy written to make fun of it. By this time, I had begun to think that it did not much matter what he read, so I did not trouble to explain the mistake. I asked, instead, what he thought of the book. 'Well,' he replied, 'there was only one statement in the book that I could understand, and that I did not agree with.' 'What statement was that?' I asked, expecting that it would have to do with some deep philosophical doctrine. 'It was', he replied, 'the statement that Julius Caesar is dead.' I am accustomed to having my remarks disputed, but this particular remark seemed to me innocuous. 'Why did you disagree with that?' I asked in surprise. At this point he underwent a sudden transformation. He had been sitting in an armchair in a melancholy attitude and as though the weight of the world oppressed him, but at this point he leapt up. He drew himself up to his full height, which was five foot two. His eyes suddenly ceased to be mild, and flashed fire. In a voice of thunder, he replied: 'BECAUSE I AM JULIUS CAESAR!' It dawned upon me suddenly that this had been the purport of the mystic voices and that he was hoping to re-establish the empire which had temporarily toppled on the Ides of March. Being alone with him, I thought that argument might be dangerous. 'That is very remarkable,' I said, 'and I am sure that Arthur Balfour will be much interested.' I coaxed him to the door and, pointing along the street, said, 'that is the way to the Foreign Office.'

What Mr Balfour thought of him when he got to the Foreign Office I never learnt, but an obscure footnote to a subsequent new edition of that eminent thinker's *Foundations of Belief* led me to wonder.

II

The Right Will Prevail or The Road to Lhasa

Have we eaten on
the Insane Root
that takes the reason
prisoner?

1

I HAD decided that Westminster Bridge was the best place
from which to end it all. It was a dark November evening with
a penetrating drizzle and a cold fog. The pavement was covered
with a film of slimy mud, and looking down from the bridge
I could not see the river. The water will be very cold, I thought
with a shiver of fear. But then another thought came to me:
if earth hath not anything to show more fair, there is not much
point in staying on such a dismal planet. Nerved by this
thought, I climbed upon the parapet. But while I was summon-
ing the necessary last ounce of resolution, a firm hand seized
my collar, and a quietly determined voice said, 'Oh no, that's
not really necessary'. I turned in a fury, although beneath the
fury the instinct of survival brought a surprising surge of
relief. I saw before me a tall and massive gentleman of rather
foreign appearance, wrapped in a very opulent fur coat. 'My
friend,' he said, 'I saw what you were about to do. But I
make it my mission, whenever I can, to prevent useless tragedy
and to offer to the despairing new hopes of happiness. Come

163

with me; tell me your troubles; and I shall be much surprised
if I cannot alleviate them.'

With a submissiveness that surprised me, although he took
it for granted, I obeyed his suggestion. He hailed a passing
taxi and gave an address on Campden Hill. Throughout the
drive neither of us spoke a word. The house, when we reached
it, was large and isolated and surrounded by a garden. He took
me into his study, a vast room lined with books and warmed
by a blazing fire. He set me down in a very comfortable chair,
gave me a cigar and supplied me with a generous whisky and
soda. I had arrived shivering with cold and despair, but when
the fire and the whisky had begun to warm me, he turned to
me with a smile and said, 'Now, I think, the time has come
for you to tell me your troubles'. The whisky, the cigar, and
the warmth, combined with the relief from intolerable tension,
broke down my defences, and I found myself telling everything
to this total stranger as unreservedly as if he had been my
father-confessor.

It was a miserable and discreditable story. My father is rich
and universally respected. I had been a civil servant, not
without ability, and having before me every prospect of a
successful, if not distinguished, career. But, unfortunately for
me, I met that unbelievably beautiful lady, Arabella Main-
waring. From the first moment of my seeing her, she dominated
my waking thoughts and haunted all my dreams. I forgot my
work, I forgot my friends, I forgot the importance of retaining
my father's good opinion, and thought only of how I might
win Arabella's favours—not her heart, for I knew that she had
none. In spite of many generations of honourable ancestors,
she cared for nothing but money and luxury. For these she
had a craving which was almost insane, and it was only as a
means of satisfying this craving that she valued her physical
attractions. All this I knew, and it should have made me
despise her; but it did not. I soon discovered that it was only
necessary to spend money upon her in order to secure a

temporary semblance of love. I spent my savings. I gambled dishonestly, and with my winnings purchased an exquisite ruby pendant which secured me a night of bliss. The fact that I had cheated at cards was discovered, and in desperation I forged a cheque on my father's account. When this came to his knowledge, he refused to shield me from prosecution. Arabella, as was to be expected, coldly taunted me with my folly. It was from this situation that I had seen no escape except by suicide.

2

When I had finished my confession, I turned a despairing look upon my host and said, 'I think you will admit that my position is one in which hope is impossible!' 'Nonsense, my dear Sir,' he replied, 'I can put it all right. My hobby is preventing suicide. All shall be well if you will work for me.' 'What work do you require?' I asked. 'Only a little research', he replied. With tears in my eyes, I grasped his hand and thanked him. 'Oh, my dear Sir,' he said, 'it is nothing to make a fuss about. Every man has his little hobby, and I have mine.' I asked him what I was to do. 'The first step', he said, 'is isolation in my house with a view to disguise. During the period of isolation, you shall grow a beard, have your bushy eyebrows plucked, and wear heavy horn-rimmed spectacles. For public purposes, you shall have a new name, and I will supply you with a pass-port capable of passing the severest scrutiny of the immigration officials. While your beard is growing, you shall live in my house, and I will instruct you as to the part you are to play in return for my protection.'

Throughout the ensuing month, my initiation continued. I learnt that my host's name was Aguinaldo Garcinacia, that he was a native of the small republic of San Ysidro in the foothills of the Andes, that he was distressed by the spread of subversive ideas and believed that only rigid adherence to tradition could preserve the human race from disaster. He had, therefore, founded a fraternity which he called *The League of the Fight for the Right*. He explained that he meant Right as opposed to Left, not right as opposed to wrong. He said that he had seven immediate subordinates who dined with him every Saturday night to consider the strategy of the campaign. His aims, so he assured me, were noble and public-spirited, and not even the most tender conscience need hesitate to assist him. My conscience, as he knew from my confession, is not one of the most tender; and, as the alternative to his proposal was ruin and prison, I did not hesitate to enrol myself as his disciple.

The month of seclusion, while my beard was growing, would have been tedious but for the gradual process of initiation to which Aguinaldo subjected me. At first, I had been inclined to regard his projects as those of a fantastic visionary, but gradually, as he told me more and more of the sources of his power, I realized that his success was not impossible. In the small village which was his birthplace—so he informed me—there grows a herb which has a very peculiar property: when eaten in small quantities, it produces extreme indiscretion in which even the most profound secrets are confessed; in larger doses, it produces permanent insanity; and in still larger doses, death. The herb grows nowhere else. The villagers, in the course of many generations, have become immune to its deleterious properties. They were, in fact, totally unaware of these properties, as strangers hardly ever penetrated to their remote fastness. Once, however, when Aguinaldo was still a young man, a Bolivian official with a staff of surveyors, in the course of a frontier dispute with Peru, visited the village. The official and his staff were given a salad containing the fatal herb. They all blabbed the most secret intentions of the Bolivian Government. Aguinaldo, who had studied medicine in the United States, suspected the cause of their indiscretions and confirmed his suspicions by subsequent experiments. He quickly realized the power which had been placed in his hands. By means of blackmail, he soon acquired an enormous fortune.

He swore all the inhabitants of his native village to secrecy, giving them all, in return, a comfortable livelihood. Out of the 'Insane Root', he made a powder that looked like pepper. When he wished to get a man into his power, he would invite him to dinner and induce him to sprinkle some of the food with what seemed to be pepper. From that moment, the man was in Aguinaldo's power, and had to obey him or suffer disaster. 'And all this immense power', he concluded, 'I use in furtherance of human welfare, which demands the dispelling of subversive and anarchic myths and adherence to the ancient and tried wisdom of the stable ages of the past. You will admit, I am sure, that you are fortunate in being allowed to contribute to this great work.'

The month of probation was devoted, not only to the growth of my beard, but also to indoctrination. Aguinaldo was a powerful personality. He appeared to be completely untroubled by any doubts as to the wisdom of his crusade. His culture was very wide; his knowledge of history, amazing. But, in addition to these assets, his large and piercing eyes had an almost hypnotic quality which held my will in suspense while he conversed. At the end of the month, he was satisfied. 'Next Saturday', he said, 'you shall join our hebdomadal dinner and be introduced to my immediate colleagues.'

3

Saturday evening came and I found a company of seven, in addition to my host. All the seven, I was informed, had for public purposes Spanish names and San Ysidran passports. I, also, had been similarly provided. But in the house of Aguinaldo, we knew each other by our real names. Since all of us were wanted by the police in our own countries, if not elsewhere, this mutual knowledge made treachery impossible and linked us in a chain of unbreakable confederacy. At this first dinner, Aguinaldo informed the company of my difficulties and of my reasons for joining the Order. Turning to me, he said: 'During the coming week, each of our guests shall confide in you reciprocal secrets which shall place you on an equality with the older members of our Sacred Brotherhood.'

Two of them, who were close friends, came to see me the next day. They were Count Cesare Altogrado and Baron Schambok. Count Cesare, I learnt, was a Count of the Holy Roman Empire; by birth a Venetian; dapper, and well dressed; a man whom, at first sight, you would not suspect of seriousness about anything. But, in this, you would have been mistaken. There was one thing about which he was in earnest, and that was the Holy Roman Empire. He adored the memory of the Emperor Frederic II, and never ceased to lament the defeat of this great man by the money-grabbing merchants of the Lombard cities. For a moment, he had hoped that Mussolini might revive the ancient glories; but the rise of Hitler reminded him that the Hohenstauffen were Germans, and he urged Mussolini to abdicate in favour of Hitler. Neither Dictator was grateful to him, and, but for Aguinaldo, he would have suffered the penalty of his idealism.

Baron Schambok had much in common with Count Cesare. He was a short man, whose appearance was redeemed from insignificance by magnificent and ferocious mustachios. Fiery energy showed in all his movements, and one felt that he ought to have a knout in his hand. He looked back nostalgically to the days of the original Baltic Barons from whom he was descended. He remembered how they had introduced Teutonic civilization to the still pagan inhabitants of northern regions. The Teutonic Knights dwelt in his imagination as the shining champions of chivalry and Christendom in a dark, difficult land. Though he had been an exile since 1917, he still hoped: some turn of the wheel of fortune, so he dreamt, might restore his family and friends to their former greatness. Meanwhile, to prove to the world that he was not a fanatic, he had allowed himself to enter into relations with the Soviet Government.

'And what', I inquired, 'brought you two into relation with Aguinaldo?'

'Well,' they told me, 'the story is rather curious. He invited us both to dinner, and, after dinner, asked us if we would like to listen to some gramophone records. We both said that we would prefer to talk. "Well," he said, "I think you are making a mistake. I am sure that you would be interested in the particular records that I wish you to hear." So we acquiesced; and the result amazed us. We had met secretly in the depths of the Black Forest at midnight to arrange a pact between the Kremlin and the Vatican, to be kept a complete secret lest the adherents of either should be revolted by thoughts of friendship with the other. We had conversed, as we believed, in complete solitude, and, as plenipotentiaries, we had concluded the desired pact. But Aguinaldo had realized that something was up, and had set his spies upon us. He has, in fact, a vast secret service, everywhere on the look-out for valuable secrets. The record which he played to us was a verbatim report of the whole of our midnight conversation. If this were published, we should be ruined. He promised not to publish it if we joined his crusade. We approved his objects, and therefore, agreed.'

4

The next member of the Fraternity to visit me was the Egyptian Ahmes, whose name had been Suleiman Abbas. He had changed his name in order to purge it of everything that was not Egyptian in origin. His nationalism had secured him considerable success, but his opposition to Islam had brought him the enmity of the Egyptian Government. He believed passionately that everything good is Egyptian in origin and that everything evil is alien to the clear spirit of the dwellers on the Lower Nile. He was convinced, with a quite unshakable certainty, that all would be well with the world if the Pharaonic Empire and culture could be restored. 'Consider', he said, 'what we, in our great days, contributed to world culture. Your education is still based upon what you call "the three R's". But you do not tell the helpless children committed to your charge that all three R's owe their origin to my country. How many of you Westerners will recognize the source of the name that I have adopted? Do you realize that Ahmes was the author of the oldest extant textbook of arithmetic? And, to pass to another department of culture, have you realized how, in the days of the Pharaohs, pictorial art spread from Egypt throughout what is now the empty and desert Sahara? You Westerners are in the habit of praising the Greeks, but have you reflected that it was only after contact with my country that Greek civilization began to blossom? The long night that my country has suffered began with the madman Cambyses, continued under the drunken Alexander and the uxorious Antony. Two Semitic religions proceeded to oppress the Egyptian spirit. And, to this day, even those who proclaim themselves champions of Egyptian nationalism are willing to abase themselves before the superstitions invented by an ignorant Arab and spread by savage, invading hordes. My ancestors, the Pharaohs, imagined that they had done with Semites when they sent Moses into the desert. Alas, they did not foresee the conquests of Christ and Mohammed. Persians, Macedonians, Romans, Arabs, Turks, French, and British have in turn oppressed my unhappy land. It is not enough to secure political freedom. It is, above all, cultural freedom that I seek to restore to Egypt; and it is this that has caused my troubles. The ungrateful Government of Cairo, which still abases itself before the Semitic conqueror of fourteen centuries ago, opposes with un-Egyptian fanaticism every attempt to restore the worship of Ammon-Râ. Nor is my Egyptian nationalism more welcome outside the confines of Egypt. Everywhere, I have found myself in conflict with governments, and, if it had not been for the helping hand of Aguinaldo, I should have languished miserably under a régime inspired by one of the three Semitic impostors—Christ,

Mohammed, and Marx. To my intense joy, Aguinaldo realized that my crusade was an integral part of his world-wide Fight for the Right; and in this sacred Brotherhood I have found scope for my well-justified hatreds. I can now allow myself to dream of the not very distant day when Aguinaldo's campaign will be crowned with success, and Egypt can once more become the inspirer of all that is noblest in the life of Man.'

When he was speaking, I allowed myself to be carried along sympathetically on the stream of his eloquence, but when he left me, I rubbed my eyes and seemed to awaken from a dream. 'It is all very fine', I said to myself, 'to praise the dwellers on the Nile, but has he not forgotten the Euphrates, the Tigris, and the Indus—not to mention the Yellow River and the Yangtse? I am afraid his view of history is somewhat myopic, but as I am committed to Aguinaldo, I must learn to work with his lieutenants.'

While I was still meditating on the rivers of Asia, I was visited by another of Aguinaldo's lieutenants, the Mexican Carlos Diaz, whose name had now been changed to Quetzalcoatl. Like Ahmes, he wished to revive the past, but a somewhat less distant past than that of the Pharaohs; and like Ahmes, he had had considerable success amongst his own countrymen with his propaganda. It was pre-Columban Mexico, and especially the Maya civilization, that he admired. He considered the Spaniards, and white men generally, as barbarians who had destroyed the peaceful and prosperous civilization of his country and had displayed a fanatical vandalism which (so he maintained) every lover of art and beauty must profoundly deplore. He had found only one European teacher with whom he could in any degree sympathize. This one was Karl Marx. In Mexico, the Spaniards were the upper class and the Indians were the proletariat. Marx, therefore, appeared to him as the champion of the Indians. I could not but think that, in this opinion, he was justified. Perhaps, also, Marx might have not objected to the Aztec system of human sacrifice

171

provided that the victims had all been rich. The dreams of Carlos Diaz, like those of Ahmes, were of a somewhat violent character. He hoped to see a great confederation of Indians from the Rio Grande to Cape Horn ousting the White Man, acquiring modern weapons, and, perhaps, ultimately restoring even the northern portions of their continent to the descendants of those who had roamed the great plains before the advent of Columbus. The more bloodthirsty of his visions he revealed seldom and reluctantly, but it was clear that he hoped for a day when the skyscrapers would topple and Manhattan would revert to forest. These hopes were suspected in Washington and did not enhance his popularity. His admiration of Marx made it possible to treat him as a Communist, and his somewhat unguarded advocacy of revolution gave the governments of the world a pretext for his incarceration. On the very day of his impending arrest, he was rescued by Aguinaldo. A forged passport supplied him with a new name and plastic surgery supplied him with a new face. He had disliked his old name because it was Spanish, and with joy he decided that his new name should be Quetzalcoatl. Henceforth, as one of Aguinaldo's lieutenants, he was able to pursue his propaganda in secret by the devious methods which Aguinaldo had perfected.

In the course of my interviews with Dr Aguinaldo's lieutenants, I soon discovered that they fell into two classes: there were those who genuinely believed in the Fight for the Right and hoped that Aguinaldo's methods would prove successful; but there were others who were purely cynical and attached to Aguinaldo solely by his power of blackmail. With one exception, all of them, of both kinds, were in Aguinaldo's power owing to some hold which he had acquired through his agents. But those who agreed with his professed aims worked with him enthusiastically, while the others were only concerned to save their own skins. The most important in the second class was Dr Mauleverer, whom I found at once interesting and repulsive. As a student of scientific medicine, he had won a great reputation, especially as regards the cause and cure of cancer. It soon became obvious in the course of our talk that he was avid for both power and money, and cared for nothing else. While he was still undetected, suspicious people observed that those of his patients who were very rich were apt to die of cancer unless they paid him enormous fees. Police investigation had made a criminal prosecution imminent; and, but for Aguinaldo's timely rescue, he would have faced ruin and prison, if not death. Dr Aguinaldo, after changing Mauleverer's name and appearance, supplied him with new medical diplomas from San Ysidro and with the opportunity of acquiring a new medical reputation. In return for this help, he undertook to diagnose cancer in any patient whom Aguinaldo disliked. If such a patient did not alter his politics or retire from public life, Dr Mauleverer saw to it that he did in fact die of cancer. His victims were of two kinds: those who were effective opponents of the Fight for the Right and those who were enemies of the Republic of San Ysidro. But care was taken to make it seem that these two kinds were one. Dr Mauleverer explained all this to me with complete *sang froid*. The sufferings of his victims were a matter of entire indifference to him. For the present, he was content with the money and power which he acquired in the service of Aguinaldo, but it was clear to me that, if ever opportunity offered, he would seek a career of independent crime. No such opportunity had as yet presented itself, but I sensed that he had not given up hope. He made a medical discovery which he hoped would prove useful, namely, that the immunity to the effects of the Insane Root enjoyed by the natives of Aguinaldo's village wore off gradually if they went to live elsewhere.

I was much interested by the Russian member of Aguinaldo's fraternity. His name was General Zinsky, and he had enjoyed the favour of the Soviet Government until 1945, but at the time of Potsdam and in the immediately following months, he had urged a lenient policy towards Germans on the ground that they might again become allies of Russia as in 1939. This brought him into disfavour, and he was about to be purged when Aguinaldo's secret emissaries rescued him. He was a very useful man in the organization because of his intimate knowledge of Soviet secrets. Although in his heart he still accepted Communist ideology, personal indignation made him willing to work against the Soviet Government, and self-preservation compelled him to do so in the service of Aguinaldo.

There was another ex-Communist among Aguinaldo's lieu-tenants: namely, the American Woodrow Bordov. He was a man with one very simple desire: he wished to see himself in the headlines as often as possible. At one time he had thought that Communism would conquer the world and had become a member of the Communist Party. When this proved dangerous, he became an Informer and told whatever stories about American Communists the fervent anti-Communists wished to hear. After a time, nevertheless, the newspapers had had enough of him, and he no longer rated their front pages. He then turned round and retracted, on oath, all that he had pre-viously said on oath. It was brought home to him, however, that perjury is only tolerated in defence of the Right, and that, in defence of the Left, it is a crime. While in a state of terror, he was approached by one of Aguinaldo's agents and skilfully rescued. Aguinaldo found him useful because of his knowledge of Western Communist agents. Under the new name bestowed upon him by Aguinaldo, he achieved headlines in the more extreme organs of Western anti-Communism. What he achieved in this way was less than he had hoped and less than he still desired, but so far it was all that was possible while Aguinaldo's hold on him remained.

5

At the dinner at which I was introduced to the fraternity, my attention had been attracted to the only woman in the company, but, at that time, I learnt nothing about her except what I could see. She was exquisitely beautiful, rather tall, with jet black hair and large, compelling eyes. Her demeanour was proud and dominating. At this first dinner she said little, and I did not see her again until after I had seen all Aguinaldo's other lieutenants, but I had learnt from them that she was his closest collaborator and knew more of his secrets than any of the others knew. I looked forward with lively interest to the interview with her, which was to complete my initiation. I learnt that her name was Irma d'Arpad, and that she was a descendant of ancient Hungarian kings. During my interview with her, I felt as though I were having an interview with royalty. Unlike the others, she evidently did not feel herself to be in Aguinaldo's power. On the contrary, she seemed to feel that Aguinaldo was fortunate in being allowed to work with her. Unlike the others, she was not held to him by any tie of blackmail. She was a complete, and even fanatical, believer in the professed principles of the Fight for the Right; and it was this belief, alone, which caused her to work with Aguinaldo. All this she explained to me. 'You cannot wonder', she said, 'that I favour the Fight for the Right. I am descended from many generations of Hungarians, and the blood of Attila flows in my veins. For those of humble origin, it must be difficult to imagine the burning shame which I suffer from the spectacle of my country under the heel of vulgar upstarts whose ancestors trembled at the name of Attila and were proud of the opportunity to support him against the majesty of Rome. What do they know of the pride bestowed by ancient lineage? What do they know of the linking of past and future that this pride brings with it? I cannot and will not endure subjection to such riff-raff. While life remains, I will stand for majesty and tradition. It is because I believe that Aguinaldo's principles are the same as mine that I have joined him in his great enterprise. I am aware that some of his methods are such as the morality of our age deplores, but the spirit of my great ancestor supports me, and I do not shrink from what would have been thought right by the justly named Scourge of God.'

From Irma, who knew, or thought she knew, all Aguinaldo's secrets, I learnt more than I had previously been told about his methods of work. The 'Insane Root' had provided him with immense opportunities of blackmail of which he had taken full advantage. He spent the greater part of his vast resources on an international secret service which supplied him with the preliminary information as to possible victims. In every non-Communist country, he concentrated most of his attention upon those who seemed to be effective champions of the Left. The public was astonished over and over again by defections towards the Right. Men whom Progressives had trusted appeared suddenly to lose heart and to abandon beliefs to which they had seemed particularly wedded. In Communist countries, a somewhat different technique was attempted, but, as yet, with only very moderate success. In these countries, evidence was produced or manufactured that So-and-so, a man prominent but not supreme in the Soviet hierarchy, had been for some considerable time an object of investigation by the secret police and was now on the point of being liquidated. If he was successfully persuaded, attempts were made to smuggle him across the Iron Curtain and find him employment as an anti-Communist agent.

'I suppose', I observed, 'that what you have said explains a remark of Aguinaldo's of which, when he made it, the meaning remained obscure to me. When I asked him what he wanted from me in return for saving me from disaster, he replied, "Only a little research". Am I right in assuming that the researches which he wished me to make are such as will bring discredit upon Left-wing politicians and upon such officials as, in his opinion, have a bad effect upon the decisions of politicians?'

'Yes,' she replied, 'that is exactly what he will wish you to do. Your previous experience must have made known to you many weaknesses of eminent men. Some have been financially corrupt, some have been guilty of sexual aberrations of a sort which the public condemns, others have had indiscrete relations with Communist Governments. You will be expected to make such men acquainted with Aguinaldo, who will put the finishing touches to the work, if necessary, with the help of the Insane Root.'

Although I do not pretend to be particularly squeamish, I must confess that I was repelled by this programme of work. Although my conduct had been far from irreproachable, I did not much like the prospect of devoting my time and skill to the business of forcing eminent men to act in violation of their beliefs. Irma perceived my reluctance, and it stimulated in her a flood of eloquent and passionate conviction. 'Do you not see', she said, 'that, for lack of the old stabilities, the world is sinking into an abyss where either all must perish or, at best, a few miserable survivors can live the life of the beasts of the field? Do you not see that monarchy, religion, respect for the Great, and complete faith in the well-tried dogmas of past centuries, are the only forces that can keep in check the turbulent creeds and cruelties of the swinish multitude? Consider the lessons of history. The ancient empires of Egypt and China persisted for forty centuries. In our day an empire is fortunate if it survives for two decades. Men have become restless, anarchic, impatient of discipline. The best are full of doubt, and the rest are governed by rapacity. It is not by gentle means, or by a conventionally virtuous campaign, that these dreadful evils can be eradicated. The day for squeamishness is past; and it is Aguinaldo whose methods can, alone, bring a cure.'

While she spoke, her eyes flashed fire and her voice vibrated with passion. Not unwillingly, I fell under her spell, influenced partly by her powerful personality, and partly by very compelling motives of self-interest. In that moment, I vowed myself to the work and decided to close my eyes to its distasteful aspects.

M 177

6

After the occasion on which I had been formally admitted to membership of the Brotherhood, I was free to live a normal life under my new name and with my new personality as a Latin American. The only restriction upon my freedom was a vow which had been imposed upon me by Aguinaldo that I would not seek the company of the Siren who had brought me to the brink of ruin. Every Saturday evening, at our weekly dinners, we began with a general discussion of policy and then proceeded, under the guidance of Aguinaldo, to the allotting of suitable tasks to the various members. Our ultimate aims were clear, but it was often difficult to think of any means by which they could be achieved. We wished, of course, to restore monarchy wherever it had been replaced by a republic. Even in Spain, much as we admired Franco's valiant championship of religion and censorship, we could not ignore our obligation to the ancient Royal Family. Even when this was decided, there still remained a problem: should we seek out the heirs of Don Carlos and revive the Carlist Party, or should we be content with the restoration of the Royal Family whom the Revolution of 1930 had dispossessed? Germany, likewise, presented a problem. We could not feel that the German Empire established by Bismarck had sufficient antiquity to command our respect; and, after some debate, we decided in favour of the restoration of all the separate Principalities and Dukedoms that had existed before the achievement of German unity. In Italy, we of course supported the restoration of the Papal States, the Grand Duchy of Tuscany, and the rest. In regard to Russia, we had a vehement debate in which Irma took one side and the rest of us took the other. All the rest of us would have been content with the restoration of the Romanovs, but Irma, who felt herself a Mongol, passionately protested that the Imperial Family of Russia were subversive rebels against the Empire established by Genghis Khan. In view of this division of opinion, we decided that, for the present, we would leave Russia except for occasional pin-pricks.

The problem of Russia was one example of a difficulty which arose in many of our discussions. How far back should we go in our attempt to recreate the past? In regard to India, for example, should we attempt to recreate something like the Empire of Asoka, or should we be content with the Great Mogul? And in China, should we accept the Manchu dynasty? We debated such problems with great earnestness at our Saturday meetings, and in general we ended by accepting the judgment of Aguinaldo. There were, however, two problems as to which we found agreement impossible. One of these, already mentioned, was Irma's championship of the Mongols; the other, which proved even more serious, was a disagreement between Aguinaldo and the Mexican Diaz—now Quetzalcoatl. Aguinaldo prided himself on his descent from the Conquistadores, whereas Diaz hated the Spaniards and wished to recapture Mexico and South America for the descendants of their pre-Columban inhabitants. Most of us, in this dispute, sympathized with Diaz. Irma, in particular, whose Mongolian ancestry had inclined her to antipathy towards Europeans, could not bring herself, on this point, to accept the authority of our Chief. She was deeply in love with him and would have given way on almost any other issue, but, when she heard him upholding European domination, the blood of Attila boiled in her veins and she found submission impossible. Gradually, his influence over her declined—the more so, as he showed a complete indifference to her advances. Coldly inflexible, he appeared wholly devoted to The Cause. Not for him were any of the softer joys that she longed to provide. In all his discourses, he endeavoured to instil an implacable, ascetic fanaticism and an entire indifference to everything except victory. At first, Irma had accepted this complete immolation of self; but she could not carry it to the length of accepting the subjection of non-Europeans. This rift became gradually more and more serious and increasingly threatened the success of the Great Enterprise.

The trouble was increased by disquieting facts which Diaz secretly brought to the notice of the rest of us. It appeared that, in dealings with Latin-American States, Aguinaldo was dominated, not by the avowed principles of the Brotherhood, but by the attitude of these various States to his own Republic of San Ysidro. He would make friends with revolutionary leaders if they were prepared to co-operate with his country, but would be hostile to reactionaries if they opposed increases in the power of San Ysidro. Diaz was the only member of the Brotherhood, except Aguinaldo, who understood the complex politics of Latin America, and first Irma and then the rest of us, came gradually to think that his misgivings were not unfounded. Could it be that Aguinaldo was not all that we had thought? Was it possible that he was using the Insane Root, not for the glorious impersonal ends which he had put before us, but for his own aggrandizement and that of San Ysidro? Obscure dealings with dope merchants in the United States accidentally came to light, in spite of Aguinaldo's endeavours to conceal them, and it did not seem that these dealings had any connection with the Fight for the Right.

7

Week by week, our misgivings increased. Diaz, after carefully instructing us about the doings of some South American Governments, set traps for Aguinaldo, who assumed that most of us were ignorant as to the points in dispute. At last, we all agreed that there was only one thing to be done. We must secretly administer to him a very small dose of the Insane Root—not enough to make him mad, still less to cause his death, but just enough to give him an attack of that dangerous disease first diagnosed by Belloc, and by him christened *Veracititis*. This was not a difficult matter. It was our custom to keep a powdered form of the Insane Root in special pepper pots which our occasional influential guests were encouraged to use. We had only to transfer the powder to an ordinary pepper box and provide a dish for which we knew that Aguinaldo would desire a peppery flavouring. The success of our plot was facilitated by his unusual addiction to pepper. In the deepest secrecy, we made our preparations. In breathless suspense, we watched him shake the fatal pepper box. As the Saturday dinner proceeded, he became gradually more excited, more boastful, and less restrained. At last he burst out into a loud harangue:

'What do you know of ME? What do you understand of my plans? Do you think, you poor deluded fools, that I care tuppence about all this jargon of Right and Left? Do you really suppose that I care about monarchy in the abstract? No, indeed! It is monarchy in the concrete that I care about—monarchy with me as the Monarch; monarchy with the whole world at my feet; monarchy with subjects imploring my mercy, and often not obtaining it. You have helped me, you patient idealistic or criminal tools, to acquire a hold over the governments of the world. The secrets which you have helped me to unearth are such as would cause the populations of all the countries of the world to turn upon their rulers in savage fury. The rulers, to escape this fate, must bow to my will. The time is almost ripe. I, Aguinaldo—I, who began as a humble citizen of the tiny Republic of San Ysidro—I, whom men have regarded as a harmless fanatic of reaction—I shall soon be Emperor of the World. It is to this end that I have built up our organization. It is for this end that your researches will be used. Those who oppose me will die raving from unexpected doses of the Insane Root. Under me, the world shall be united and the silly politics of this age shall be forgotten.'

We listened in horror, but, in obedience to a resolution which we had made in advance, we concealed our horror and pretended to applaud the new revelation. We knew that when

181

the intoxication passed he would not remember what he had said and would suspect no change in our relation to him. But when the time came for the next Saturday dinner we repeated our previous performance, but this time we put the powdered Root into the food as well as into the pepper box. Again he became excited, but more recklessly than before. 'Bow down before me, slaves,' he shouted. 'If you are faithful, I, the Emperor of the World, will reward you as you may deserve. If you are not faithful, you will perish.' Gradually, his speech became inarticulate. He writhed in strange contortions and, finally, fell dead.

A bewildered silence fell upon us. The unity which we had owed to service under a common chief was dissolved. As separate units, without aim or purpose, none of us could think how to proceed. Irma alone remained calm.

'Well, friends,' she said, 'we have been deceived. The leader whom we revered was a charlatan, and the aims to which we gave allegiance were visionary absurdities. Can any of you suggest a course of action not wholly futile?'

At these words, a curious transformation came over us. All of us had been deeply and passionately devoted to Irma, but her love for Aguinaldo and our respect for him had kept our feelings towards Irma in the region of humble adoration. We all began to speak at once, and the substance of what we said was the same for each one of us. In the resulting babel, I was only dimly aware of what the others said, but I gathered afterwards that it differed little from my own speech: 'Irma,' I cried, 'in the shipwreck of all that we have believed and hoped, there remains for me one immovable rock: I love you, and if you can reciprocate my feeling, my life may still possess purpose and joy.'

When we discovered that all the others had been saying just the same thing, we turned upon each other in a fury. 'You miserable worms, do you suppose that you are worthy to share the life of the Imperial descendant of Attila? Can you imagine that she would look upon any of *you* with favour?' Very soon, we came to blows, and an unmannerly brawl took place in the presence of the corpse. But Irma once more took command.

'Stop!' she cried. 'Cease your unseemly quarrels. I love you all, my Colleagues in an enterprise which has suffered momentary eclipse. Your trouble has a solution as simple as it is radical. You know that one of our greatest successes has been the restoration of the ancient régime of Tibet, and that among the institutions which the shameless Communists endeavoured to sweep away was that of polyandry. We will go to Lhasa, and I will marry you all.'

*   *   *

EDITOR's NOTE: They went—but what became of them is unknown.

III

Newly Discovered Maxims
of La Rochefoucauld

INTRODUCTION

THE FOLLOWING, hitherto unknown, maxims of La Rochefoucauld were lately discovered at the bottom of a well in the
garden of a chateau in France that had, at one time, been
inhabited by Lord Bolingbroke. It seems probable that the
manuscript was given by La Rochefoucauld's descendants to
this English philosopher whom they regarded as their ancestor's
spiritual descendant.

I cannot pretend that, at all points, I am in agreement with
the epigrammatic Duke. Indeed, there is only one of the ensuing
maxims in which I wholeheartedly and unreservedly believe.
This one is the nineteenth. Some readers may feel that to accept
it completely is to incur a logical paradox. To them, I can only
say: remember that life is greater than logic.

1. Men do as much harm as they dare, and as much good as
   they must.
2. The purpose of morals is to enable people to inflict suffering without compunction.
3. The advantage of duty is that it can always be neglected.
4. People never forgive the injuries they inflict nor the
   benefits they endure.

5. Since the effects of all actions are incalculable, actions intended to do harm, do good, and actions intended to do good, do harm. It follows that evil intentions should be encouraged.

6. Manners is the pretence that you think your interlocutor is as important as yourself.

7. Liberty is the right to do what *I* like; licence, the right to do what *you* like.

8. A pacifist is one who is always determined to annoy everyone.

9. Discipline and indiscipline are the twin children of Authority.

10. Pythagoras and Plato thought to get the better of Zeus: but they forgot that Aphrodite as well as Pallas Athene is his daughter.

11. 'Truth' is a governmental concept.

12. Religion is a department of politics.

13. Friendship may be defined as a common enmity.

14. Arithmetic is a dastardly attempt of the Administrator to impose His authority upon the flux.

15. Vagueness is the rebellion of truth against intellect.

16. We must let our opponents think—if they can.

17. Philosophy is the art of using in an impressive manner words of which you do not know the meaning.

18. An eminent philosopher has stated: 'That all knowledge begins with experience is not open to doubt.' But he would have been hard put to it to say what he meant by 'knowledge' and what by 'experience'. Familiarity with the words made him mistakenly suppose that he knew what they stood for.

19. It matters little what you believe, so long as you don't altogether believe it.

20. A Realist is a man who confirms the prejudices of the man who is speaking.

IV

Nightmares

(1) THE FISHERMAN'S NIGHTMARE OR 'MAGNA EST
VERITAS'

SIR PETER SIMON had been from early youth passionately fond
of fishing and, although he became a very busy and successful
professional man, he always devoted the summer holidays to
his favourite sport. After testing various regions, he finally
came to prefer the Highlands of Scotland. He was, however,
deeply distressed by what he considered the vulgar notoriety
conferred by the Loch Ness Monster. Although he had often
fished in that Loch, he had never come upon any sign of this
curious animal, and his nature was such that he thought everything not visible to himself must be mythical.

One evening, after reading in Izaak Walton about respectable
fishes such as the chavender or chubb, he fell asleep, and his
waking thoughts took shape in the form of a strange nightmare.
He dreamt that the Loch Ness Monster had inspired some
ingenious people who lived on a loch in a nearby glen. These
people—so he dreamt—were actuated by a motive, that of
ambitious competition, which he could but applaud. The influx
of tourists from the degenerate South following upon the
discovery of the Loch Ness Monster had been noted by the
hardy Highlanders of the neighbouring glen, and they had
observed with envy that the development of tourism had
brought whole swarms of chars-à-bancs that made the month

of August hideous but, for the dwellers on Loch Ness, extremely lucrative. Sir Peter's sleeping imagination presented these people as having manufactured a monster to inhabit their own lake who was made in part like a car tyre, but with the addition of a long tail that waved in the current like seaweed. This horrid creature was provided with a cleverly contrived device by which, when the air was let out, he uttered loud and dismal howls, at the same time 'Swinging the scaley horror of his folded tail'. On dark nights, especially when there was a thunder storm, this device succeeded in inspiring terror among the more timorous fishermen—a terror far greater than the Loch Ness Monster had ever created.

But, alas, the land-owners of the neighbourhood, who had invented the monster, though they soon succeeded in out-doing the Loch Ness Monster, had underestimated the scientific curiosity of our impertinent age. A rather young FRS, Mr Jonas MacPherson, who had been born and bred in the neighbourhood and who was a fanatic votary of fishing, discovered the hoax by circumambulating the lake on stormy nights and observing the presence of a rowing boat in the neighbourhood of the dreadful howls. In the works of that eminent Lord Chancellor Francis Bacon, he had come across the statement that knowledge is power, and it occurred to him that his knowledge about the Monster gave him power of a very useful kind. Being by no means well-off, he had, hitherto, had great difficulty in paying for his Highland holidays. But now he went to the local hotel-keeper telling of his discovery and promising to keep silence if he was allowed fishing rights and free board and lodging at the hotel. The hotel-keeper, who was one of the ring-leaders in the plot, summoned the committee of conspirators; and Mr MacPherson's terms were reluctantly accepted.

For a time, all went well, but the fame of the new monster continued to grow, and, at last, the pressure of the sensational press combined with the desire of Sir Theophilus Thwackum to add the beast to his private zoo, compelled the Royal Society to send a deputation to investigate the phenomena. The deputation consisted of ten eminent men of science who, it was confidently believed, would not easily be taken in by any hocus-pocus if, indeed, something of the sort were involved. Mr MacPherson, who was not without gratitude to the conspirators and also wished to preserve his free holidays, felt that he should earn his keep. He therefore proceeded to supply the creature with howls and yells far more horrible than before; and he inserted in its inside tape-recordings which loudly wailed, 'Repent, Ye Unbelievers!' All the ten Fellows heard the dreadful message on a dark night of thunder and lightning. Alas, each one of them was deeply conscious that there was that in his past which called for repentance. All ten feared that if they repeated the experiment the awe-inspiring monster would no longer be content with generalities, but would specify the items in which these hitherto respected citizens had sinned. All returned to London with hair completely white. Their cronies would endeavour on social evenings to elicit at least some hint of what had occurred on those northern waters, but not one of these great men could be induced to make even the smallest revelation. All of them, when compelled to speak of their experiences, remarked in grave and awe-stricken tones: 'There are some things which it is not for mortals to investigate.'

And there the matter might have rested if good taste and proper reticence had had due sway. Unfortunately, the results of the investigation seemed unsatisfying to a certain rash young scientist, Mr Adam Monkhouse. Mr Monkhouse was even younger than Mr MacPherson, and, although on the road to scientific success, had not yet become a Fellow of the Royal Society. He had a personal grudge against Mr MacPherson who had adversely criticized a hypothesis of his which he was very loath to abandon. He spent a month at the hotel with which Mr MacPherson had his agreement, and devoted himself to the cultivation of friendly relations with the hotel-keeper.

Late one evening, by the expenditure of considerable sums on the very best Highland whisky, he succeeded in producing in the hotel-keeper a mellow mood in which, for the moment, nothing seemed worth concealing. The hotel-keeper told all; and Mr Monkhouse returned jubilant from the gloomy glens and fastnesses which his cheerful soul abominated. He published the results of his researches, with unkind remarks about the investigating committee. The result, however, was not what he had hoped. The Royal Society was indignant at the slur upon ten of its foremost members, and it became clear that he no longer had any hope of himself becoming one of that August Body. All the ten members of the investigating committee sued him for libel. All ten were supported by the whole body of organized science. All ten were awarded heavy damages, which at first he saw no means of paying. But, being a resourceful person, he found a way out: he saw the error of his ways, and joined the Society for Psychical Research.

Sir Peter Simon awoke. The sweat was cold upon him. But with awakening came warmth and understanding. 'Ah', he cried, 'how useful is faith when properly directed! How more than useful is even curiosity—is investigation—when properly curbed by faith!'

NOTE: After writing the above, I learnt, from the following article in the *Guardian*, that my fantasy was nearer to the truth than I had supposed.

IN HOSPITAL AFTER LOCH NESS DIVE

Search for 'monster'

John Newbold, aged 31, of Stafford, known as Beppo, the clown, was detained in hospital yesterday after diving into Loch Ness in a frogman's outfit to try to get evidence about the 'monster'.

He made a dive lasting ten minutes and surfaced in a semiconscious state. He was taken aboard a yacht belonging to Mr Bernard Mills, the circus proprietor, and recovered partly after artificial respiration had been applied.

Mr Newbold, who was unable to say what had happened while he was underwater, is an experienced high diver and swimmer. He had made several practice dives to a depth of more than 30 feet before yesterday's attempt. The water is several hundred feet deep at this part of the loch.

The late Mr Bertram Mills offered £10,000 before the war for the capture of the 'monster' and nine years ago his sons, Bernard and Cyril, increased the offer to £20,000.

(2) THE THEOLOGIAN'S NIGHTMARE

The eminent theologian, Dr Thaddeus, dreamed that he died and pursued his course toward heaven. His studies had prepared him and he had no difficulty in finding the way. He knocked at the door of heaven, and was met with a closer scrutiny than he expected. 'I ask admission', he said, 'because I was a good man and devoted my life to the glory of God.' 'Man?' said the janitor, 'What is that?' And how could such a funny creature as you are do anything to promote the glory of God?' Dr Thaddeus was astonished. 'You surely cannot be ignorant of man. You must be aware that man is the supreme work of the Creator.' 'As to that,' said the janitor, 'I am sorry to hurt your feelings, but what you're saying is news to me. I doubt if anybody up here has ever heard of this thing you call "man". However, since you seem distressed, you shall have a chance of consulting our librarian.'

The librarian, a globular being with a thousand eyes and one mouth, bent some of his eyes upon Dr Thaddeus. 'What is this?' he asked of the janitor. 'This', replied the janitor, 'says that it is a member of a species called "man", which lives in a place called "Earth". It has some odd notion that the Creator

190

takes special interest in this place and this species. I thought perhaps you could enlighten it.' 'Well,' said the librarian kindly to the theologian, 'perhaps you can tell me where this place is that you call "Earth".' 'Oh,' said the theologian, 'it's part of the Solar System.' 'And what is the Solar System?' asked the librarian. 'Oh,' said the theologian, somewhat disconcerted, 'my province was Sacred Knowledge, but the question that you are asking belongs to profane knowledge. However, I have learnt enough from my astronomical friends to be able to tell you that the Solar System is part of the Milky Way.' 'And what is the Milky Way?' asked the librarian. 'Oh, the Milky Way is one of the Galaxies, of which, I am told, there are some hundred million.' 'Well, well,' said the librarian, 'you could hardly expect me to remember one out of so many. But I do remember to have heard the word "galaxy" before. In fact, I believe that one of our sub-librarians specializes in galaxies. Let us send for him and see whether he can help.'

After no very long time, the galactic sub-librarian made his appearance. In shape, he was a dodecahedron. It was clear that at one time his surface had been bright, but the dust of the shelves had rendered him dim and opaque. The librarian explained to him that Dr Thaddeus, in endeavouring to account for his origin, had mentioned galaxies, and it was hoped that information could be obtained from the galactic section of the library. 'Well,' said the sub-librarian, 'I suppose it might become possible in time, but as there are a hundred million galaxies, and each has a volume to itself, it takes some time to find any particular volume. Which is it that this odd molecule desires?' 'It is the one called "the Milky Way" ', Dr Thaddeus falteringly replied. 'All right,' said the sub-librarian, 'I will find it if I can.'

Some three weeks later, he returned, explaining that the extraordinarily efficient card-index in the galactic section of the library had enabled them to locate the galaxy as number XQ 321,762. 'We have employed', he said, 'all the five thousand clerks in the galactic section on this search. Perhaps you would like to see the clerk who is specially concerned with the galaxy in question?' The clerk was sent for and turned out to be an octohedron with an eye in each face and a mouth in one of them. He was surprised and dazed to find himself in such a glittering region, away from the shadowy limbo of his shelves. Pulling himself together, he asked, rather shyly, 'What is it you wish to know about my galaxy?' Dr Thaddeus spoke up: 'What I want is to know about the Solar System, a collection of heavenly bodies revolving about one of the stars in your galaxy. The star about which they revolve is called "the Sun".' 'Humph,' said the librarian of the Milky Way, 'it was hard enough to hit upon the right galaxy, but to hit upon the right star in the galaxy is far more difficult. I know that there are about three hundred billion stars in the galaxy, but I have no knowledge, myself, that would distinguish one of them from another. I believe, however, that at one time a list of the whole three hundred billion was demanded by the Administration and that it is still stored in the basement. If you think it worth while, I will engage special labour from the Other Place to search for this particular star.'

It was agreed that, since the question had arisen and since Dr Thaddeus was evidently suffering some distress, this might be the wisest course.

Several years later, a very weary and dispirited tetrahedron presented himself before the galactic sub-librarian. 'I have', he said, 'at last discovered the particular star concerning which inquiries have been made, but I am quite at a loss to imagine why it has aroused any special interest. It closely resembles a great many other stars in the same galaxy. It is of average size and temperature, and is surrounded by very much smaller bodies called "planets". After minute investigation, I discovered that some, at least, of these planets have parasites, and I think that this thing which has been making inquiries must be one of them.'

At this point, Dr Thaddeus burst out in a passionate and indignant lament: 'Why, oh why, did the Creator conceal from us poor inhabitants of Earth that it was not we who prompted Him to create the Heavens? Throughout my long life, I have served Him diligently, believing that He would notice my service and reward me with Eternal Bliss. And now, it seems that He was not even aware that I existed. You tell me that I am an infinitesimal animalcule on a tiny body revolving round an insignificant member of a collection of three hundred billion stars, which is only one of many millions of such collections. I cannot bear it, and can no longer adore my Creator.' 'Very well,' said the janitor, 'then you can go to the Other Place.'

Here the theologian awoke. 'The power of Satan over our sleeping imagination is terrifying', he muttered.

V

Dreams

THE FOLLOWING dreams are exactly as I dreamt them. I offer them to the psychoanalysts in the hope that they will make the worst of them.

(1) JOWETT

I sometimes had dreams which had, perhaps, rather more of literary quality than one expects of dreams. I can remember several of these: one, when I was just at the end of adolescence. I had suffered, as many adolescents do, from melancholy, and I thought that I was on the verge of suicide. I don't think I really was, but that was what I thought. And, just as I was beginning to feel rather less of this sort of melancholy, I dreamt that I was dying and that Benjamin Jowett was watching by my death-bed. In my dream, I said to him in a die-away voice: 'Well, at any rate, there is one comfort. I shall soon be done with all this.' To which Jowett, in his squeaky voice, replied, 'You mean life?' And I said, 'Yes, I mean life'. Jowett said, 'When you are a little older, you won't talk that sort of nonsense'. I woke up; and I never talked that sort of nonsense again.

(2) GOD

Another time, when I lived in a cottage where there were no servants at night time, I dreamt that I heard a knock on the front door in the very early morning. I went down to the front

door in my night shirt—this was before the days of pyjamas—
and, when I opened the door, I found God on the doorstep.
I recognized Him at once from His portraits. Now, a little
before this, my brother-in-law Logan Pearsall Smith had said
that he thought of God as rather like the Duke of Cambridge—
that is to say, still august, but conscious of being out of date.
And, remembering this, I thought, well, I must be kind to Him
and show that, although of course He is perhaps a little out
of date, still I quite know how one should behave to a guest.
So I hit Him on the back and said, 'Come in, old fellow'. He
was very much pleased at being treated so kindly by one whom
He realized to be not quite of His congregation. After we had
talked for some time, He said, 'Now, is there anything I could
do for you?' And I thought, 'Well, He is omnipotent. I suppose
there are things He could do for me'. I said, 'I should like you
to give me Noah's Ark', and I thought I should put it somewhere in the suburbs and charge sixpence admission, and I
should make a huge fortune. But His face fell, and He said:
'I am very sorry, I can't do that for you because I have already
given it to an American friend of mine.' And that was the end
of my conversation with Him.

(3) HENRY THE NAVIGATOR

On another occasion, I dreamt that I was a friend of Henry
the Navigator, and that I went to see him one day and said,
'Can you give me lunch?' And he said, 'Well, I'm sorry, I can't
give you lunch here because I have to go to a diplomatic
Congress, but I can take you to the Congress if you like'. So
I said that I should be delighted, and he took me to the
Congress. When we got there we found all the other delegates
already assembled under a Chairman. When Henry the
Navigator came into the hall, they all stood up as he was the
only royal personage at the meeting, and the Chairman, in a
kind of ecclesiastical, intoning voice, said, 'What is the price

of Royalty?' And the congregation replied, 'Royalty has no price'. To which the Chairman rejoined, 'But it has inestimable value'. Whereupon, they sat down, and the proceedings continued.

(4) PRINCE NAPOLEON LOUIS
(Dreamt by Bertrand Russell, night of July 5, 1960)

I dreamt that I was travelling (as observer from the House of Lords) in a train containing the whole House of Commons, and that I was sitting next to the Speaker. The time was 1879. The train broke down on the borders of Zululand. The Speaker informed me that he would there and then call a meeting of the House of Commons. I inquired, sceptically, whether he possessed the right to do so. Somewhat indignantly, he informed me that he could call a meeting of the House anywhere, at any time. He then began a speech to the assembled Members, but had not got beyond the introductory platitudes when we all observed a man running at great speed from our ranks towards those of the Zulus. A moment's observation showed that he was Prince Napoleon Louis, the son of Napoleon III. The assembled House of Commons concluded that he intended to promise the protection of France against British arms and therefore, as one man, we all pursued him.

I woke up before the issue was decided.

(Major Chard (?) hero of the Zulu War came to Pembroke Lodge and told of his campaign, much to the joy and excitement of the young Bertie.)

(5) THE CATALOGUE

I dreamt that I was staying in an hotel which was at the top of a three-thousand-foot precipice. It had a balustrade from which the descent was sheer. I heard a man call out in a piercing voice, 'Death to John Elmwood, Communist and Atheist!' A confused noise of fierce assent came from people whom at first I did not notice. On looking round, I observed a man tied by a rope to the balustrade, and I realized that he was John Elmwood. Again and again, I heard the same fierce denunciation, and, each time, the crowd, which I could now see, advanced a little further towards the bound man. At last, with a savage cry, they all rushed towards him. He struggled, and broke the rope that bound him. As it broke, he fell over the precipice. I watched his fall, which seemed to continue endlessly and to be slow, like the fall of a feather. At last, he fell upon tree-tops, and broke. Everybody seemed happy except a little girl some ten years old, who was crying bitterly. One of the lynchers spoke to her, and she answered. I could not hear what was said. But he announced to the assembled crowd: 'She is crying because she has not got a catalogue.' I realized that the death which I had seen was only one of many that had been arranged as a public spectacle.

P.S. This dream was occasioned by my having to listen to a panegyric on free speech in Western countries by the Father of the H-bomb.

VI

Parables

(1) PLANETARY EFFULGENCE[1]

SCIENCE IN MARS had been making extraordinarily rapid progress. The territory of Mars was divided between two great Empires, the Alphas and the Betas, and it was their competition, more than any other one cause, which had led to the immense development of technique. In this competition neither side secured any advantage over the other. This fact caused universal disquiet, since each side felt that only its own supremacy could secure the future of life. Among the more thoughtful Martians, a feeling developed that security required the conquest of other planets. At last there came a day when the Alphas and the Betas, alike, found themselves able to despatch projectiles to Earth containing Martian scientists provided with means of survival in a strange environment. Each side simultaneously despatched projectiles, which duly reached their terrestrial target. One of them fell in what the inhabitants of Earth called 'The United States', and the other in what they called 'Russia'. To the great disappointment of the scientists, they were a little too late for many of the investigations which they had hoped to make. They found large cities, partially destroyed; vast machines, some of them still in operation; store-houses of food; and large ships tossing aimlessly on stormy seas. Wherever they found such things, they also

[1] The *New Statesman*, 1959.

found human bodies, but all the bodies were lifeless. The Martian scientists, by means of their super-radar, had discovered that on Earth, as in Mars, power was divided between two factions which, on Earth, were called the A's and the B's. It had been hoped that intercourse with the curious beings inhabiting Earth might add to Martian wisdom. But, unfortunately, life on Earth had become extinct a few months before the arrival of the projectiles.

At first the scientific disappointment was keen; but before very long cryptologists, linguists, and historians succeeded in decyphering the immense mass of record accumulated by these odd beings while they still lived. The Alphas and the Betas from Mars each drew up very full reports on what they had discovered about Tellurian thought and history. There was very little difference between the two reports. So long as each of the two factions remained unidentified, what A said about itself and about B was indistinguishable from what B said about itself and about A. It appeared that, according to each side, the other side wanted world dominion and wished all power to be in the hands of heartless officials whom the one side designated as bureaucrats and the other as capitalists. Each side held that the other advocated a soulless mechanism which should grind out engines of war without any regard to human happiness. Each side believed that the other, by unscrupulous machinations, was endeavouring to promote world war in spite of the obvious danger to all. Each side declared loudly: 'We, who stand for peace and justice and truth, dare not relax our vigilance or cease to increase our armaments, because the other side is so wicked.' The two Martian reports, drawn up by the Alphas and the Betas respectively, had similarities exactly like those of the A's and B's whom they were describing. Each ended up with a moral to its government. The moral was this: 'These foolish inhabitants of Earth forgot the obvious lesson that their situation should have taught them, namely, that it is necessary to be stronger than the other side. We hope that the government to which we are reporting will learn this salutary lesson from the awful warning of the catastrophe on our sister planet.'

The Governments of the Alphas and the Betas, alike, listened to the reports of their Tellurian experts and, alike, determined that their faction should be the stronger.

A few years after this policy had been adopted by both the Alphas and the Betas, two projectiles reached Mars from Jupiter. Jupiter was divided between the Alephs and the Beths, and each had sent its own projectile. Like the Martian travellers to Earth, the Jovian travellers found life in Mars extinct, but they soon discovered the two reports which had been brought from Earth. They presented them to their respective governments, both of which accepted the Martian moral with which the two Martian reports had ended. But as the Rulers of the two rival States of Alephs and Beths were finishing the drawing up of their comments, each had a strange, disquieting experience. A moving finger appeared, seized the pen from their astonished hands, and, without their co-operation, wrote these words: 'I am sorry I was so half-hearted at the time of Noah. (Signed) Cosmic President.' These words were deleted by the censor on each side and their strange occurrence was kept a profound secret.

(2) THE MISFORTUNE OF BEING OUT OF DATE

The last years of the second millennium, like the last years of the first, were filled with prophecies of the end of the world, but with somewhat more reason than at the earlier date. The cold war had been steadily getting hotter, and was felt to be rapidly approaching explosion point. Attempts had been made by both sides to make use of various heavenly bodies as bomb-sites. Astronomy, both in the East and in the West, had been made a department of the Air Ministries, and all recent astronomical knowledge was 'classified'. Each side continued to hope that the other knew less than it did, but so far this hope had proved vain. Each side had hopefully sent an expedition to the Moon and, after a few days of jubilation, had discovered that the other side had also landed there in full force. The two parties had instantly engaged in nuclear warfare and had wiped each other out. But what they had not foreseen was that the Moon was made of more explosive materials than the Earth. The brief H-bomb war started a chain reaction on the Moon. The Moon began to crumble and, within a month, was reduced to a cloud of tiny particles. A few poets regretted the loss, but they were considered subversive. The British Poet Laureate wrote a verse obituary of the Moon, pointing out that she had been the source of lunacy, and we were well rid of her. An eminent Soviet scientist published a very learned memoir pointing out the advantages of having done with tides.

Since the Moon had proved unsatisfactory, the next war effort on both sides was directed to reaching Mars and Venus. Both were reached simultaneously by both sides; but, again, the space-travellers considered it their duty to ideology to exterminate each other. But, alas, Mars and Venus, like the Moon, disintegrated under the influence of the powerful nuclear solvents that the voyagers from Earth had brought with them. Nothing daunted, the apostles of the rival faiths proceeded to Jupiter and Saturn. But even these enormous planets disappeared as the Moon and Venus and Mars had done.

The solar system, so the zealous governments on either side decided, is too small for our cosmic warfare. We cannot hope to win a decisive superiority over our dastardly foes, unless we can find a means of enlisting the stars.

Meanwhile, astronomy pursued researches which, both in the East and in the West, were shrouded in the utmost secrecy. Radar had proved that the distances of the nearer stars had been quite wrongly estimated, and this wrong estimate was explained as due to the bending of light rays by the gravitational effect of dark matter in the inter-stellar spaces. Each side decided that the nearest habitable spot, outside the solar system, was the Dark Companion of Sirius, which, in view of the new data, was estimated to be at a distance of fifty light-years from the Sun. Each side hoped that it alone possessed this knowledge. True, there was one astronomer in the West, and one in the East, who was suspected of treacherously revealing secret information, but it was hoped that the leak had been stopped in time. Both in the West and in the East, it was found possible to launch a projectile with a velocity not far short of that of light, and it was calculated that this projectile should reach the Dark Companion of Sirius eighty years after its launching. The expense was so great that food in both East and West had to be rationed to the bare minimum demanded by health, and all new capital investment had to be forbidden unless it contributed to the Grand Design. Since it could not be expected that the passengers originally embarked in the projectile would survive their eighty years' journey, it was necessary to make provision for new passengers to be born *en route*, although this entailed a much larger projectile than would otherwise have been necessary. All this was successfully accomplished, and, with a cargo of adequately indoctrinated boys and girls, each projectile was sent on its journey on the last day of the second millennium. On Earth each side came to know that the other side also had launched a projectile towards Sirius, but, as this was only discovered after the launching, the passengers did not know it and believed that they had stolen a march on their enemies.

Year after year each projectile sailed on its way through the darkness of interminable night. The boys and girls, instructed by wise elders and removed from all subversive influences, were cheered throughout the dreary years of their imprisonment by the hope of the ideological benefit which would ultimately accrue to those whom they had left behind on Earth. The boys and girls grew to manhood and womanhood, and children were born to them. Indoctrinated by their parents, the children equally felt themselves dedicated to the sacred task. They, in turn, had children, and it was this second generation, now in the prime of life, which found itself at last on the firm ground of the Dark Companion. They proceeded at once to set up radar and send triumphant messages to Earth—triumphant, because neither knew that the other party also had landed. 'Communism vanquished', said one message: 'Wall Street over-whelmed', said the other. Fifty years after these messages were despatched, they duly reached the Earth.

But during the hundred and thirty years that had elapsed since the projectiles had been despatched, affairs on Earth had taken a new turn. Capitalism and Communism had, alike, disappeared into the archives of history. The division of man-kind into separate nations had ceased. In an uncommitted nation a great Prophet had arisen who had taught that enough to eat could bring even more pleasure than simultaneous death to our enemies and ourselves. But he had not confined himself to this hedonistic argument. He had revived an older and almost forgotten ideology which taught that people should love one another, and even that they should love their enemies. Oddly enough, this idealistic doctrine did as much to convert public opinion as did the appeal to self-interest. In Eastern and Western lands alike, mobs assembled, shouting: 'Let us all live in peace. We will not hate. We will not believe that we are hated.' At first the mobs were small and were easily dispersed by the police, but gradually the words of the Prophet found more and more of an echo, until only governments were left preaching the old doctrines. At last even they surrendered to the immense wave of liberation and goodwill that swept over the world. Mankind had established a single government, and had forgotten the old divisions that had kept the human race in bondage to strife. The new generations knew little of the cold war period, since all knowledge of it had been kept secret while the danger of war remained, and very few in the new world of joy cared to plunge back into the gloomy abyss in which their grandparents had thought themselves compelled to live.

The messages from the Dark Companion were almost unintelligible except to historical students. They had the same musty, old-world flavour as we should feel if we got messages from Wessex and Mercia denouncing each other's abominable wickedness. When the messages from the Dark Companion reached the Earth, the World Government considered them and at last sent a brief reply. The reply said: 'Come home together and forget all this nonsense.' The reply reached the Dark Companion a hundred years after the immigrants sent their triumphant messages. Warned by the fate of the Moon and the Planets, the two parties on the Dark Companion had established an uneasy truce which was kept in being by the Great Deterrent. But neither side had abandoned hope of ultimate triumph, or had ceased to regard the other as the progeny of Satan. Each side, throughout the century since their landing, had been inspired by a great faith, the faith that themselves were good and the others were bad. The dreadful message from Earth showed that the ideologies in which they had lived were outmoded. When it appeared that the government not specially representing either East or West had sent identical messages to both groups, the faith of each side collapsed, and each side felt that it had nothing left to live for. In sorrow, both groups met in no man's land, and both decided that life had nothing more to offer to either. In a joint harangue, the leaders of the two sides proclaimed their common loss of faith. Sadly and solemnly, in the sight of the two assembled groups of immigrants, they set a light to two very small nuclear weapons, and after a solemn moment of waiting all were reduced to dust.

(3) MURDERERS' FATHERLAND: A FABLE

There was once, a very long time ago, a country where the murderers banded together for mutual protection. Their first step was to murder anybody who testified against a murderer. They then founded a murderers' club, open only to those who had committed a murder without being condemned. Members were expected to marry rich widows and murder them after they had made wills in favour of their beloved husbands. The club committee kept all files and by blackmail acquired half of every murderer's gains. The president of the club was the member who had the greatest number of unpunished murders to his credit. In the end, the club became so rich that it was able to decide elections and control the government. It made a law that murder should not be illegal, but it should be illegal to call anybody a murderer, however good the evidence might be, which enabled the members of the club to proclaim loudly their detestation of murder. All went well until the president and vice-president of the club had a quarrel. They murdered each other, and the club committee, which was evenly divided, was wiped out in the resulting quarrel.

I cannot think where this country was. My historical friend, who gave me the information, omitted to tell me the date. Some malicious and ill-disposed person rashly asserted that it was the twentieth century, but, I am happy to say, he was clapped into gaol where he remains.

PART FOUR

Peace and War

I

Psychology and East-West Tension[1]

THE HOSTILITY between East and West, as it exists at the present day, is a cause of the gravest anxiety to all sane men. It involves the catastrophic possibility of an all-out nuclear war and, short of that, demands continually increasing expenditure upon continually more deadly and more expensive weapons of war to which no end can be seen except reducing both East and West to subsistence level. In view of these obvious facts, a great many people perceive the desirability of producing more friendly relations, especially between Russia and America. But efforts in this direction have hitherto proved fruitless, and their failure has, if anything, augmented the general danger. It seems, therefore, that, if peaceful co-existence is to be successfully promoted, some fresh diagnosis must be found and other methods must be sought.

It is my belief that the source of the trouble lies in the minds of men and not in any non-mental facts. I think that the place where conciliation ought to begin is in the beliefs of statesmen and plain men as to the true character of the conflict. I think that, if these beliefs were changed, the difficulties which at present make disarmament congresses abortive would melt away. At each present, side is firmly persuaded of the other's wickedness, so firmly as to believe that any concession by one's

[1] From a forthcoming book of essays edited by Quincy Wright, William M. Evan and Morton Deutsch, to be published by Bell Telephone Laboratories, New Jersey.

o   209

own side, however slight, has the character of surrender to Absolute Evil. While this mood persists, it is obvious that no negotiations can succeed.

In analysing the present troubles, there are two kinds of facts to be borne in mind. There are what might be called hard facts, concerned with armaments, risks of unintended war, Western obligations to West Berlin, Russian tyranny in Hungary, and so on. There are also what, in comparison, may be called soft facts. These consist of the hopes and fears that have inspired actions which have increased hostility. There is a continual inter-action between these two sets of facts, and to debate which set should come first may seem like the old problem of the hen and the egg. I think, however, that a smaller effort is needed to change the soft facts than to change the hard ones, and that the easiest way to change the hard facts is to tackle the soft facts first.

Let us, for the moment, consider the matter from the point of view of human welfare rather than from that of the victory of either side. It is obvious that, if the feelings of East and West towards each other were friendly and neither had any wish to exterminate the other, both sides would perceive the futility of immense expenditure on weapons of mass destruction. Both sides would emerge from the cloud of fear which now darkens every moment in the life of every thinking person. Both sides could combine to lessen the load of poverty and malnutrition which still weighs down the majority of the population of the globe. All the immense and truly remarkable skill which is now employed in the technical business of new armaments could be employed, instead, in inventions that would make human life happier and more prosperous. What is needed to bring about this change? Only that both East and West should have friendly, instead of hostile, feelings towards each other.

'But', both sides will say, 'how is it possible to have any friendly feeling towards people so abysmally wicked as the other side?' The rest of this speech, from our side, is sadly familiar. 'Do you not know', we shall be told, 'that the Soviets are atheistical materialists? Do you not know that they permit no individual freedom in any country that they dominate? Have you not heard of their brutal tyranny in Hungary and Eastern Germany? Were you unaware of their barbarous expulsion of Germans from formerly German territory in 1945? Can you ask us to tolerate the monsters who put in Arctic concentration camps every man and woman throughout Communist territory who showed one spark of independence?' So much for the Western case. But the East, also, believes that it has a case, which is the only one that its subjects are allowed to hear. The East maintains that the West is incurably imperialistic and that, while it prates of individual liberty, it suppresses national liberty wherever it can in Asia, Africa, or Latin America. Communists, we are assured, stand for world peace, which the imperialistic West is continually threatening. And as for the supposed love of freedom in the West, how about its ally Franco who established a brutal military tyranny by the help of Hitler and Mussolini, and to this day enforces a censorship against all the beliefs by which the West pretends that it is inspired. Moreover, they assure each other that American wage-earners to this day are as badly off as the British wage-earners of 1844 whose plight was so eloquently depicted by Engels.

Each of these speeches is a mixture of truth and falsehood. Each produces furious vituperative retorts from the other side. Both speeches are made by eminent statesmen at meetings of the United Nations, but, to everybody's astonishment, they do not generate friendly feelings between East and West.

Propaganda, however, is seldom a prime cause of the emotions which it is intended to stimulate. At the beginning of the First World War, stories of German atrocities, however untrue, were eagerly absorbed and repeated throughout Britain. At the end of the Second World War, far worse atrocity stories about German concentration camps, though completely authenticated, were shrugged off by the British public as unrealistic propaganda. The difference lay solely in the popular mood. In 1914, the great majority of the British public felt warlike and was glad of reasons to justify its feelings. In 1945, with victory assured, war-weariness caused an exactly opposite reaction. The moral of these two sets of facts is that what is believed about an opposing group depends upon prevailing fashions much more than upon what is happening.

It would be idle to deny that both East and West have had reasons for mutual hostility such as, in an earlier state of armaments, might, without complete insanity, have been thought to justify a war. In 1917 and 1918, the new Bolshevik Government did several things that annoyed the West: it made a separate peace treaty with Germany; it repudiated the Czarist national debt; and it confiscated the Lena gold fields. As a consequence of these acts, Britain, France, Japan, and Czechoslovakia joined in an attack on Russia. Unfortunately for the governments which ordered this attack, the soldiers and sailors felt no hostility to the Bolsheviks and mutinied so vigorously that they had to be withdrawn. The baffled governments tried to sway public opinion by invented stories of the nationalization of women and similar fables, but they did not at that time succeed in rousing hostility to Russia among wage-earners. They did succeed, however, in rousing a deep-seated and passionate hostility to Western governing classes in most politically conscious Russians.

All this might have simmered down in time if it had not been for nuclear weapons. These produced, first in Russia and then in the Western world, a new feeling of terror and a new conviction of each other's wickedness. This was, of course, the sort of reaction that psychiatrists study in mentally afflicted patients who, when they are in danger, are apt to do everything possible to increase the danger. Governments have always acted in this way. When I was a boy, the British Government was afraid that Russia, advancing through central Asia, would be in a position to invade British India. It was feared that

Afghanistan might help them in this project, and the British therefore made two wars on Afghanistan under the impression that this would cause Afghans to love the British. This was a folly, but a little one. The present folly is psychologically very similar, but on a global scale, and may well bring disaster to the whole world.

The present trouble is caused by the vast mass emotions of fear, hate, and suspicion which each side feels towards the other. I do not deny that on each side there are grounds for these feelings. What I do deny is that acts which they inspire are such as to diminish danger. They are, on both sides, essentially insane reactions in the sense that they make the danger immensely greater than it would otherwise be. If both sides were capable of thinking rationally about the danger, they would minimize the ground of conflict instead of using all the arts of propaganda to inflame it.

Take, as a very noteworthy part of the conflict, the difference of ideologies between East and West. We are told that the Russians are atheists, and that it is our religious duty to oppose them in every possible way. In our time this accusation has an old-fashioned sound. Socrates was accused of atheism, and this was one of the grounds on which he was put to death. The early Christians were accused of atheism because they did not believe in the Olympic Gods. As Gibbon states it: 'Malice and prejudice concurred in representing the Christians as a society of atheists, who, by the most daring attack on the religious constitution of the Empire, had merited the severest adimadversion of the civil magistrate' (*Decline and Fall*, Chapter XVI). But in later times atheism, like other kinds of unorthodox theology, has come to be tolerated. The Chinese became atheists in the eleventh century, and remained so until Chiang Kai-shek came to power, but this was never alleged as a ground for fighting the Chinese, even at times when we were at war with them. The ideological differences between Christianity and Islam were thought, for many centuries, to make peace between the two impossible. When it was found that neither side could win, it was realized at last that adherents of the two ideologies could live together without any difficulty. Britain had the same hostility to Russia as it has now from 1854 to 1907, although at that time the Russian Government was earnestly Christian and a whole-hearted supporter of capitalism. When I was a boy, hostility to Russia was taken for granted in England until Gladstone excited the country against the Turks. One of my amusements in those days consisted of demolishing nettles, which I, and all other English boys, called 'Russians'. But in 1907, it was decided by the British Government that we were to hate the Germans and not the Russians. All the disputes that caused a half-century of enmity between Russia and Britain were solved by a month or two of negotiation, and from then until 1917 any criticism of the Czarist Government was frowned upon. At the present day, if China increases in power and becomes a threat to Russia, the ideological conflict between Russia and the West will be quickly forgotten.

Another of the grounds alleged for hostility to Russia is the question of freedom versus dictatorship. There is one curious fact about this, which is that those who profess the greatest eagerness to defend Western freedom against the Communist menace are the very men who are doing the most to diminish Western freedom and produce an approximation to the Soviet system, whereas those in the West who have a genuine love of freedom are, for the most part, those who are most firmly persuaded that peaceful co-existence with Communism is both possible and desirable. The spectacle of McCarthyism in defence of freedom is so ludicrous that, if a fiction writer had invented it, he would have been thought unpardonably fantastic. To anyone not deafened by slogans, it should be obvious that the lack of freedom in the East and the grave threat to freedom in the West are both products of fear, and that the first step towards increase of freedom must be diminution of fear. Perhaps, without being accused of paradox, one might add that freedom is not very useful to corpses, and that any defence of freedom conducted by means of a nuclear war can only be supported by those who deserve to be patients in psychiatric wards. To an impartial observer, it must, therefore, be obvious that the professed love of freedom in the West is a pretext, usually unconscious, to cover up aims which are not avowed.

Militarists, in the past, have often been able to achieve their aims. History, in fact, may be viewed as a long series of imperialistic conquests. The Persians subdued the Ionian Greeks, the Romans subdued everybody who lived near the Mediterranean. When Rome fell, hordes of barbarians established new kingdoms and, in many cases—for example, in Britain—exterminated most of the former inhabitants. For a time, imperialist leadership was acquired by the Mohammedans, but, with Columbus and Vasco da Gama, it returned to the West. There was no shadow of legal justification for white dominion over Indians, either in the Western hemisphere or in India. The pursuit of world dominion inspired successively the Spaniards, the French, the British, and the Germans. This long history, from the time of Cyrus to the time of Hitler, has become deeply imbedded in the unconscious aspirations of militarists and statesmen both in the East and in the West— and not only of militarists and statesmen, but of a very large part of the general population.

It is difficult, especially for those accustomed to power at home, to realize that the happy days of successful slaughter have been brought to an end. What has brought them to an end is the deadly character of modern weapons of war. The influence of weapons of war on social structure is no new thing. It begins at the dawn of history with the conflict between the horse and the ass, in which, as was to be expected, the horse was victorious. The age of chivalry, as the word implies, was the age of the horse. It was gunpowder that put an end to this

215

age. Throughout the Middle Ages, barons in their castles were able to maintain freedom against the central governments of their countries. When gunpowder was able to demolish their castles, the barons, though they made all the speeches in defence of freedom which are being repeated in our own day, were compelled to submit to the newly strengthened monarchies of Spain, France, and England. All this is familiar. What is new is the impossibility of victory. This new fact is so unpalatable that those in whom history has inspired a belief that the defeat of enemies is noble and splendid are totally unable to adapt themselves to the modern world. Fabre describes a collection of insects which had the habit of following their leader. He placed them on a circular disc which their leader did not know to be circular. They marched round and round until they dropped dead of fatigue. Modern statesmen and their admirers are guilty of equal and very similar folly.

There are those in the Western world, and presumably also in the East, who carry folly a step farther than it was carried by Fabre's insects. When forced to acknowledge that victory in a general war is no longer possible, they take refuge in applauding the heroism of those who die fighting, and they, almost invariably, conclude their rhetoric by quoting Patrick Henry. It does not occur to them that Patrick Henry, if he should die in the struggle, expected to leave behind him others who would enjoy the fruits of his heroism. His modern would-be imitators profess to think that one should fight for the Right even if assured that the only outcome will be a world without life. Although many of the people who take this extreme view profess to be democrats, they nevertheless consider that a small percentage of fanatics have a right to inflict the death penalty upon all the rest of mankind. This morbid view involves an extreme of religious persecution surpassing all that previous ages have known. I do not doubt that it would have horrified Torquemada almost as much as it horrifies me. It is scarcely possible to doubt that there is an element of unconscious insin-

216

cerity in those who would prefer the end of Man to the victory of a faction which they dislike. It seems probable that they find the impossibility of victory through war so intolerably painful that in a corner of their minds they reject it and continue to believe that in a nuclear war some miracle will give the victory to what they consider the Right. This is a common delusion of fanatics. But it is a pity when such men control the policy of a great State.

The first step towards the recovery of sanity in our mad world should be the public and solemn recognition by both sides that the worst thing that can possibly happen is a general nuclear war. I should like to see the statesmen of East and West declare that the success of their opponents would be a smaller misfortune than war. If this were acknowledged sincerely and after due study, it would become possible for the two sides to come together and examine how peaceful co-existence could be secured without sacrifice of the vital interests of either. But it seems hardly worth while to prolong the tedious process of negotiations while each side hopes that negotiations will continue to end in failure and secretly cherishes the belief that, against all the evidence, its own side would, in war, achieve a victory in the old-fashioned sense. I am credibly informed that the young men who undergo military training in the United States are instructed as to what to do *when* war comes, not *if* war comes. I have little doubt that the same is true in Russia. This means that young men at an impressionable age are encouraged by the authorities of their country to expect, if not to desire, a course of events which must be utterly catastrophic, although all imaginable pains are taken to prevent the young men from becoming aware of the magnitude of the disaster towards which they are told to march. This sort of thing will have to be changed if the danger of war is to be diminished.

How can such a change be brought about? I think it will have to begin at the summit. Publicity and propaganda have now such influence that the majority in any powerful country is pretty sure to believe whatever its government wishes it to believe. It is unlikely that what the government wishes us to believe will be what the government believes to be the truth, and it is still more unlikely that it will be what, in fact, is the truth. Power impulses in great States have such a hold upon men's desires and instincts that it is very difficult to secure acknowledgment of facts when such acknowledgment thwarts the impulse to dominion. This is the psychological truth which underlies the warlike preparations of East and West. The mutual talk about each other's wickedness is merely a smoke-screen behind which conscience can hide. I do not mean that either East or West is impeccable. On the contrary, I think the governments of both are deeply criminal. But I do not think that this fact, if it be a fact, is a reason for desiring the extermination of the populations of both and also of neutral countries. Propaganda which promotes mutual hate serves no useful purpose, and those who indulge in it are encouraging mass murder.

I believe, I repeat, that conciliation will have to begin at the top. Camp David might have been a beginning, but was sabotaged by the militarists of West and East who continued the U-2 flights and their interception during the preparations for the Summit Meeting which consequently proved abortive. What I should like to see is the establishment of a very small body, which might be called the Conciliation Committee, consisting of eminent men from East and West and, also, certain eminent neutrals, who should spend some time in each other's company until they had become accustomed to thinking of each other as individuals and not as emissaries of Satan. This committee could be appointed by the United Nations, given the previous admission of China. I should wish these men, in the early stages of their association, to make no attempt at concrete and definite proposals. I should wish them, at first, only to arrive at a state of mind in which agreement seemed possible and the necessity of reaching agreement had become evident. After the mellowing influence of propinquity had produced this state of mind, it would then become possible to proceed to the tackling of questions as to which agreement is difficult.

It may be thought that nothing would come of such a procedure except renewed quarrels and increased bitterness. There is, however, some evidence to the contrary. The Pugwash Conferences in which scientists, Eastern and Western and neutral, all meet, have found it possible to preserve good personal relations and to arrive at unanimous resolutions. The melodramatic picture of each other which East and West have created through the years does not easily survive close personal contact. In the course of such contact, people become aware of each other's common humanity. They share sensations of heat and cold, of hunger and thirst, and even, at long last, an appreciation of each other's jokes, and it comes gradually to be felt that the political part of each of us is only a small part, and that the common humanity which we share covers a larger area than the abstract creeds in which we differ. Such a group of men as I have in mind, if encouraged by their governments, could gradually become a source of sanity, and accustom East and West, alike, to admit the limitations of their power which have resulted from the modern possibility of mass destruction and have made victory in the old-fashioned sense impossible for either side.

Perhaps the first work which such a body should recommend to governments would be the spread of truthful knowledge about each other. At present such knowledge is regarded on both sides as dangerous. In America, books giving truthful information about Russia are banned from public libraries. In Russia, there is almost complete prohibition of accurate knowledge about the West. At the end of the Second World War, Russian soldiers who had been prisoners in the West were all suspect to the Russian Government because they knew that the West is not what Russian propaganda presents it as being.

The governments of East and West should do what lies in their power to moderate the virulence and untruthfulness of the Press and to use the Press to refute such popular misconceptions as are calculated to inflame suspicion.

The primary motive in any attempt at conciliation should be the prevention of war, and correct information about what a war would mean should be widely disseminated. It should be made clear to the nations of both East and West that survival is not to be secured by multiplying weapons of war or by exacerbating hatred and suspicion.

The world at present, not only that of Communists and anti-Communists, but also that of uncommitted nations, is living in daily and hourly peril of complete extinction. If this peril is to be lessened, it will be necessary to diminish the autonomy of those who control the major weapons of war. The present state of tension has made it seem necessary to both sides to be prepared for instant retaliation, since each side believes the other to be capable of an unprovoked attack and has devised fallible methods of detection which may cause a false belief that such an attack has been perpetrated. The life of each one of us is at the mercy of those who control technical inventions of marvellous ingenuity. These men, as is humanly inevitable, tend to regard the modern triumphs of technique as ends in themselves and to deplore anything that would divert technical skill into less dangerous channels. While the tension between East and West persists, those who have technical control are thought to be the guardians of our safety, whereas, in fact, they are the exact reverse. They will not be felt to be a danger until the feelings of East and West towards each other have grown less suspicious and less filled with fear. The dangerous state of the world is caused, I repeat, by the dangerous passions of ordinary men and women, which have been inflamed by unwise propaganda on both sides. It is these widespread passions that must be assuaged if we are to be no longer exposed to the imminent risk of total annihilation.

If the governments of East and West were at last persuaded that the safety of each demands successful negotiations, many things would quickly become possible. I should put first the total abolition of nuclear weapons under a system of inspection conducted by neutrals, for, until this is achieved, the present state of popular terror on both sides is difficult to mitigate. If this had been achieved, I should invite the Conciliation Committee to approach both sides with a view to finding acceptable solutions of difficult problems such as that of Germany and Berlin. Such solutions should not alter the balance of power between East and West, and should be such as each side could accept without loss of face, for, if these conditions are not fulfilled, there will be little hope of both sides accepting the suggested solutions. The Conciliation Committee should have only an advisory capacity, but it may be hoped that it would in time acquire such moral authority as would make resistance to its proposed solutions difficult. If it achieved success and had been appointed by the United Nations, the United Nations should take up its work and might lead the way to the creation of a real World Government endowed with the only powerful armed forces in the world. In any case, only a World Government affords a long-term hope of the survival of the human race. In the present temper of the Great Powers, World Government is not possible, but for all friends of Man it must remain the goal towards which our efforts should tend.

II

War and Peace in My Lifetime[1]

MY ADULT LIFE has been passed in a very gloomy period, and what has made it gloomy is war and the fear of war. When I was very young, under the influence of the Sidney Webbs, I was not averse from British imperialism, and I was even tolerant of the Boer War. But, while it was in progress, my feelings changed completely. I was horrified by the concentration camps which the British invented and which have since been developed by the Nazis and the Communists. It was during that war that British statesmen became persuaded of the need of Continental allies although the alliances then concluded led, as statesmen should have foreseen, to increasingly hostile relations with Germany and ultimately to the First World War. I first heard the policy of the Entente advocated in a private discussion club by Sir Edward Grey in 1902, two years before it became the policy of the British Government. I vehemently opposed the policy then and there and saw no reason to change my opinion when it produced its inevitable consequences in 1914. I thought, and still think, that it would have been better for the world and for our own country if Britain had been neutral in that war. We were told—for example, by H. G. Wells—that it was a war to end war and a war against militarism. It had, in fact, exactly the opposite effect. It led directly to Communism in Russia and, through the punitive vindictiveness of the Versailles Treaty, to Nazi

[1] Talk on the BBC Asian Service, 1959.

domination in Germany. The world since 1914 has been one in which civilized ways of life and humane feeling have steadily decayed; and there is, as yet, little sign of a contrary tendency.

I have never been able to adopt an attitude of complete and absolute pacifism. There have been wars that have done good, such as the American War of Independence, though they have been fewer than is generally supposed. I cannot see how the Second World War could have been avoided, though unfortunately it has led to a situation in which a third world war is not unlikely.

The danger of a third world war, with which we are now threatened, arises from the strange inability to learn from experience. Before the First World War, there was a very intense naval arms race between Britain and Germany. Each side proclaimed that, since its love of peace was indubitable, the peace of the world would be preserved if only it (the peace-loving side) remained stronger than the other side. The arms race led, as such competitions always do, to increasing animosity ending in war. (I do not mean to suggest that arms races are the only cause of war. I do not think that the Second World War was caused in this way. Wars have many causes, but among these, arms races stand out because they are advocated in the name of peace.) Both Russia and the West are repeating the fatal process that took place before 1914, although the dangers involved are now many thousand times greater than they were then. It is despairing to observe how high-placed men, who in other respects are not devoid of intelligence, can believe, both in the East and in the West, that peace is to be preserved by one's own side being always stronger than the other side. What makes this view now even more absurd than it was at an earlier time, is that either side, even if weaker than the other, may be capable of completely obliterating the 'enemy'. It may well be that the next war will end with the stronger side still possessing H-bombs, but neither side possessing live human beings. This is the consummation to which the arms race, if pursued to the bitter end, must inevitably lead the embattled nations.

One of the evil effects of war is that populations and politicians become accustomed to horrors, and contemplate with equanimity abominations which would have seemed unthinkable in quieter times. This has become increasingly true with the development of modern weapons. Our powers of destruction have been enormously increased and are pretty certain to increase much further in the near future. Our methods of conciliation and avoidance of war have not, however, increased by one iota. They are the same as the methods employed in the eighteenth century, and as ineffectual as they were then. We find sober men officially employed in making forecasts, debating whether, after one day of war, survivors in the United States can be hoped to amount to half the population. In Western Europe, including our own country, no serious student of modern war would venture upon anything like so optimistic a prophecy. One might have thought that such a prospect would rouse in every country an indignant protest and a determination to have done with outmoded methods of statecraft. Unfortunately, this has not, so far, occurred. Paralysed by the maxims of traditional power politics, the statesmen find no way out of the impasse. Passive populations, meanwhile, in a strange, fascinated apathy, accept the approach of doom as though it were inevitable and not decreed by human volition.

The fault lies not only with statesmen, but also with populations. And the fault with populations does not consist *only* in apathy. It consists even more in the fact that political feeling is concerned with national groups, although nations from an economic and from a military point of view have become a dangerous anachronism. In the days of the Heptarchy, the men of what is now Oxfordshire doubtless hated and abominated the men of what is now Hampshire. 'Do you suggest', they would have exclaimed indignantly, 'that we ought to live at peace with these degraded beings?' Gradually, however, this kind of local patriotism faded, to be replaced by national patriotism. The men of Oxfordshire and Hampshire replaced their mutual hatred by a common hatred of the French. Everywhere, advancing technique increased the size of social units. In our own day, an attempt has been made to substitute loyalty to NATO or to the Powers of the Warsaw Pact for national loyalties. This is, on each side, a substitution of a loyalty to an ideology in the place of loyalty to a nation. There is nothing new in this. In the time of the Crusades, there was loyalty to Christianity on one side and to Islam on the other. In the wars of the sixteenth and seventeenth centuries, loyalty to Catholicism or Protestantism often outweighed national loyalty. What is new in our day is, not this way of feeling, but the amount of harm that it can do. There is more need than there ever was at an earlier time of ideological toleration and freedom from fanaticism. In this respect the opposing ideologies of East and West present a danger which is different from that of nationalism. NATO and the Warsaw Pact fail of what the world needs not only through the bitterness of the ideological opposition between them, but also because, for technical reasons, both military and economic, no organization which is less than world-wide is sufficient for modern needs.

It may be that the kind of co-operation which produced, first, nations, and then, alliances is only psychologically possible if directed *against* somebody or something. If this is the case, we have to learn a somewhat new way of feeling. At present, the West fears the East and the East fears the West. Each fear is well-founded so long as hostility remains. But there is an entirely different way of viewing the situation, in which we do not think of the East or of the West—as the case may be—as constituting our peril, but think, instead, of the common peril of both East and West which arises from the destructive capacities of modern war. It is a sober truth that nine-tenths of the interests of East and West are identical and not competitive. Their supreme common interest is to find a method of international organization which shall liberate both from the fear of mutual annihilation. In theory, this is not difficult. What is needed is as clear as noon-day. What is needed is an International Authority with power to arbitrate disputes and to settle disagreements without resort to war. The difficulty is not to see what is needed, but to rise above the self-assertions of creeds and power politics to a consideration of mankind as a whole.

But this sort of thing, we are told, is Utopian. Let us muddle along until we all perish, for that is less painful than disinterested thought. And so, for lack of energy, for lack of the instinct towards life, we allow ourselves lazily to drift towards disaster.

This is an unworthy and feeble way of reacting to danger. Mankind has slowly climbed a difficult ascent from primitive barbarism to a measure of intellectual and moral awareness which should be felt as part of the steady advance towards the full development of human capacity. Each human generation inherits a certain capital of civilization from its predecessors and each should feel its historic obligation to hand on the capital, increased and not diminished. This present generation seems unaware of itself as a stage in history. Its vision is myopically concentrated upon the passing contests of our own time. There have been contests in the past, many of them, which seemed at the time as important as the contests of our time seem to the present generation. But the men of former times did not possess the skill in evil-doing that we have acquired. They could be wicked, and still leave hope for the future. We can not. If we persist in wickedness, there is no future for our species.

I must admit that this is disputed and that among those who dispute it are some very influential people both in the East and in the West. Mr Krushchev has repeatedly expressed the conviction that the Communist Powers might 'win' a world war. Mr Dulles has stated that the West might 'win' the hot war. Each of these two eminent men meant the word 'win' to be understood in an old-fashioned sense. They did not mean that, at the end of the war, there might be ten people alive on their side and only five on the other. It is difficult to be sure that their optimism was sincere, but I think one can be sure that it was mistaken. I do not think it can rationally be maintained that a great war could lead to a result which either side would consider tolerable, and, in spite of some eminent opinions such as those that I have mentioned, the view that victory in a great war is now impossible is held by the great majority of those who have studied the facts.

There are others—some of them high-placed and respected—who admit the risk that total war might end in total death, but who think this risk worth running, since they consider the end of mankind a smaller evil than submission, however temporary, to an enemy whom they regard as utterly abominable. They are prepared to see the human race destroy itself rather than forgo the pleasures of fanaticism. Such men are blind to the continuing possibilities of human excellence and heartless towards those who do not share their bigotry.

This is not how life should be lived. Men collectively, if they will allow human sympathy to extend beyond the narrow bounds of creed or colour, are capable of contributing to each other's happiness, and not only to terror and death. Why should we use knowledge to destroy each other? It can equally be used to bring happiness to all. The darker our world becomes, the more imperative is our duty to keep hope alive, to hold before the weary spirit of man a shining vision of populations freed from ancient excess of toil and from the modern nightmare of fear, developing what is splendid in human faculty, in knowledge, in the creation of beauty, and in the emotions of friendship in which happy societies can flourish.

III

The Social Responsibilities of Scientists[1]

SCIENCE, ever since it first existed, has had important effects in matters that lie outside the purview of pure science. Men of science have differed as to their responsibility for such effects. Some have said that the function of the scientist in society is to supply knowledge, and that he need not concern himself with the use to which this knowledge is put. I do not think that this view is tenable, especially in our age. The scientist is also a citizen; and citizens who have any special skill have a public duty to see, as far as they can, that their skill is utilized in accordance with the public interest. Historically, the functions of the scientist in public life have generally been recognized. The Royal Society was founded by Charles II as an antidote to 'fanaticism' which had plunged England into a long period of civil strife. The scientists of that time did not hesitate to speak out on public issues, such as religious toleration and the folly of prosecutions for witchcraft. But although science has, in various ways at various times, favoured what may be called a humanitarian outlook, it has from the first had an intimate and sinister connection with war. Archimedes sold his skill to the Tyrant of Syracuse for use against the Romans; Leonardo secured a salary from the Duke of Milan for his skill in the art of fortification; and Galileo got employment under the Grand Duke of Tuscany because he could calculate the trajectories

[1] Address to Pugwash on CND scientists, 1959; reprinted from *Science*, February 12, 1960.

of projectiles. In the French Revolution the scientists who were not guillotined were set to making new explosives, but Lavoisier was not spared, because he was only discovering hydrogen which, in those days, was not a weapon of war. There have been some honourable exceptions to the subservience of scientists to warmongers. During the Crimean War the British Government consulted Faraday as to the feasibility of attack by poisonous gases. Faraday replied that it was entirely feasible, but that it was inhuman and he would have nothing to do with it.

AFFECTING PUBLIC OPINION

Modern democracy and modern methods of publicity have made the problem of affecting public opinion quite different from what it used to be. The knowledge that the public possesses on any important issue is derived from vast and powerful organizations: the press, radio, and, above all, television. The knowledge that governments possess is more limited. They are too busy to search out the facts for themselves, and consequently they know only what their underlings think good for them unless there is such a powerful movement in a different sense that politicians cannot ignore it. Facts which ought to guide the decisions of statesmen—for instance, as to the possible lethal qualities of fall-out—do not acquire their due importance if they remain buried in scientific journals. They acquire their due importance only when they become known to so many voters that they affect the course of the elections. In general, there is an opposition to widespread publicity for such facts. This opposition springs from various sources, some sinister, some comparatively respectable. At the bottom of the moral scale there is the financial interest of the various industries connected with armaments. Then there are various effects of a somewhat thoughtless patriotism, which believes in secrecy and in what is called 'toughness'. But perhaps more important than either of these is the unpleasantness of the facts, which makes the general public turn aside to pleasanter topics such as divorces and murders. The consequence is that what ought to be known widely throughout the general public will not be known unless great efforts are made by disinterested persons to see that the information reaches the minds and hearts of vast numbers of people. I do not think this work can be successfully accomplished except by the help of men of science. They, alone, can speak with the authority that is necessary to combat the misleading statements of those scientists who have permitted themselves to become merchants of death. If disinterested scientists do not speak out, the others will succeed in conveying a distorted impression, not only to the public but also to the politicians.

OBSTACLES TO INDIVIDUAL ACTION

It must be admitted that there are obstacles to individual action in our age which did not exist at earlier times. Galileo could make his own telescope. But once when I was talking with a very famous astronomer he explained that the telescope upon which his work depended owed its existence to the benefactions of enormously rich men, and, if he had not stood well with them, his astronomical discoveries would have been impossible. More frequently, a scientist only acquires access to enormously expensive equipment if he stands well with the government of his country. He knows that if he adopts a rebellious attitude he and his family are likely to perish along with the rest of civilized mankind. It is a tragic dilemma, and I do not think that one should censure a man whatever his decision; but I do think—and I think men of science should realize—that unless something rather drastic is done under the leadership or through the inspiration of some part of the scientific world, the human race, like the Gadarene swine, will rush down a steep place to destruction in blind ignorance of the fate that scientific skill has prepared for it.

It is impossible in the modern world for a man of science

to say with any honesty, 'My business is to provide knowledge, and what use is made of the knowledge is not my responsibility'. The knowledge that a man of science provides may fall into the hands of men or institutions devoted to utterly unworthy objects. I do not suggest that a man of science, or even a large body of men of science, can altogether prevent this, but they can diminish the magnitude of the evil.

There is another direction in which men of science can attempt to provide leadership. They can suggest and urge in many ways the value of those branches of science of which the important practical uses are beneficial and not harmful. Consider what might be done if the money at present spent on armaments were spent on increasing and distributing the food supply of the world and diminishing the population pressure. In a few decades, poverty and malnutrition, which now afflict more than half the population of the globe, could be ended. But at present almost all the governments of great states consider that it is better to spend money on killing foreigners than on keeping their own subjects alive. Possibilities of a hopeful sort in whatever field can best be worked out and stated authoritatively by men of science; and, since they can do this work better than others, it is part of their duty to do it.

As the world becomes more technically unified, life in an ivory tower becomes increasingly impossible. Not only so; the man who stands out against the powerful organizations which control most of human activity is apt to find himself no longer in the ivory tower, with a wide outlook over a sunny landscape, but in the dark and subterranean dungeon upon which the ivory tower was erected. To risk such a habitation demands courage. It will not be necessary to inhabit the dungeon if there are many who are willing to risk it, for everybody knows that the modern world depends upon scientists, and, if they are insistent, they must be listened to. We have it in our power to make a good world; and, therefore, with whatever labour and risk, we must make it.

IV

Three Essentials for a Stable World[1]

THOUGHT ABOUT public affairs in recent years has been so completely absorbed by the problem of relations between Russia and the West that various other problems, which would remain even if that one were solved, have not received as much attention as they deserve. The world during the last one hundred and fifty years has been undergoing transformation so rapid that ideas and institutions have been unable to keep pace with modern needs. And, what is proving in some ways even more serious, ideas which might be beneficent if they spread slowly have spread with the rapidity and destructiveness of a prairie fire.

When Rousseau preached democracy, it appeared after some two hundred pages of rhetoric that there was only one small corner of the world where democracy could be successfully practised, namely, the city of Geneva. His disciples gave it a somewhat wider extension: it was permitted in America and for a few bloodstained years in France. Very slowly it was adopted in England. By this time Rousseau's moderation and caution had been forgotten. Democracy was to be a panacea for all the ills of all the countries in the world.

But somehow it looked a little different when it acquired new habitats. In a certain Balkan country, where the elections had produced an almost even balance, one party came into the

[1] Reprinted from the *New York Times Magazine*, August 3, 1952.

chamber with loaded revolvers and shot enough of the other party to secure a working majority. Neither Locke nor Rousseau had thought of this method. In Latin America, where the original insurgents against the power of Spain were fervent disciples of Rousseau, there was a system of checks and balances quite different from that advocated by Montesquieu. The party in power falsified the register, and after a while the party out of power conducted a successful revolution.

In the period of United States imperialism after the Spanish-American War, this system was upset by the intrusion of Jeffersonian legality. The falsification of the register was still tolerated; but revolution was frowned upon. In various ways, in various regions that lay outside the purview of eighteenth-century Liberals, the orderly process of parliamentary government, in accordance with general elections, broke down. The idea of democracy persisted, but the practice encountered unforeseen difficulties.

The same kind of thing happened with the idea of nationality. When one reads the works of Mazzini, one finds one's self in a tidy little world which he imagines to be the cosmos. There are about a dozen European nations, each with a soul which, once liberated, will be noble. The noblest, of course, is Italy, which will be the conductor of the wholly harmonious orchestra. It is only tyrants, so Mazzini thought, that cause nations to hate one another. In a world of freedom, they will be filled with brotherly love.

There was only one exception and that was Ireland, because the Irish supported the Pope in his opposition to Italian unity. But except for this tiny chink, the light of reality was not permitted to penetrate the dim halls of his utopia. But in regard to nationality, as in regard to democracy, although the reality has offered unpleasant problems to traditional Liberalism, the ideal has remained unchallenged and none of us can resist the appeal of a nation rightly struggling to be free, whatever oppressions and barbarities may be the goals for which freedom is desired.

Scientific technique is another of these ideals that seem to have gone astray. The world has not developed as Cobden imagined that it would. He imagined two industrial nations, America and Britain, supplying by machine production a great wealth of goods to grateful agriculturists distributed throughout the less civilized parts of the world. Commerce and division of labour were to secure universal peace; and each nation would love every other, since each would be the customer of every other.

But, alas, this dream proved as utopian as Mazzini's. As soon as the power of machine industry had been demonstrated, other countries than those in which it had originated decided to become competitors. Germany, Japan, and Russia, each in turn, have developed large-scale industry. And every nation which has the faintest chance of following their example attempts to do so. The consequence is that a very large part of the productive capacity of every advanced nation is devoted to the production of engines for the destruction of the inhabitants of other advanced nations. So long as this system persists, every improvement in technique is a misfortune, since it enables nations to set aside a larger proportion of the population for the purpose of mutual extermination.

Owing to the spread of education, Western ideals have come to be accepted, though often in distorted forms, in parts of the world that have not had the previous history needed to make these ideals beneficent. Old-style imperialism has become very difficult, because those who are subjected to it know much better than they formerly did what it is that their imperialistic masters are keeping to themselves. And the formerly imperialistic nations themselves have so far accepted the watchwords of Liberalism that they cannot practise old-style imperialism without a bad conscience, even when it is obvious that its sudden cessation will bring chaos.

When the Romans taught military discipline to the barbarians the result was the fall of Rome. We have taught industrial discipline to the barbarians of our time; but we do not wish to suffer the fate of Rome. Our world inevitably includes self-determining nations whom the eighteenth and nineteenth centuries never thought of as independent powers. We cannot return to the security and stability that was enjoyed by our grandfathers until a way has been found of satisfying the claim of hitherto subject peoples without, in the process, producing universal chaos. If this is to be achieved, the ideals of Liberalism, however valid they may remain, are insufficient, since they offer no obstacle to anarchical disaster.

There are three things that must be achieved before stability can be recovered: the first of these is a world government with a monopoly of armed force; the second is an approximate equality as regards standards of life in different parts of the world; the third is a population either stationary or very slowly increasing. I do not say that these three things will be achieved. What I do say is that unless they are, the present intolerable insecurity will continue. There are those who imagine that, if once we had defeated the Russians, all would be well. In 1914–18, they thought this about the Germans. Ten years ago they thought it about the Germans and Japanese. But no sooner were they defeated than we had to set to work to restore their power. Defeat of enemies in war, however necessary, is not a constructive solution of social problems.

A monopoly of armed force is quite obviously the only method by which the world can be secure against war. In the short run, any single Government of the world, however oppressive, would secure this result; but it cannot do so in the long run unless it wins the acquiescence of the governed. I find a curious reluctance to acquiesce in the idea of world government. People use arguments against it which are, equally, arguments against government in general. It is of course true that governments exist to limit freedom, but if we are to achieve the security at which we aim when we establish a police force, we must be as ready to suppress nations that indulge in murder or burglary as we are to suppress individuals who do so.

Economic equality in the different parts of the world may seem a very distant ideal, and it would be folly to approach it too suddenly. There would be no gain to mankind if Western nations had their standard of life reduced to equality with the standard in China or India. Equality must be approached not by lowering the standards of the fortunate but by raising the standards of the others. In the nineteenth century the arguments for raising the standard of life in backward countries would have been merely humanitarian. Now they involve our own self-preservation. So long as some nations are very much poorer than others the poorer nations will inevitably feel envy and will be a source of unrest. It is no longer possible, as it was formerly, to go on living in the kind of world in which we are living now, in which from day to day we can have no assurance against vast disaster.

If there is to be secure peace two things are necessary: first, that no important group of nations should have any just grievance against any other; and second, that there should not be opportunities for military conquest by predatory nations. I do not think that these conditions can be fulfilled until approximate economic justice has been established throughout the world. I do not pretend that this is easy. It must be a long time before India and China can achieve the diffused prosperity of the United States. And perhaps in Africa the time required will be even longer.

The third requisite of stability—namely, an approximately stationary population—is intimately bound up with the second. So long as all improvements in the technique of production are swallowed up by an increasing population, money spent in the development of backward areas might just as well be thrown into the sea. In India this has been recognized by Nehru; and I think that general recognition need not take so long as is sometimes supposed. In the meantime raising the standard of life will probably prove in the East, as it has proved in the West, a powerful means of checking unduly rapid growth of population.

I do not wish to be thought discouraging in suggesting the necessity of these large and difficult reforms. It is not necessary that they should be all achieved at once. It will be enough if their necessity is recognized and active steps are taken to bring them about.

Real stability, such as the world imagined itself to be enjoying before 1914, is not to be achieved quickly. But if the way to achieve it is realized, and if it is clear that the world is moving in the right direction, confidence in the future will revive and the danger of a paralysis of hope will disappear. It is obvious that the first necessity is the creation of a system in which attack by either side will be no longer a pressing danger. But this is only the first step. Asia and Africa will remain to be dealt with and the aim must be to find ways of admitting them to equality without anarchy. I do not suggest that this is easy, but it will become gradually possible when both East and West have ceased to be a menace to new freedom. For it will then be possible, in spite of propaganda to the contrary, to persuade Asia and Africa that we have both the power and the will to benefit them.

V

Population Pressure and War[1]

THE WORLD is faced at the present day with two antithetical dangers. There is the risk, which has begun to sink into popular consciousness, that the human race may put an end to itself by a too lavish use of H-bombs. There is an opposite risk, not nearly so widely appreciated, that the human population of our planet may increase to the point where only a starved and miserable existence is possible except for a small minority of powerful people. These risks, though diametrically opposed to each other, are nevertheless connected. Nothing is more likely to lead to an H-bomb war than the threat of universal destitution through over-population. It is with the nature of this threat and with the means for averting it that I shall be concerned in what follows.

Wars caused by pressure of population are no novelty. Four times—so the historians of antiquity assure us—the population of Arabia was led to over-run neighbouring countries by drought at home. The results were many and of many kinds. They included Babylon and Nineveh, the Code of Hammurabi, the art of predicting eclipses, the Old Testament, and finally Islam. The barbarians who destroyed the Roman Empire did not keep accurate vital statistics, but there can be little doubt that population outgrew the resources of their northern forests and that this pressure precipitated them against the rich

[1] From *The Human Sum*, ed. C. H. Rolph, London, Heinemann, 1957.

Mediterranean lands. During the last few centuries population pressure in Europe has been relieved by emigration to the Western hemisphere, and, as Red Indians do not write history, we have thought of this process as peaceable. The East, however, has enjoyed no such outlet. It was mainly population pressure that precipitated Japan's disastrous excursion into imperialism. In China, the Taiping Rebellion, civil war, and Japanese aggression, for a time kept the population in check. In India, the population grew and grows unchecked, producing a downward plunge towards misery and starvation.

But, although population pressure has been a vital element in human affairs from time immemorial, there are several new factors which make the present situation different from anything that has preceded it. The first of these is the utter disastrousness of scientific warfare which means that war makes the survival of anything doubtful and the survival of any good thing almost certainly impossible. The second is the absence of empty or nearly empty lands such as those into which the White man overflowed from the time of Columbus to the present day. The third, which has an immense importance but has hardly begun to be recognized, is the success of medicine in diminishing the death rate. These three factors taken together have produced a situation which is new in human history. It must be coped with if utter disaster is to be avoided. The East has been awakening to this necessity; the West, largely for ideological reasons, has been more backward.

A few facts are necessary to make the situation clear, but I shall deal with them briefly as Professor Huxley's previous article[1] has dealt with most of them. The population of the world, which at most periods has been very nearly stationary, began to grow with unprecedented rapidity about the year 1650. Since then the rate of growth has been not merely maintained but continually increased and is now much more rapid than it was even twenty years ago. The present rate of increase in

[1] 'World Population' in *The Human Sum.*

the population of the world is, roughly, one a second or eighty thousand a day or thirty million a year, and there is every reason to think that during the next decade the rate of population growth will become even greater. As a consequence of the growth in numbers during the last twenty years, human beings, on the average, are less well nourished than they were before the Second World War. It is considered that 2,200 calories is the least upon which health and vigour can be maintained and that those who have less than this are under-nourished. Adopting this standard, half the world was under-nourished during the 'thirties and two-thirds of it is under-nourished now. To this process of deterioration no limit can be set except by a slowing-up of the increase in numbers. A careful survey of the world's resources in the matter of food leads to the conclusion that technical advances in agriculture cannot keep pace with the great army of new mouths to be fed. Moreover, technical advances can barely hold their own against the deterioration of the soil which results from a desire for quick returns. There is yet another matter of policy which has played a great part in the USSR and is destined to play a great part in China as well as in various other countries. This is the determination, for reasons of national power and prestige, to industrialize very quickly and even at the expense of agriculture. In the existing state of the world, one can hardly blame countries for this policy. Before the First World War, Russia had little industry but was an exporter of grain. Before the Second World War, Russia had much industry and had ceased to export grain. Russia was defeated in the First World War and was victorious in the Second. In view of such facts, we cannot wonder at the race towards rapid industrializing on which many under-developed countries have embarked.

All these reasons make it nearly certain that poverty and under-nourishment will increase in many of the most important parts of the world during at least the next twenty years, even if everything possible is done to prevent this result. The downward trend will continue until the growth of population has been slowed up. The deterioration in living conditions must be expected to produce increasing discontent and increasing envy of the more prosperous parts of the world. Such feelings tend to produce war even if, on a sane survey, no good can come of war to anybody.

In regard to the population problem there is an enormous difference between the white and non-white parts of the world. In most white countries there has been a continual decline in the birth rate during the last eighty years and, at the same time, such a rapid advance in technique that the growth in population has not been incompatible with a rise in the standard of life. But in the East, in Africa, and in tropical America the situation is very different. While the death rate has declined enormously, the birth rate has remained nearly stationary and the nations concerned have not enjoyed those outlets which enabled Western Europe to prosper during the nineteenth century. Let us consider the three most important countries of the East: India, China, and Japan. These three countries, between them, contain two-fifths of the population of the world. China, where the vital statistics are somewhat uncertain, is estimated to have a population of 583 million and an annual increase of 11·6 million. India has a population of 372 million and an annual increase of 4·8 million. Japan has a population of 86·7 million and an annual increase of 1·2 million. All these three countries, as well as the USSR, have recently undergone a change of policy in regard to population. In India and Japan, this change has been very notable. Nehru inaugurated the change by a pronouncement which had no precedent among the leading statesmen of the world: 'We should', he said, 'be a far more advanced nation if our population were about half what it is.' In pursuance of this policy, his government inaugurated a birth control campaign. Unfortunately, so far, economic and ideological reasons combined have led to the adoption of ineffective methods, but there is every reason to hope that better methods will be adopted before long. The Japanese Government in an official bulletin published in December, 1940, just one year before Pearl Harbour, said: 'If we think of the distant future of mutual prosperity in Asia, and if we give heed to the glorious mission of the Japanese race, the one thing of which we can never have enough is the number of superior people belonging to the Imperial nation.' Defeat in war has changed the attitude of the Japanese Government, which is now doing everything in its power to lower the rate of population growth. In the absence of birth control information, abortions in Japan have become extremely prevalent. According to Dr Yasuaki Koguchi there were between one million eight hundred thousand and two million three hundred thousand induced abortions in the one year 1953. So desperate is the economic situation that large numbers of women have resorted to sterilization. The Japanese Government, although it does not forbid abortion, is aware that contraception would be preferable and does what it can to encourage it.

Both China and Russia have been compelled by hard facts to take up an attitude not consistent with what Communists have hitherto regarded as Marxist orthodoxy. They have been in the habit hitherto of proclaiming that only under Capitalism does a population problem exist and that under Communism over-population cannot occur in any foreseeable future. In Russia abortion, which Stalin had made illegal, was made again legal by a decree of November 23, 1955. China, during the past two years, has permitted and even encouraged propaganda for scientific methods of contraception avowedly 'at the general request of the masses' and in the hope of bringing about a steady fall in the Chinese birth rate.

In all these four countries—Russia, India, China, and Japan—the main difficulty is not now the opposition of government or of public opinion to birth control, but the lack of the necessary appliances and the extreme poverty which would prevent their purchase even if they were obtainable. It is for this reason that abortion is common in spite of the danger to health that it involves. But, however great the difficulties may be, there is good reason to hope that in all four countries the birth rate will be much reduced within a generation.

In under-developed countries that are still under Western domination, a less enlightened policy prevails. In Africa, the West Indies and the tropical part of Central and South America nothing is done to check the increase of population, and the standard of life is, in consequence, continually falling. Western nations, and especially the United States, spend great sums of money in the hope of benefiting under-developed nations, but the hoped-for benefit does not result because it is not accompanied by control of population. On the balance, what the West spends philanthropically on under-developed regions merely increases the number of sufferers and augments the terrible sum of human misery. It is a humiliating reflection for those who are inclined to feel complacent about what are called 'Western Values' that on this supremely important question, upon which the whole future of mankind depends, the West is less enlightened than the East and less capable of rational adjustment to circumstances. This is due, no doubt, in large part to the fact that the most powerful Western countries, owing to their low birth rates, do not have a serious domestic population problem. Western practice at home is at variance with Western theory. What people do is right, but what they think they ought to do is wrong. What they think they ought to do has disastrous consequences, not at home, but wherever Western nations dominate less developed regions either directly or through financial and medical assistance. By their superstitious and benighted policy, they are breeding great areas of discontent and hostility.

There are in the world at present sharply marked divisions between areas of prosperity and areas of poverty. In Western Europe and North America and Australia, the immense majority of the population are adequately nourished. In Africa, India, and China, a large majority have less food than is necessary for health and vigour. This situation is not getting better. On the contrary, it is getting worse. The poorer countries are growing poorer, while the richer ones grow richer. It is mainly the increase of population that causes the poverty of the poorer countries. The resulting situation is explosive. It is hardly to be expected that the less prosperous parts of the world will tamely acquiesce in the continually widening inequality. The situation is of just that kind that in the past has always led to war and conquest. However irrational a resort to war in modern circumstances may be, hunger and sullen anger may, in desperation, produce an outbreak that can end only in utter disaster. There cannot be secure peace in the world while the present economic inequalities persist. If peace is to become secure, it can only be through an improvement in the standard of life in undeveloped regions, and this improvement will have to be so great and so long-continued as to give a prospect of ultimate economic equality. As things are at present, if the world's supply of food were divided equally among all the populations of the world, there would have to be a catastrophic decline in the Western standard of life, and it is obvious that Western nations would not submit to such a decline except as a result of defeat in war. Hopes of peace, therefore, must rest on measures designed to benefit the East without injuring the West, and such measures are impossible unless they involve a very great fall in the birth rate of the more prolific countries.

It is difficult not to be filled with despair when one contemplates the blindness of statesmanship and of everyday popular thought on the issues with which modern man is faced. The leading powers of the world spend enormous sums and devote their best brains to the production of methods of killing each other. Eminent moral leaders give their blessing to such efforts, and at the same time tell us that it is wicked to prevent the births which, by their excessive number, drive the nations on to the invention of H-bombs. I could wish to see it generally recognized in the West, as it is coming to be recognized in the East, that the problem of over-population could probably be painlessly solved by the devotion to birth control of one-hundredth or even one-thousandth of the sum at present devoted to armament. The most urgent practical need is research into some method of birth control which could be easily and cheaply adopted by even very poor populations. There is, at present, only an infinitesimal research on this all-important matter, although it is in the highest degree probable that rather more research and rather more public encouragement could produce incalculably beneficial results.

Given a successful outcome to such research, there should be in every town and village of the more prolific countries centres of birth control information and public assistance as regards the supply of birth control apparatus. The Western nations have a special responsibility in this matter, for it is the discoveries of Western medicine that have so lowered the death rate as to produce a lack of balance that, on a global scale, is a wholly new phenomenon. I will give two illustrations out of many. In Ceylon, when DDT was introduced to combat malaria, the death rate fell within two or three years to the level of Western death rates, while the birth rate remained constant, with the result that there is at present an increase of population at the rate of $2 \cdot 7$ per cent per year. The figures of the death rate in Japan are even more remarkable. In the five years before the Second World War, the average death rate in Japan was $17 \cdot 4$. In 1946, it had risen to $17 \cdot 6$. In the following years it fell with extraordinary suddenness: in 1951 it was $10 \cdot 0$ and, in 1954, $7 \cdot 9$. A large part of this fall is attributable to American methods of public health. In spite of the very highest motives, those Western medical missions and medical scientists who have with extraordinary suddenness brought about the great decline in the death rate, have incidentally done very much more harm than good. The desirable remedy does not lie in restoring the death rate to its former level. It does not lie in the promotion of new pestilences. Least of all does it lie in the vast destruction that a new war may bring. It lies in adapting births to deaths. The stern limits of the earth's fertility will see to it before long that the balance between births and deaths is restored. It will see to it with an arithmetical inevitability which is independent of human wisdom or folly. But if the balance is restored by human folly, immense suffering throughout the world will be involved; while, if it is restored in accordance with the dictates of good sense and humanity, there can be an end to poverty and an end to the vast hopelessness of female lives devoted to the production of children who ought not to exist and whose existence must almost inevitably be filled with misery.

During what remains of the present century, the world has to choose between two possible destinies. It can continue the reckless increase of population until war, more savage and more dreadful than any yet known, sweeps away not only the excess but probably all except a miserable remnant. Or, if the other course is chosen, there can be progress, rapid progress, towards the extinction of poverty, the end of war, and the establishment of a harmonious family of nations. It seems that the East is becoming alive to the problem, but the West, in its theories and in its external dealings, lags behind. Of all the long-run problems that face the world, this problem of population is the most important and fundamental for, until it is solved, other measures of amelioration are futile. It is too late to escape from great hardship in the near future, but there is good reason to believe that, if war can be averted meanwhile, the pressing needs of the world will bring amelioration before it is too late.

VI

Formal Address to the Congress of the Pugwash Movement at Vienna September 20th, 1958

I T I S a very great and sincere pleasure to have this opportunity of expressing the thanks of this Congress for the generous hospitality extended to it by the Austrian Government. At this difficult time they have shown an enlightened liberality in encouraging free and serious discussion amongst men of varied nations and political creeds of matters that are of fundamental importance to the whole future of the human race.

It may be not without interest to mention that 103 years ago, during a war between Russia and the Western Powers, my grandfather, at that time British Foreign Minister, attended a diplomatic Conference in your famous city which, it was hoped, would lead to peace. He favoured terms which the Russian Government was willing to accept, but Napoleon III, envious of his uncle's military fame, insisted upon another twelve months of senseless slaughter. I, alas, cannot speak for the British Government, but I equally stand for peace.

The movement represented by this Congress has grown with surprising rapidity owing largely to the generous assistance of Mr Cyrus Eaton and to the energy and organizing ability of Professors Rotblat and Powell. The movement had a very small beginning. In 1955, ten eminent scientists joined with me in signing a pronouncement on the dangers of nuclear war and the importance of finding ways to prevent it. A great many scientists found themselves in sympathy with this pronouncement. Science, unintentionally and almost accidentally, has caused by its discoveries an unforeseen possibility of vast disaster. Many men of science have, in consequence, felt it a matter of conscience to do what lay in their power to prevent the evils which science has rendered possible. It is this feeling which has caused the growth of organizations such as ours, and of organizations with similar purposes in various countries. Men of science, however, were quick to perceive that much of what needs to be done lies outside the sphere of their special competence, and that the search for measures to avert the danger requires a wide co-operation. The combination of scientific and political questions which is involved in the problem of nuclear warfare causes a difficulty: it is difficult for scientists to think politically and for politicians to think scientifically. But some mingling of the two ways of thought is essential and must be attempted in spite of its difficulties.

It is surprising and somewhat disappointing that movements aiming at the prevention of nuclear war are regarded throughout the West as Left-Wing movements or as inspired by some -ism which is repugnant to a majority of ordinary people. It is not in this way that opposition to nuclear warfare should be conceived. It should be conceived rather on the analogy of sanitary measures against epidemics. The peril involved in nuclear war is one which affects all mankind and one, therefore, in which the interests of all mankind are at one. Those who wish to prevent the catastrophe which would result from a large-scale H-bomb war are not concerned to advocate the interests of this or that nation, or this or that class, or this or that continent. Their arguments have nothing whatever to do with the merits or demerits of Communism or Democracy. The arguments that should be employed in a campaign against nuclear weapons are such as should appeal, with equal force, to Eastern and Western blocs and also to uncommitted nations, since they are concerned solely with the welfare of the human species as a whole and not with any special advantages to this or that group.

It is a profound misfortune that the whole question of nuclear warfare has become entangled in the age-old conflicts of power politics. These conflicts are so virulent and so passionate that they produce a wide-spread inability to understand even very obvious matters. If we are to think wisely about the new problems raised by nuclear weapons, we must learn to view the whole matter in a quite different way. It must be viewed, as some new epidemic would be viewed, as a common peril to be met by concerted action.

Let us take an illustration. Suppose that a sudden outbreak of rabies occurred among the dogs of Berlin. Does anybody doubt that Eastern and Western authorities in that city would instantly combine to find measures of extirpating the mad dogs? I do not think that either side would argue: 'Let us let the dogs loose in the hope that they will bite more of our enemies than of our friends; or, if they are not to be let completely loose, let them be muzzled with easily detachable muzzles and paraded on leashes through the streets so that, if at any moment the "enemy" should let loose its mad dogs, instant retaliation would follow.' Would the authorities of East or West Berlin argue that 'the other side' could not be trusted to kill its mad dogs and that, therefore, 'our side' must keep up the supply as a deterrent? All this is fantastically absurd and would obviously not occur to anybody as a sane policy, because mad dogs are not regarded as a decisive force in power politics. Unfortunately, nuclear weapons are regarded, quite mistakenly, as capable of securing victory in war; and because they are so regarded, few men think of them in a manner consonant with sanity or common sense.

Let us take a, perhaps, more apt illustration. In the fourteenth century the Black Death swept over the Eastern hemisphere. In Western Europe it destroyed about half the population, and in all likelihood it was about equally destructive in Eastern Europe and in Asia. In those days, there did not exist the scientific knowledge necessary to combat the epidemic. In our day, if there were a threat of such a disaster, all civilized nations would combine to combat it. No one would argue, 'Perhaps this pestilence will do more harm to our enemies than to us'. Anybody who did so argue, would be considered a monster of inhumanity. And yet neither the Black Death nor any similar pestilence has ever offered as terrible a threat as is offered by the danger of nuclear war. The countries of NATO, the countries of the Warsaw Pact, and the uncommitted countries have precisely the same interest in this question. The same interest, in fact, as they would have in combating a new Black Death. If this were realized by the statesmen and populations of East and West, many difficulties which now seem insuperable, or nearly so, would disappear. I am, of course, supposing that the point of view which I am advocating would be adopted by both sides equally. Given a sane and sober consideration of what is involved, this harmony on the problems of nuclear weapons would inevitably result. It would not be necessary to invoke idealistic motives, although they could be validly invoked. It would be necessary only to appeal to motives of national self-interest, for, owing to the nuclear peril, the interests of each have become the interests of all, and it is only in co-operation that any can survive. If nations can be brought to realize this fact, we may be on the threshold of a happier era than any previously known in human history.

VII

Address to the C.N.D. Meeting at Manchester, May 1st, 1959

BEFORE ENTERING upon the rather painful matters which this meeting is called to consider, there is one very pleasant topic with which I should wish to begin. It is the expression of deep gratitude to our Chairman[1] on the part of all who are concerned in the Campaign for Nuclear Disarmament. What he has done in Manchester and the neighbourhood is, no doubt, known to all of you at least as well as to me. His work on the nuclear problem in general has been valuable in many ways, but more particularly through the obvious sanity of all that he had to say. I had the privilege of being closely associated with his work in connection with the Motion that he introduced in the House of Lords. I was impressed alike by his energy and his skill. We are indeed fortunate to have him with us in our difficult campaign.

It is the purpose of those who support the Campaign for Nuclear Disarmament to seek out and advocate such measures as may diminish the risk of nuclear warfare. Before considering the measures which this campaign puts forward, and the reasons in their favour, it will be well to face the whole of the questions involved in their setting in relation to the history of mankind. Man, like other meat-eating animals, has always been ferocious, but unlike most other carnivora, his most effective ferocity has

[1] The late Lord Simon of Wythenshawe.

been directed against his own species. In the past, however, he has not possessed the skill that was needed for the complete extirpation of his enemies. Now, he has acquired this skill. There is no limit to the destruction which he can inflict upon those whom he dislikes. Unfortunately for those who enjoy mass murder, it is pretty certain that they will suffer as much injury as they inflict. And the injury will not be confined to belligerents, but will fall also, though in a diminished measure, upon nations which wish to be neutral. No one knows what would happen if a nuclear war broke out tomorrow. It seems probable that there would be survivors in the Southern Hemisphere, at any rate in Patagonia and the South Shetland Islands. But, with every year that passes, the power of mutual destruction increases and, if nuclear weapons should prove insufficient, there are biological and chemical weapons in reserve which may complete the evil work.

As a result of increase in skill, mankind has arrived at a point where the continued existence of the species can only be secured by new maxims of statecraft and new ways of thinking and feeling. The habits of many millennia cannot be changed in a moment. The most that can be expected in the field of day-to-day practical politics, is the avoidance of immediate war by such expedients as may be available. But I think we should all remember that man will not long continue to exist unless means are discovered, and adopted, for the total prevention of large-scale wars.

The danger of a nuclear world war in the present state of the world is greater than most people realize or Western Governments admit. The side which has the initiative in a nuclear attack will have a great advantage over the other side. Each side, therefore, expects the other side to be the aggressor, and prepares itself for instant retaliation. Eastern and Western H-bombs are continually in the air, and are to be employed at once if the other side is thought to be attacking. The risks incurred in this policy are such as no sane man can contemplate calmly. Suppose a plane carrying an H-bomb encounters a meteor and explodes. The meteor will certainly be mistaken for an enemy missile, and, within a few minutes, a full-scale nuclear attack will be in progress. It will, of course, provoke retaliation. What will be the result? Let us not be too abstract as to this. One bomb on Manchester will destroy all the houses within some miles of the place where it falls. All the people in the streets will be killed instantly. Those who are *less* fortunate may find momentary shelter from the blast, and will die in slow agony during the coming hours or days. The same sort of thing will be happening in almost every part of Britain and in all the great cities of Eastern and Western Europe. Perhaps some statesmen may remain alive, and will 'console' the dying with the thought that there are just as many deaths among the 'enemy'. I wonder how much consolation this reflection will afford to those who see their children perishing and know that all hope is at an end.

You may say that a meeting between a plane and a meteor is not very probable. True; but there are many more probable things which might have similar consequences. A technical defect in radar equipment might cause belief in the approach of enemy missiles. Nerve-strain might cause a breakdown in some person possessed of local authority. The doctrine of instant retaliation involves local initiative. It will be impossible to wait for orders from Washington or Moscow or London since these cities may be already destroyed. When we consider the nervous strain that such a situation involves, we must admit that temporary insanity in some one or other of the many people concerned is not improbable.

Such risks, one might suppose, are bad enough, but statesmen are bent upon increasing them. At present only three Powers possess H-bombs; but, unless there is some change in Western policy, France and Germany and Switzerland and Sweden will soon join the 'Nuclear Club'. It is hardly to be supposed that China will consent to be excluded. Very soon every Power, great or small, will insist upon possessing H-bombs. If H-bombs are granted to any new Power, why not to all? It is just conceivable that, among so many Powers, there may be one which is not wholly wise; or there may, somewhere, be an insurrection of some part of the armed forces of some country, and the insurgents may seek power by threats which will be resisted. The First World War was brought about by a small band of terrorists in Serbia. The Third World War could be brought about in a similar manner.

The Bulletin of the Atomic Scientists for March of this year contains a careful article by Professor Orear, who is Professor of Physics at Cornell, on the increased risk involved in the spread of H-bombs to new Powers. He estimates that, if this spread is permitted, 'it appears probable that there will be a nuclear war within the next ten or twenty years'. He goes on to say that 'our present policy involves a practically infinite risk'. I do not see how it is possible to disagree with him.

It is for such reasons that we urge a reversal of the policy of granting H-bombs to nations which at present do not possess them, and, to facilitate such a reversal, we wish to see Britain renounce the H-bomb.

There are many matters of great importance as to which scientific opinion is divided—for instance, as regards test explosions. We wish to know how much harm is to be expected from fall-out and how easy it is to detect a test. The governments which favour the continuation of tests are optimistic as regards fall-out, and pessimistic as regards detection. Scientists employed by governments tend to agree with their employers. Governments tend to base their policies upon whichever opinion suits them on any doubtful matter, and invite us to acquiesce in risks which no one would think of running if politics were not involved. If you ask, for example, 'how many children will die as a result of tests carried out last year?' you will probably be told, 'Oh probably not very many; so why worry?' Although this is considered to be statesmanship, it would, in any other sphere, be considered reckless folly.

There are those who say: 'All this desire for survival is cowardly. Heroes are ready to die for their Cause, and what nobler cause can there be than the extirpation of Communism?' —or 'Capitalism?' (the choice between these two depending upon your longitude). I cannot bring myself to admire the so-called 'heroism' inspired by this brand of fanaticism. It is all very well to die for a cause yourself. But is it not rather a different matter to kill your children and grandchildren, your friends and neighbours, and all the many millions throughout the world who take no interest in the conflict of Communism and Capitalism? Those modern worshippers of Moloch who think such a course justified are not heroes, but utterly terrifying criminals.

The prevention of the spread of H-bombs to new Powers is only a first step—and, some will say, a very small step— towards our ultimate goal. We must hope to see all existing nuclear weapons destroyed, and the manufacture of new weapons of the same kind prohibited. If the abolition of nuclear weapons is not to involve a change in the balance of power, it will have to be accompanied by a serious diminution in conventional armaments. Hitherto, this kind of problem has enabled both East and West to advocate disarmament in the secure belief that their advocacy will be unsuccessful. If any good is to come of disarmament conferences, they will have to be conducted in a different spirit. The aim will have to become that of actually reaching agreements, and not merely that of making proposals the rejection of which by the other side is disadvantageous to that other side from the point of view of propaganda.

It is not yet the business of the Campaign for Nuclear Disarmament to look further than the abolition of nuclear weapons by agreement and with an adequate system of inspection. But I think we should remember that, even if we had achieved this immense measure of success, the danger would not be at an end. Whatever agreements may have been concluded, they would be null and void if war should break out. Since the knowledge would still exist, both sides would proceed to the manufacture of nuclear weapons. We cannot, therefore, feel the future of mankind assured until measures have been adopted which make large-scale war very improbable.

I have been speaking of reasons for fear, but there are also reasons for hope—and I could wish that they were more prominent in the minds of statesmen. The interests of East and West are almost wholly identical, though, unfortunately, the emphasis is placed upon the few points where they differ. Their interests are alike, first and foremost, as regards survival. If East and West hate each other, both will perish. If they do not, they can co-operate in common purposes. Their interests should, also, be identical in agriculture and industry, in medicine and in the arts and sciences. Whatever divergences at present exist in any of these spheres are unnecessary, and would be swept away by a little wisdom. They differ mainly in the competition for power; if each wants to be supreme, one *must* be disappointed, and both, almost certainly, will be. This sort of competition, therefore, is an outdated folly. If their community of interest came to be realized, they would acquiesce in a system designed for the welfare of all, rather than for the disaster of supposed enemies. The immense resources of science and scientific technique could then be used to promote human happiness, and not to manufacture engines of death. Age-old evils, such as plague, pestilence and famine, could be ended or enormously diminished. The ancient empire of fear could cease, and a new energy could fill human life with hitherto unknown joy. All this is possible. But there is one great change which it demands: we must cease to hate and fear each other, and must regard each other as allies in the realization of what man can be.

VIII

What Neutrals can do to Save the World[1]

MANKIND at the present time is faced by dangers to the whole species so great that the avoidance of them ought to be the common aim of all the Powers. The facts are known to everybody who chooses to know them, but for reasons of propaganda they are not adequately emphasized on either side of the Iron Curtain. It is true that they have been stated in Western countries, but not in such a manner as to influence policy. They have been stated more clearly and forcibly in America than in any other country, but they do not seem to have made any impact upon the average Congressman or the average American voter. The *Bulletin of the Atomic Scientists*, month by month since Hiroshima, has published detailed and reasoned warnings, but this journal has a very small circulation since it appeals only to those who wish to know rather than to shout. It is true that some influential people who are not scientists have become aware of the situation brought about by the new methods of warfare. Ernest T. Weir, for example, who represents what is most intelligent in Big Business, has said at the end of an irrefutable piece of reasoning: 'In short, even if we defeated Russia—Communism would win.'[2]

[1] From *Britain Today*, September 14, 1954.
[2] In an article 'Peace must be Pursued', *U.S. News and World Report*, March 18, 1954.

The supreme fact, that governments cannot bring themselves to face, is that their aims can no longer be achieved by war. This applies equally to Communist and anti-Communist Powers. Perhaps Mr Weir may be right in saying that *if* the United States were victorious in a great war Communism would win, but it should be added that there is no probability of anybody being victorious. Consider what is likely to happen in the first week of a world war. New York, Washington, London, and Moscow will probably be wiped out. A great deal of the Caucasus oil will be set a-blaze and communications will be disrupted both in Russia and in Western Europe. Such parts of the populations as survive bombs will starve, and ordered government will be replaced by anarchic violence. All great States will disintegrate, as Rome disintegrated in the fifth century. Communism and modern capitalism alike will disappear. The United States, Western Europe, Russia, and China will all suffer catastrophically, and nothing will emerge that any of these governments desire. This is obvious to anyone who takes a little trouble to study the situation. We have all had Clausewitz's dictum dinned into our ears that war is the continuation of policy. This is no longer true. War cannot further the aims of either Communist or anti-Communist Powers. Whether you are a Communist or an anti-Communist, you have to face the unpleasant fact that your aims cannot be realized by fighting.

Why is it that, although this is obvious to anyone who takes even a little trouble to study the situation, governments and public alike continue to talk and think in terms of war? Among the Western Powers, this is largely due to the fact that any talk about the futility of war sounds like defeatism and may be regarded as an argument for appeasement. I suppose that the same considerations apply to the politically active part of the population of the Communist countries. It seems, on both sides, as if the only alternative to war were abject surrender. There is, however, another alternative. It is that both sides should recognize, and should be known to recognize sincerely, that war has become futile. Neither side alone can be vigorous in urging the futility of war since to do so gives an impression of weakness. It is here that Neutrals can, if they will, save both camps from mutual destruction.

Neutrals have two advantages over the Powers in either camp. The first advantage is that they can urge the destructiveness and futility of war without incurring the odium of seeming to advocate cowardly submission. The second advantage is that they can speak to governments on both sides without being thought to be actuated merely by bias. This is especially important as regards Communist countries, for in them public discussion and controversy play no part. While relations between East and West remain as strained as they are at present nothing that the Western Democracies can say to Russia or China has any weight if it is an appeal to reason rather than to force. Neutral governments, on the contrary, can speak in identical terms to both Communist and non-Communist Powers, and can avoid the suspicion that they are concerned to promote the success of either side.

If I belonged to one of the neutral countries, I should urge upon my government, and upon any other neutral government that might be willing to listen, the taking of very active steps to persuade both sides simultaneously to abandon the threat of war as an instrument of policy. The first step should be to appoint a commission to investigate the probable effects of a world war upon Neutrals. I should hope that a number of Neutrals would join in this, but the work could be done by any one or more of them: for example, by India and Sweden, jointly or separately. Nobody can doubt that a world war would bring great hardships to Neutrals, perhaps as great as those which would be suffered by belligerents. It would therefore be a rational act from a traditional point of view to investigate these possible hardships and to inquire whether they could be averted or mitigated by anything except the prevention of world war. I should hope that such a commission, if appointed, would find it impossible to confine its inquiries to the effects of war upon Neutrals. I believe that it would very soon find the problems of Neutrals inextricably bound up with those of belligerents, and that it would be forced into some kind of forecast of the course of the war if it took place.

I do not mean that the Neutrals should predict the victory of this side or that. I believe that such a victory for either side is out of the question, and I think this would be evident to of any intelligent Neutral not blinded by the passions which are producing the East–West tension. The commission should be concerned with the evils of war, not with the chances of victory. It should preserve a most meticulous impartiality and should never betray even by the faintest word any greater sympathy for the one side than for the other. Its inquiries should be technical and dispassionate. Its members should be few and should be eminent in various relevant directions. There would have to be military, naval, and air experts, a first-class nuclear physicist, a bacteriologist, an economist, and a man of experience in international politics. A body so composed could, I am convinced, draw up a report which would make the futility of world war entirely undeniable by anybody who had studied it.

The report should be presented by the government or governments that had caused it to be drawn up to all the governments likely to be belligerent in a world war. All these governments should be invited to express their opinion on the report. If the governments concurred in its findings—and it would be very difficult for them to do otherwise—the Powers on each side would be informed of the opinion of the Powers on the other side. I do not believe that at the present moment either side desires a great war: even Malenkov has expressed the opinion that it would be a disaster. But on each side there is a suspicion that the other side is not sincere. Neither Russia nor the United States is convinced that the other will not start aggressive war at any moment. It is this mutual suspicion which must be allayed if war is not to break out sooner or later through some rashness or some inadvertence. I think that this mutual suspicion could be very much diminished if on both sides simultaneously agreement were expressed with the findings of the Neutral Commission.

It may be feared that neutral governments will shrink from a task which is sure to offend all the most powerful nations of the world, but there is one matter on which all the powerful nations appear to be agreed and that is that neutrality is an offence against morality and decency. For this reason any neutral nation undertaking such a task will need courage. But courage is needed in order to stay alive. Passive poltroonery leads straight to death. Courage for war is common to the greater part of mankind. Is it Utopian to hope that some neutral nation or nations may show a much smaller degree of courage in the interests of peace? I will instance two nations which I think might possibly be induced to act in the sense that I have been advocating. They are Sweden and India. Neither is perhaps wholly neutral. Sweden's sympathies are Western and India's sympathies are Eastern; but both are legally neutral, and in co-operation they might display a genuine impartiality. I have encountered among Swedes a sentiment which, though irrational, is not unnatural. Sweden has never been at war since 1814, and there are not a few in Sweden who have a sort of shame in the thought that they have had no share in the arduous heroisms of this turbulent century. But if Sweden were to undertake such a work for peace as the suggested commission could perform, Sweden would appear at once in the very forefront of heroism, and of a heroism which would be constructive, non-violent, and in the service of humanity as a whole. I do not see that national self-respect could demand anything better. The Government of India, while not strictly pacifist, is profoundly affected by the doctrine of non-violence as preached by Mahatma Gandhi. To show to the world convincingly that war will not only be horrible and cruel and destructive, but will also be futile from a governmental point of view, would be a fitting tribute to the memory of Gandhi, and one which would enhance the moral stature of India among the nations.

The scheme which I have been proposing, even if completely successful, would be only a first step. If each side were convinced that the other side realized the uselessness of war from the point of view of its own aims and ambitions, it would become possible to negotiate with some hope of reaching solutions. I do not venture to suggest what these solutions should be. There are problems which, in the present temper of the world, appear insoluble. Perhaps the most intractable of these is the unification of Germany. But no problem is insoluble where there is mutual good-will and where concessions are not regarded by one side as a triumph and by the other as a disgrace. The truth is so plain and simple that it seems as if governments must in time become aware of it: The Communist and non-Communist worlds can live together or die together. There is no other possibility. When both sides realize this, it may be hoped that they will choose to live rather than to die.

IX

The Case for British Neutralism[1]

RECENT DEVELOPMENTS, military and political, have necessitated a reconsideration of policy by the West and, more particularly, by members of NATO other than the United States. The situation is so confused and difficult that no prudent man will venture to be dogmatic as to the best policy, but I think that many people, both in the East and the West, overlook very important factors which ought to be taken account of by statesmen who have policy decisions to make. So much pride and passion is involved on both sides that clear thinking requires a great effort. In the hope of facilitating such thinking, let us begin with a coldly abstract survey such as might be made by a visitor from another planet.

The Powers of the world are, at present, divided into three groups, which we may call A and B and C. C is the group of uncommitted nations. A and B are the groups whose mutual hostility causes the threat of nuclear war. Which is East and which is West is, for the moment, to be left doubtful. There are many things which A and B have in common. Each believes, I think sincerely, that itself stands for peace and freedom, while the other stands for war and slavery. Each believes that its own ideology is immeasurably superior to that of the other group and that the world would benefit enormously if what it thinks the better ideology could achieve worldwide superiority. Each believes the other to be treacherous

[1] From the *New York Times Magazine*, 1960.

and deceitful, and suspects it of an intention to launch an unprovoked war whenever the time is thought propitious. Each, though convinced of its own sincerity, is unable to believe in the sincerity of the other side. The dangerous situation in the world is due to these common characteristics of the two groups, not to the differences between them, which are not such as to make co-existence difficult except when embittered by mutual fanaticism.

The logical possibilities existing at present fall under three heads: first, war; second, prolonged brinkmanship; and third, peaceful co-existence.

If a nuclear war occurred, there are, again, various different logical possibilities: first, the victory of one group; second, reversion to universal barbarism; third, the end of the human race. It is, I think, generally agreed that, if a general nuclear war were to break out while the present grouping of Powers persists, it would not lead to a victory of either side, unless 'victory' is defined in a quite novel manner. I suppose that, if, at the end of the few hours of war, there remained six people alive on one side and five on the other, the six might claim victory, but it would not be quite what has hitherto been meant by that word. Nobody knows, and we must devoutly hope that nobody ever will know, what would be the outcome of a large-scale nuclear war. It may be that, as a result of fall-out, the human race would become extinct within a year or so. It may be that there would be a surviving remnant, hungry, desperate, and barbarous, and so genetically damaged that their children would be idiots or monsters. It may be that, in the extreme south of the southern hemisphere, some healthy individuals would survive and that, after a thousand years or so, they would be capable of repeating the disaster from which they had learnt nothing. But I do not think that the survival of such a healthy remnant is very probable. The overwhelming probability is that a large-scale nuclear war would represent the end of everything. If this estimate of probability is right, it follows that a large-scale nuclear war is the worst thing that could possibly happen, and that no sane statesman should risk it.

Nevertheless, there are those on both sides of the Iron Curtain who advocate a continued policy of brinkmanship in the confident hope that they can go on threatening war for decades or centuries without ever arriving at actual war or causing the 'enemy' to become indifferent to the monotonous cry of 'wolf'. I do not see how anybody with even the faintest knowledge of human nature can regard such a view of the future as realistic. The risk of unintended war, although perhaps not very great at any one moment, becomes almost a certainty over a period of years. I have read a number of very careful, expert investigations of the possible causes of unintended war. All the investigators who were not in the pay of some government came to the same conclusion—namely, that continuation of existing policies in East and West was almost certain to lead to an unintended war, if not to an intended one.

Apart from this danger, there are others that are involved in the policy of brinkmanship. This policy involves, of necessity, a continued increase of armament on both sides with a continually mounting expenditure augmented by every new invention. Before very long, the upper air will be full of manned satellites, each containing at least one H-bomb and each liable to explode intentionally or unintentionally. The countries of both East and West will be reduced to subsistence level and will live in a daily and hourly terror of complete annihilation, causing a nervous tension which must, sooner or later, explode into disastrous action.

On such grounds, every sane man, whether in the East or in the West, must hope that a policy of peaceful co-existence will prevail on both sides.

Although this general conclusion cannot be rationally contested, the West is faced with some new problems, which are by no means simple and demand a considerable amount of fresh thinking. As a sequel to the U-2 episode, Russia has threatened that, in certain circumstances, satellites of the United States will be obliterated if they grant certain favours to the United States. The satellites of the United States have, therefore, to decide whether they will continue to co-operate with the United States in ways which Russia has declared intolerable, or whether they will establish limits to what they would grant the United States, or whether they shall withdraw completely from alliance with the United States. There is a growing doubt as to whether a Russian attack upon one member of the Western group—say Pakistan—would cause the United States to bring about a general nuclear war by coming to the defence of the attacked satellite. The conventional argument in the West is that Russia would be deterred from any attack on a Western satellite by the fear of United States retaliation. But, if the Soviet Government thinks that such retaliation will not take place, the argument fails, and the Soviet Government might decide to take the risk. The United States Government would then have to decide: shall we abide by our obligations and so destroy the human race, or shall we allow the Soviet Government a partial victory? If I were President of the United States and had to make this decision, I cannot think that I should consider it my duty to decide for the extermination of my own country and all other countries; and I think it quite possible that the Soviet Government might be willing to gamble on the United States acquiescing rather than causing total disaster.

The most careful and dispassionate discussion of this problem that I have seen occurs in an article by Mr Herman Kahn originally published in the Stanford Research Institute *Journal* and reprinted with some alterations in Vol. II, No. 2, of *Survival*. This article is entitled 'The Feasibility of War and Deterrence'. It discusses various problems, but I am only concerned with what it says about American obligations to allies. It begins by quoting a statement by Mr Herter on the occasion of the hearing on his nomination. He said: 'I cannot conceive of any President involving us in an all-out nuclear war unless the facts showed clearly we are in danger of all-out devastation ourselves, or that actual moves have been made towards devastating ourselves.' Mr Kahn goes on to say: 'I find it difficult to believe that under these circumstances any President of the United States would initiate a thermonuclear war by retaliating against the Soviets with the Strategic Air Command. There is no objective of public policy that would justify ending life for everyone. It should be clear that we would not restore Europe by our retaliation; we could only succeed in further destroying it, either as a by-product of our actions or because the Soviets would destroy Europe as well as the United States.' He mentions that he discussed with many Americans the question, what would an American President do when faced with a serious Russian attack upon an ally of America if he had twenty-four hours to come to a decision and had reason to believe that, in an all-out nuclear war, one hundred and seventy-seven million Americans would be killed. The people of whom he asked this question, at first, replied instinctively that of course America must fulfil her obligations, but all of them, after fifteen minutes' discussion, concluded that there was a limit to the price that America should be willing to pay. Some put the acceptable price as low as ten million deaths; some, as high as sixty million. He concludes that 'no American that I have spoken to who was at all serious about the matter believed that United States retaliation would be justified—no matter what our commitments were—if more than half of our population would be killed'. We may add that nobody who has seriously studied the effects of nuclear warfare believes that the casualties in America could be as low as half the population.

A discussion of this kind, when it comes to the notice of statesmen allied to the United States, cannot but produce feelings of profound dismay. It is true that the State Department on June 1st issued a statement renewing the promise of

American support in the event of a Russian attack upon a Western satellite, but, nevertheless, uneasiness persists. The reason for its persistence is not any doubt as to America's intentions to keep faith, but as to what would actually happen at the critical moment. The decision which the American Government would have to make would be this: shall we acquiesce in the destruction of one satellite, or shall we spread equal destruction throughout the whole world? I do not envy the administration that has to make this decision. The reactions of Western satellites have been various. Some of these countries, it is true, have their own reasons for hostility to Russia. This is notably the case in Germany. But most of the allies of the United States became allies in the pursuit of safety and have no other *compelling* reason for hostility to Russia. It now appears that the American alliance, so far from bringing safety to an ally, immensely increases its danger. To take the case of my own country: if Britain were neutral, Russia would have no motive for attacking it; but, while Britain is useful to the United States, Russia has such a motive, which may well become decisive if it is believed in Russia that the argument of the Great Deterrent does not apply because America would do nothing if Britain were destroyed. From the point of view of a patriotic Briton, it seems that there is no gain, and possible disastrous loss, through the American alliance. Russia could exterminate the population of Britain in an hour or two and, after allowing a suitable period for radioactivity to die down, could repopulate the country with members of Communist States after the pattern inaugurated in East Prussia. Such a course of events would serve no purpose that America or any other non-Communist States could welcome.

We are sometimes called upon, in rhetorical terms, to be willing to die for a great cause without stopping to consider whether the great cause will be in any degree furthered by our death. That is unmitigated nonsense. We proved in 1940 our willingness to die if any purpose was to be served thereby. But willingness to die without serving any purpose is merely morbid.

For my part, both as a patriot and as a friend of humanity, I should wish to see Britain officially neutral in the conflict between America and Russia. The patriotic argument is a very obvious one. No sensible man would wish to see his country obliterated without any gain to the kind of way of life that makes his country valuable. And, as things stand, so long as Britain remains allied to America, there is a serious risk of extermination without the slightest advantage either to America or to the Western way of life. From the point of view of humanity in general, the hostility between Russia and America is what threatens disaster, and anything tending to mitigate this hostility is a service to Man. Owing to the destructive character of nuclear weapons, it is no longer useful to point to the wickedness of the side to which we do not belong. Whether you are of the East or whether you are of the West, the side to which you are opposed does not present so great an evil as does the enmity between the two sides. I should like to see this recognized by the two giants. Meantime, more than half the population of the world belongs to neither group and waits in impotent fear for the death which the two groups may inflict, not only upon each other, but also upon the bystanders. The bystanders need not be so wholly impotent as they have hitherto been. They can influence public opinion in both East and West. They can suggest solutions to vexed problems which both East and West can accept. They can bring their weight to bear in United Nations' discussions of disarmament. They can, not improbably, be the decisive force turning men aside from collective suicide. It is in this work that I should like to see my country helping.

ANSWERS TO OBJECTIONS

'Do you urge submission to Russia?'

No. If the alternative were 'submit or fight', I think that either East or West, if wise, would submit. But that is not the alternative. What I urge is negotiation designed to reach agreement, as opposed to a deadlock that can be exploited for propaganda.

'Do you urge United States Unilateral disarmament?'

No. I urge agreed disarmament of United States and USSR, with help of neutrals, and neutral inspectors. Kahn (*Thermonuclear War*, p. 474) says: 'I would prefer to see some pressure on the West to run risks by trying to do too much, rather than to play too cautious a role, since the biases the other way are extremely large. For this reason even ill-considered pressures by "peace" groups can still have a good effect.'

'Do you wish Britain to abdicate, and make no further efforts to prevent Russian world domination?'

No. I consider that a neutral Britain can do more to make peaceful co-existence possible than can be done by Britain as a member of NATO. Kahn agrees (*op. cit.*, pp. 178–9).

'Is a nuclear war likely?'

As to the likelihood of a nuclear war by accident, Mr Oskar Morgenstern, a politically orthodox American defence expert, in an article reprinted in *Survival*, Vol. II, No. 4, says: 'The probability of thermonuclear war's occurring appears to be significantly larger than the probability of its not occurring.' The Ohio State University inaugurated a study of the possible causes of unintended war, which are numerous and have already, on several occasions, very nearly resulted in disaster. The moon, once, and flights of geese, repeatedly, have been mistaken for Russian missiles. Mr Adlai Stevenson has said: 'There can be no deterrent to war by accident.' I suppose it is proneness to such remarks which caused him to be thought unfit to be President. I refrain from further quotations on the subject of war by accident.

'What would occur in a nuclear war?'

The United States Secretary of Defense in 1958, summarizing a Pentagon report, maintained that in a nuclear war there would be 160 million deaths in the United States, 200 million in the USSR, and, in the United Kingdom, everybody. Some authorities are more optimistic. Mr A. G. Field, our Civil Defence expert, has stated, 'It cannot be said categorically that in these countries [i.e. NATO allies of the United States] there would be no survivors after a nuclear attack.' (*Fifteen Nations*, No. 14.) I should certainly agree that this cannot be *categorically* asserted. Until the experiment is made, doubt is permissible, but it seems somewhat remarkable that the British Government, with the connivance of a majority of the Labour Front Bench, should support a policy of which the best that can be said is that it *may* leave a few Britons alive. We were impressed by the seriousness of Hitler's threat to Britain in 1940, but it was not nearly so serious as the United States and USSR threat to Britain at the present moment.

This threat arises not only from a possibility of a general war, but also from an entirely different source, namely, the risk that we might be dragged by the United States into acquiescence in measures regarded by the USSR as provocative, and that we might, in consequence, be subjected to a completely destructive attack directed against Britain alone, and not, also, against the United States. Some are surprised that I should consider this not unlikely. I cannot understand their surprise. At the time of the U-2 crisis, and again in connection with Polaris, Krushchev and Malinovsky loudly proclaimed that this would be their policy if incidents such as the U-2 flight continued. Malinovsky said of any NATO nation other than the

United States which tolerated such incidents, 'We shall deal them such a blow that nothing will be left of them'. He uttered on this occasion no similar threat against the United States. All the British newspapers, especially on May 10 and 11, 1960, were full of these threats, which were headlined. But apparently many on both Front Benches failed to see them.

Some find fault with me as to the expense of the arms race. At present (to quote p. 13 of Sir R. Adam's *Assault at Arms*) we in Britain spend only thirty pounds per head per annum for every man, woman, and child, but already we are being told that the estimates will have to be increased, and in America the Democrats have adopted a programme rejecting any attempt at a ceiling for expenditure on armaments. I think many people seriously underrate the ingenuity of armament experts of both East and West in inventing new weapons. The manned bomber is obsolescent; the guided missile is to have its little day; but clearly the future lies with manned satellites containing H-bombs. My arithmetic does not run to computing what *they* would cost.

As regards the economic consequences of disarmament, I find Big Business in America does not take the gloomy view that is often taken. *Nation's Business*, the organ of the United States Chamber of Commerce, published an article in October, 1959, called 'What Peace would do to you'. This article was surprisingly optimistic, but gave what seemed to be good reasons for its views. Another article appeared in *Think* for January 1960, by Senator Hubert H. Humphrey, called 'After, Disarmament, What?' This took the same optimistic view. I think one must conclude that the leaders of Big Business in America do not consider the present level of armaments production essential to American prosperity. I hope they are right. In any case, on this point their voice is authoritative. They argue that conversion of plant to peace-time uses will not be very difficult.

Most of my opponents reject my view that ideological

differences play a very small part in the hostility between East and West. I do not believe that, even if Russia became as liberal as our ally Franco Spain, we should become friendly to the Soviet régime. We have been sometimes friendly with Russia, sometimes hostile, without any change in the Soviet governmental system.

I do not wish to think that the whole world will become Communist, but I wish even less to see mankind obliterated. Neither disaster need occur. Many who speak favourably of disarmament fail to note that the most serious approaches to disarmament have been made by the USSR and have been foiled by niggling opposition from the West. Western policy, through blindness, has done everything to pose the alternative 'Red or Dead'. Those who advocate a policy which would evade this alternative are regarded as fellow travellers. As to this, however, public opinion in Britain is changing, and there seems now some hope that, in spite of our 'patriots', there may be Britons alive at the end of the present century.

X

Can War be Abolished?[1]

IS IT POSSIBLE to induce mankind to live without war? War is an ancient institution which has existed for at least six thousand years. It was always wicked and usually foolish, but in the past the human race managed to live with it. Modern ingenuity has changed this. Either Man will abolish war, or war will abolish Man. For the present, it is nuclear weapons that cause the gravest danger, but bacteriological or chemical weapons may, before long, offer an even greater threat. If we secure the abolition of nuclear weapons, our work will not be done. It will never be done until we have secured the abolition of war. To secure this, we need to persuade mankind to look upon international questions in a new way, not as contests of force, in which the victory goes to the side which is most skilful in massacre, but by arbitration in accordance with agreed principles of law. It is not easy to change age-long mental habits, but this is what must be attempted.

There are those who say that the adoption of this or that ideology would prevent war. I believe this to be a profound error. All ideologies are based upon dogmatic assertions which are, at best, doubtful, and at worst, downright false. The fanaticism with which they are believed makes their adherents willing to go to war in support of them. Christians assure us that theirs is a religion of love, but the adoption of Christianity by the Roman State in the time of Constantine did nothing to diminish war

[1] From Russian journal, *Science and Religion*, 1960.

and, in our own day, many of the most fanatical warmongers have been Christian. I do not think, however, that the dogmatic adoption of an ideology different from Christianity would be any improvement. The evil lies in the dogmatic temper, not in the particular character of the dogma. Since modern weapons leave us with no choice except all to live together or all to die together, the preservation of the human species demands a greater degree of mutual tolerance than has ever before been necessary.

The movement of world opinion during the past two years has been very largely such as we can welcome. It has become a commonplace that nuclear war is to be avoided. Even the most bellicose now repudiate emphatically the policy of 'brinkmanship' which, a little while ago, was widely regarded as the acme of statesmanship. There have been marked and very welcome changes in the policies of Britain and Russia, and a considerable softening in the policy of the United States. Very intractable problems remain in the international sphere, but the spirit in which they are being approached is a better one than it was some years ago. It has begun to be thought, even by the powerful men who decide whether we shall live or die, that negotiations ought to reach agreements even if the agreements that can be reached are not wholly satisfactory to either side. It has begun to be understood that the important conflict nowadays is not between East and West, but between Man and the H-bomb. The human race is faced with a peril of its own creating, a peril which is getting out of hand and is in danger of growing in a *quasi*-independent manner which no one had intended, but which, as yet, no government has had the wisdom to prevent. A lamentable example of this tendency is the French test explosion in the Sahara which, it is to be feared, will soon be followed by German nuclear weapons and, at no distant date, by an even more formidable armament in China. All such steps increase the peril of utter disaster. Unless some drastic change in policy takes place fairly soon, the march towards race suicide will continue with a blind momentum. If this prospect stood alone, the outlook would be dark indeed. Only a world-wide movement of public opinion can reverse the trend. With every day the danger grows more obvious, but, as it grows more obvious, those who realize the danger find a continually diminishing hostility on the part of several important governments. There are notable peace movements in almost all civilized countries. Their power, if they can co-operate, may before long become irresistible. In many countries there are several such peace movements. Movements which are genuinely and honestly in favour of peace ought to be able to work together to that end in spite of differences as to methods and immediate objectives. Movements which genuinely tend towards the preservation of peace should be welcomed without regard to Rightist or Leftist tendencies. It must, however, be admitted that there are wolves in sheep's clothing. We must not be misled by those who pretend that there are ways of making a nuclear war endurable or that we can indulge in occasional small wars without the danger of their becoming great.

I think that the advocates of peace should emphasize, not only the unspeakable disasters to which existing policies must lead, but also, and just as much, the new world of unexampled happiness which is opened to us if we can forget our quarrels. Man has risen slowly from a rare and hunted species, constantly threatened by wild beasts who were his superiors in strength, periodically decimated by disastrous famines, haunted by terrors generated by the spectacle of the apparently hostile world of nature. Man has risen to mastery over external dangers, but he has not risen to mastery over the internal dangers generated by his own passions of hate and envy and pride. The time has come when he must master these internal perils or recognize that he is himself a more dangerous wild beast than the lion or the tiger. It is unbearable to think that all the immense progress since the days of primitive man may be thrown away because we cannot acquire that last step in mastery which is the mastery over our own atavistic passions. We have the power, if we choose, to create a world quite immeasurably superior to anything that our planet has hitherto known. We have, also, the capacity, if we choose, to put an end to human and animal life. If we are to choose the better alternative, it will be necessary to discard old habits of thought and feeling, and to realize that, in our closely integrated world, our prosperity is bound up with that of others and cannot be promoted by disaster to others. To bring about such change of mental habits is not easy and cannot be achieved in a day or a year or even a decade. But it is this change, difficult as it may be to bring about, which is the aim of the friends of peace. It is a great and beneficent undertaking, and one which well deserves all the patience that it needs. It would be irrational, in such an undertaking, to expect immediate or rapid success. But, for my part, I think what has been achieved in the way of change of outlook is much more than I should have expected. The task is one to which we can, and must, all contribute. Only by generating an overwhelming public opinion can we secure victory. But in moments of discouragement, we are apt to forget that public opinion is not a vague, amorphous, external Something, but is the opinion of people like you and me. Each one of us is a unit in the making of public opinion, and each one of us can hope to win other units to our side. Human volitions have caused our troubles, and human volitions can cure them. The hope, if we succeed, is glorious. And if we can make this felt, we shall succeed.

The atmosphere of fear and horror which we have learnt to breathe can be dissipated. It will be dissipated if public opinion can be made wiser. Public opinion can be made wiser if the facts can be made known. And every convert to our way of thinking can be shown something, large or small, that he can do towards the creation of a better world. Some of the first steps towards this end are not very difficult. Public opinion should insist that in negotiations—such, for instance, as those for the abolition of tests—the negotiators should meet with a determination to reach agreement even though the agreement may not be precisely what either party would wish. Negotiations between East and West, hitherto, have been inspired by the wish to find plausible ways of disagreeing. If this could be changed, even in only one particular, such as the banning of tests, there would be a new momentum which would make further agreements less difficult. Before long each side might come to realize that the true interests of both sides are identical and that strife, in an era of nuclear weapons, must be disastrous to everybody. If war is ruled out—as it would be if men had any sanity, any capacity for pursuing their own interests, or any tiny spark of humane feeling—they would soon come to see what would be the next step. The next step would have to be the creation of some machinery for settling disagreements peaceably.

Consider, for example, the present Disarmament Conference. Russia had a plan for general and complete disarmament, which I, for my part, whole-heartedly applaud. NATO, also, had a plan, which is not without merit. It has been plain from the start that neither East nor West could win the approval of the conference for the whole of its plan. In such circumstances, the clash of public argument is much more likely to exacerbate the differences than to lead to agreement. It ought to be realized by both sides that it is more important to reach agreement than to insist upon something which makes agreement impossible. If this were realized, the two sides, instead of engaging in a public wrangle, would appoint a very small sub-committee in which East and West should have equal numbers, and it should be the business of this sub-committee to frame a compromise scheme to which both sides might agree. I believe that the work could be facilitated by the additions of two neutrals whose judgment might be acceptable as to whether a suggested compromise was fair to both sides. I am not insisting, however, on just this machinery. What I am insisting upon is that conferences should be conducted with a view to agreement rather than to propaganda victory for one's own side.

If such machinery were created, and were supported by a powerful public opinion everywhere, it would soon make war seem as obsolete as cannibalism or human sacrifice. It would soon be evident to all, except a tiny fractious minority, that science, which is being used to spread terror and hatred and death, can, instead, be used to spread joy. The age-old terrors of the days when man was at the mercy of the perils of nature have survived too long in our hearts, making fear seem natural and enemies only what we must expect. New knowledge should give strength to new emotions, emotions of freedom, of happiness, and of readiness for co-operation. It is this new expansive and less timorous way of feeling that the world needs and that can, alone, make us worthy of the mastery over nature that scientific knowledge has given us. We should all feel that what we are doing is part of a vast and world-wide movement for emancipation from ancient fears, ancient suspicions, and ancient hatreds, which are unworthy of modern man and which, if allowed to persist, must bring him to destruction. We need not be enemies, one with another. All of us can be happier by co-operation. We have to make the choice. Shall we create a dead planet of corpses? Or shall we create a glorious world where the human spirit can reach to heights never before imagined? To do something towards the happier issue lies within the power of each one of us.

XI

Human Life is in Danger

THROUGH THE deliberate action of the governments of the great Powers of East and West, it becomes every day less likely that there will be live men and women in the world at the end of the present century. Ever since the danger became evident, governments have done everything possible to increase it. Fifteen years ago, the atom bomb shocked the world. Now it is called a 'tactical weapon' and considered puny. The H-bomb followed. Everybody argued that it must not be allowed to spread to the Powers which did not yet have it, since this would increase the danger of nuclear war. Ever since this was said, it has spread, and it continues to spread.

Although the danger of accidental war is well known, absolutely nothing has been done to diminish it. Although present policies, if continued, make the end of human life imminent and almost certain, not one person in a thousand is actively aware of this fact. Governmental experts know it, but, for their personal reasons, tell lies to the governments that employ them, and the governments take care not to discover that they are lies. For reasons of power, prestige, or money, important persons, mostly elderly, take care to keep subject populations in ignorance.

Are we then to sit down and die quietly?

Some of us think this would be a mistake. But what are we to do when the major organs of publicity are hostile? The only way in which we can make the facts known is to find a form of protest which even the hostile Press will notice.

For a time, Aldermaston Marches served this purpose, but they are ceasing to be news; and the time has come, or is about to come, when only large-scale civil disobedience, which should be non-violent, can save populations from the universal death which their governments are preparing for them.

It cannot be doubted that, if the facts were generally known both in the East and in the West, the victims marked down for destruction by governments would protest with such vehemence as would make a complete reversal of policy inescapable. Those who realize the peril cannot easily make it generally known, but they can, if they choose, act in such a manner as will cause their protests to be known. As these protests become more widely known and more numerous, they may persuade the doomed ignorant battalions of men and women and children, who are now blindly marching towards death, to turn round and march instead towards life—a fuller life than mortals have ever known before because it will be a life no longer dominated by hate and fear.

Many people, who use blindness and oblivion for the purpose of remaining comfortable, say: 'Oh, but you shouldn't break the law—at any rate, not in a democratic country! You should use only such forms of persuasion as the holders of power make difficult and almost impossible for you to use. If these prove insufficient, you must allow the victims to dance gaily to their death.' This view is not one which any deeply humane person, who has realized what is at stake, can honestly adopt.

True, the law is important and not lightly to be broken, for, without respect for the law, no tolerable community is possible. But, at all times, men who could either think or feel more deeply than most have found themselves in conflict with one or more of the beliefs prevalent in their society. And many of those, who have been forced into such conflict, have come to be regarded by future ages as among those who have excelled in wisdom or in humane feeling.

Every age admits this as regards the past.

Every age denies it as regards the present.

No previous age has had as great a need as ours has of men who will proclaim how life should be lived, no matter how loudly the holders of power may howl for death. Never before has all mankind been threatened. Never before has knowledge made such murderous policies possible.

If you value your friends, your children, or the splendid achievements of which individuals and nations have been proved capable, it is your duty—or, rather, your privilege—to protest in every way likely to be effective. You are likely to suffer by doing so. But even in suffering, you will be able to preserve a deep happiness, not open to the prosperous engineers of disaster.

If you have enjoyed this book you may like to know that the following books by Bertrand Russell are also available from Routledge in paperback.

ABC of Relativity
Analysis of Matter
Analysis of Mind
Authority and the Individual
The Autobiography of Bertrand Russell
Basic Writings of Bertrand Russell
Bertrand Russell's Best
The Conquest of Happiness
Education and the Social Order
A History of Western Philosophy
Human Knowledge: its Scope and Value
Human Society in Ethics and Politics
The Impact of Science on Society
In Praise of Idleness
An Inquiry into Meaning and Truth
Introduction to Mathematical Philosophy
Logic and Knowledge
Marriage and Morals
My Philosophical Development
Mysticism and Logic including A Free Man's Worship
On Education
Our Knowledge of the External World
Outline of Philosophy
Philosophical Essays
The Philosophy of Leibniz
Political Ideals
Power
Principles of Mathematics
Principles of Social Reconstruction
Roads to Freedom
Sceptical Essays
Theory of Knowledge: the 1913 Manuscript
Unpopular Essays
Why I am not a Christian

For full details of these books please write for a Russell leaflet to the Promotions Dept, Routledge, 11 New Fetter Lane, London EC4P 4EE.